Unveiling the Core: A Comprehensive Guide to Operating System Design and Implementation

Table of Content

Chapter 1: The Foundation - Understanding Operating System Fundamentals

- Definition and evolution
- Historical overview of key operating systems
- Understanding the purpose and significance
- Relationship between hardware and software
- Processes, threads, and multitasking
- Memory management and file systems
- Overview of various OS types (e.g., real-time, distributed)
- Pros and cons of different systems
- Analysis of successful operating systems (e.g., UNIX, Windows, Linux)
- Lessons learned from historical developments

Chapter 2: Blueprinting Brilliance: Design Principles and Strategies

- Overview of key design considerations
- Balancing flexibility and efficiency
- Graphical vs. command-line interfaces
- Human-computer interaction principles
- Designing for growth and adaptability
- Handling increased system complexity
- Strategies for minimizing system failures
- Redundancy and error recovery mechanisms
- Examination of well-designed operating systems
- Extracting principles from successful implementations

Chapter 3: Building Blocks: Kernel Architecture and Components

- Definition and role in an operating system
- Types of kernels (monolithic, microkernel, hybrid)
- Process management and scheduling
- Memory management and virtual memory
- Interaction between the kernel and hardware
- Strategies for efficient input/output operations
- Design principles and file organization
- Security considerations in file management
- Common issues and solutions in kernel development
- Balancing performance and stability

Chapter 4: In the Code's Realm: Programming Paradigms for OS Development

- Imperative vs. declarative programming
- Low-level vs. high-level programming languages
- Understanding the role of assembly in OS development
- Writing basic assembly code
- Importance of C in OS development
- System-level programming techniques
- Applying OOP principles to kernel and system design
- Benefits and challenges of OOP in OS development
- Handling multiple processes and threads
- Strategies for efficient parallel programming in operating systems

Chapter 5: The Dance of Devices: Drivers and Hardware Interaction

- Definition and purpose in operating systems
- Types of device drivers and their roles
- Abstraction techniques for diverse hardware
- Ensuring compatibility and portability
- Protocols for communication
- Interrupts and their role in device interaction
- Design considerations for plug-and-play support
- Dynamic device recognition and configuration
- Strategies for improving device efficiency
- Balancing device interaction with overall system performance

Chapter 6: Securing the Citadel: Operating System Security Measures

- The critical role of security in operating systems
- Historical perspectives on security vulnerabilities
- User authentication and authorization
- Role-based access control (RBAC) and mandatory access control (MAC)
- Techniques for secure data transmission and storage
- Overview of encryption algorithms and protocols
- Securing communication channels within the OS
- Firewalls, intrusion detection, and prevention systems
- Regular updates and patch management
- Incident response and recovery strategies

Chapter 7: Performance Orchestration: Optimization Techniques and Strategies

- Defining and measuring system performance
- Key indicators for efficiency and responsiveness
- Caching mechanisms and memory compression
- Strategies for minimizing memory leaks
- Different scheduling algorithms and their impact
- Multi-core optimization and parallel processing
- Improving file access speed and data retrieval
- Reducing fragmentation and optimizing storage
- Overview of tools for performance analysis
- Real-time monitoring and profiling techniques

Chapter 8: Beyond the Horizon: Future Trends in Operating System Design

- Integration of AI and machine learning in OS design
- Quantum computing implications for operating systems
- The rise of containerized applications
- Impact on OS architecture and deployment
- Operating systems in the era of distributed computing
- Edge computing challenges and solutions
- Predictive security measures and AI-driven defenses
- Adapting OS security to evolving cyber threats
- Shaping the future of user interfaces
- Human-centric design principles in future OS development

Introduction

Welcome to "Unveiling the Core: A Comprehensive Guide to Operating System Design and Implementation." In the fast-evolving landscape of technology, where the heartbeat of progress echoes through every keystroke and algorithm, the role of operating systems stands as a silent conductor orchestrating the symphony of digital endeavors. This comprehensive guide endeavors to be your trusted companion on a profound journey into the very essence of operating systems.

As we embark on this exploration, it becomes evident that understanding the intricacies of operating systems is not just beneficial; it is fundamental in navigating the contemporary technological tapestry. The foundational concepts that underpin every operating system are akin to the roots of a mighty tree, supporting the vast branches of software applications and user experiences that flourish above. This guide unfolds these fundamental concepts, tracing the historical evolution of operating systems and elucidating their pivotal role in shaping the computing landscape.

The narrative deepens with a meticulous examination of design principles and strategies, akin to an architect crafting the blueprint of a grand edifice. "Blueprinting Brilliance: Design Principles and Strategies" takes you into the realm of choices and considerations that architects of operating systems must grapple with. From user interface design to scalability, fault tolerance to real-world case studies, the chapters weave together the threads of ingenuity that create a robust foundation for any operating system.

Moving beyond the theoretical scaffolding, we delve into the very heart of operating systems—the kernel. "Building Blocks: Kernel Architecture and Components" unveils the core components responsible for the seamless interaction between hardware and software. Here, we explore the intricacies of process management, memory handling, device drivers, and the architecture that forms the backbone of a well-crafted operating system.

Transitioning from the theoretical to the practical, "In the Code's Realm: Programming Paradigms for OS Development" immerses you in the languages and paradigms that breathe life into operating systems. Assembly languages, C, object-oriented programming, and the intricacies of concurrency become the brushstrokes that paint the canvas of operating system development. It's a journey from the low-level intricacies of machine code to the higher-level abstractions that shape modern operating systems.

"The Dance of Devices: Drivers and Hardware Interaction" beckons us into the intricate ballet between the operating system and hardware. Exploring the world of device drivers, hardware abstraction layers, and the optimization of device performance, this chapter demystifies the complexities of ensuring seamless communication between software and the myriad devices that comprise the computing landscape.

As we ascend the layers of understanding, the guide takes a pivotal turn towards security in "Securing the Citadel: Operating System Security Measures." In an era where digital fortresses face constant threats, understanding access control, encryption, and network security becomes imperative. This chapter not only delves into security mechanisms but also illuminates best practices to fortify the digital citadel against potential breaches.

Optimization becomes the central theme in "Performance Orchestration: Optimization Techniques and Strategies." Delving into the intricacies of memory optimization, CPU scheduling, and file system performance, this chapter equips readers with the tools and knowledge to fine-tune operating systems for optimal efficiency.

Finally, as we gaze "Beyond the Horizon: Future Trends in Operating System Design," the guide becomes a crystal ball, offering glimpses into the future. Emerging technologies, containerization, distributed systems, and the evolution of user experience unfold as the chapters pave the way for the next frontier in operating system design and implementation.

In essence, "Unveiling the Core" is more than a guide; it is a narrative weaving through the threads of history, theory, and practice that define the realm of operating systems. Whether you are a seasoned developer seeking to deepen your understanding or an enthusiastic explorer entering this domain for the first time, this guide aims to be your compass, guiding you through the intricate landscapes of operating system design and implementation.

Chapter 1: The Foundation - Understanding Operating System Fundamentals

Definition and evolution

The operating system (OS) serves as the foundational software that facilitates communication between a computer's hardware and the applications running on it. It plays a pivotal role in managing resources, providing a user interface, and ensuring overall system stability. The evolution of operating systems can be traced back to the early days of computing when simple batch processing systems were employed. These systems lacked user interaction and executed predefined sequences of jobs. As technology advanced, the need for more interactive and user-friendly interfaces arose, leading to the development of time-sharing systems. This paradigm shift allowed multiple users to share the computer's resources concurrently, marking a significant milestone in OS evolution.

The emergence of graphical user interfaces (GUIs) in the 1980s, epitomized by the likes of Apple's Macintosh and Microsoft Windows, transformed the user experience, making computing more accessible to non-experts. Concurrently, the evolution of operating systems saw the advent of multitasking capabilities, enabling users to run multiple applications simultaneously. This era also witnessed the rise of networked computing, with the development of distributed operating systems that facilitated communication and resource sharing across interconnected machines.

The late 20th century saw the rise of operating systems like Unix, known for its stability and scalability, and later, Linux, which embraced open-source principles. These systems gained prominence, particularly in server environments. The proliferation of personal computers in homes and offices further diversified the OS landscape, with Microsoft's Windows becoming a dominant player in the desktop market.

The turn of the millennium witnessed the rise of mobile computing, catalyzing the development of mobile operating systems such as Apple's iOS and Google's Android. These OSs were tailored to the specific needs of smartphones and tablets, emphasizing touch-based interactions and app-centric ecosystems. The concept of virtualization gained traction, allowing multiple operating systems to run on a single physical machine concurrently, ushering in new possibilities for resource optimization and management.

The 21st century also marked the advent of cloud computing, influencing the design of operating systems to better support distributed and scalable architectures. Containerization technologies, like Docker, further streamlined deployment across diverse computing environments. Security concerns prompted the development of more robust and resilient operating systems, with a focus on mitigating vulnerabilities and protecting user data.

The modern computing landscape is characterized by a variety of operating systems catering to different devices and scenarios. Windows, macOS, and Linux continue to dominate the desktop and server environments, while mobile operating systems like Android and iOS power a plethora of smartphones and tablets. Real-time operating systems (RTOS) find applications in embedded systems and critical infrastructure, ensuring precise timing and responsiveness.

Looking ahead, the evolution of operating systems is poised to be shaped by emerging technologies such as artificial intelligence (AI), edge computing, and the Internet of Things (IoT). AI integration into operating systems may enhance automation, adaptability, and predictive capabilities. Edge computing demands operating systems that can efficiently manage distributed processing across devices at the network periphery. The IoT, with its myriad interconnected devices, necessitates operating systems that can seamlessly orchestrate communication and data exchange in a secure and scalable manner.

In conclusion, the journey of operating systems from rudimentary batch processing systems to the sophisticated, interconnected ecosystems of today reflects the dynamic nature of technology and user expectations. As we navigate the ever-evolving landscape of computing, operating systems will continue to evolve, adapting to new challenges and opportunities, and serving as the cornerstone of digital experiences across diverse devices and environments.

Historical overview of key operating systems

The history of operating systems (OS) is a captivating journey that spans the entire existence of modern computing. It begins with the advent of the Electronic Numerical Integrator and Computer (ENIAC) in the 1940s, often considered the world's first general-purpose electronic digital computer. ENIAC, designed to solve complex numerical calculations, lacked what we now recognize as an operating system; its operation required manual intervention to set switches and cables for each computation.

The evolution gained momentum with the introduction of batch processing systems in the 1950s. IBM's operating system for the 701 computer, known as the Input/Output System (I/0 System), was one of the early examples. Batch processing allowed users to submit jobs in batches, which the computer executed sequentially without direct user interaction. This marked a shift from the hands-on approach of early computers to a more automated and efficient mode of operation.

In the 1960s, the concept of time-sharing operating systems emerged, epitomized by the development of the Compatible Time-

Sharing System (CTSS) at the Massachusetts Institute of Technology (MIT). Time-sharing allowed multiple users to interact with the computer simultaneously, each having their session and sharing the machine's resources. This laid the foundation for more interactive and user-friendly computing experiences.

One of the most influential operating systems of the 1960s was the IBM System/360 Operating System (OS/360). It aimed to provide compatibility across a range of IBM's System/360 mainframes. OS/360 introduced the concept of System Control Programs (OS/360 SCP), overseeing various system functions, and Job Control Language (JCL), a scripting language for defining batch jobs. However, OS/360 faced challenges due to its complexity and resource requirements.

In the same era, Multics (Multiplexed Information and Computing Service) emerged as a collaborative effort among MIT, Bell Labs, and General Electric. Multics aimed to provide a highly sophisticated and secure time-sharing system but faced challenges and ultimately did not achieve widespread adoption. However, it laid the groundwork for subsequent developments in the field.

The 1970s witnessed the birth of Unix, a landmark operating system that significantly shaped the computing landscape. Developed at Bell Labs by Ken Thompson, Dennis Ritchie, and others, Unix introduced a modular and portable design, written in the C programming language. Its simplicity, flexibility, and support for multitasking made Unix a popular choice for various applications. Unix also fostered the development of the C programming language, which further contributed to its widespread adoption.

Meanwhile, IBM responded to the challenges posed by OS/360 by introducing Virtual Machine/Conversational Monitor System (VM/CMS), a virtualization solution allowing multiple operating systems to run concurrently on a single mainframe. This innovation laid the groundwork for future developments in virtualization technology.

The late 1970s and early 1980s witnessed the emergence of personal computers, marking a shift from centralized mainframes to decentralized computing. Microsoft's MS-DOS (Microsoft Disk Operating System) became one of the first operating systems for IBM-compatible personal computers. Initially, MS-DOS lacked a graphical user interface (GUI) and relied on command-line interactions. Its success paved the way for Microsoft's dominance in the desktop operating system market.

Apple, on the other hand, introduced the Apple Macintosh in 1984, featuring the revolutionary graphical user interface. The Macintosh System Software provided a user-friendly environment with icons, windows, and menus, setting new standards for personal computing interfaces. This era marked the beginning of the graphical computing era, where user experience became a focal point of OS design.

In 1985, Microsoft released Windows 1.0, its first attempt at a graphical operating system. While not an immediate success, subsequent versions of Windows gradually improved, and Windows 3.0, released in 1990, achieved widespread popularity. Windows 3.0 introduced features like virtual memory and improved graphics, making it a viable platform for a wide range of applications.

The 1990s saw the rise of the Linux operating system, developed by Linus Torvalds. Built on Unix principles and released as open-source software, Linux gained popularity for its stability, security, and flexibility. Linux distributions, such as Red Hat and Debian, became prominent choices for server environments, challenging the dominance of proprietary Unix systems.

In the realm of mobile operating systems, the 1990s saw the development of Palm OS for personal digital assistants (PDAs) by Palm, Inc. Palm OS introduced a stylus-based interface and gained widespread popularity in the PDA market. However, it faced challenges with the advent of smartphones.

The 21st century witnessed a paradigm shift with the proliferation of smartphones. Apple's iOS and Google's Android emerged as the dominant mobile operating systems. iOS, introduced in 2007 with the first iPhone, emphasized a closed ecosystem and seamless user experience. Android, an open-source platform, offered flexibility and customization, becoming the operating system for a diverse range of devices beyond smartphones.

On the desktop front, Microsoft continued its dominance with Windows XP, Windows 7, and subsequently Windows 10. Windows XP, released in 2001, became a widely used operating system known for its stability, while Windows 7 introduced a more refined user interface and improved performance. Windows 10, introduced in 2015, marked a shift towards a more integrated and continuous update model.

The open-source movement gained momentum in the 21st century, with the Free Software Foundation releasing the GNU/Linux operating system, commonly referred to as just Linux. Linux distributions like Ubuntu, Fedora, and CentOS became popular choices for both desktop and server environments.

As cloud computing gained prominence, operating systems evolved to meet the demands of scalable and distributed architectures. Containerization technologies, led by Docker, allowed applications to run consistently across various environments, irrespective of the underlying operating system.

Looking to the future, the evolution of operating systems continues in tandem with emerging technologies. Artificial intelligence (AI) integration, security enhancements, and adaptability to edge computing and the Internet of Things (IoT) are shaping the next phase of operating system development. The journey from ENIAC to the current landscape reflects not only technological advancements but also the changing paradigms of user interaction, decentralization, and the relentless pursuit of efficiency in computing environments. As we navigate this ever-evolving landscape, operating systems remain at the core, orchestrating the complex dance between hardware and software, shaping the digital experiences of generations to come.

Understanding the purpose and significance

The purpose and significance of operating systems (OS) in the realm of modern computing are multifaceted, encompassing a vast array of functionalities that collectively form the backbone of digital interactions. At its essence, an operating system serves as the intermediary layer between the hardware components of a computer and the software applications that users interact with. This intermediary role is fundamental, aiming to provide a cohesive and standardized environment that abstracts the intricacies of hardware complexities, thereby facilitating an efficient and user-friendly computing experience.

Resource management stands out as one of the primary objectives of operating systems. In a computing environment where multiple processes and applications compete for limited resources, such as CPU time, memory, and storage, the OS plays a pivotal role in allocation and deallocation. By overseeing the distribution of these resources, the operating system ensures optimal utilization, preventing conflicts and bottlenecks that could otherwise impede the smooth functioning of the system. This orchestration of resources is not only crucial for maintaining system stability but also for enhancing overall performance and responsiveness.

Concurrently, the evolution of operating systems has seen the integration of sophisticated concurrency control mechanisms. In the early days of computing, the concept of multitasking emerged, allowing multiple processes to run concurrently. Operating systems, through their scheduling algorithms, manage the execution of these processes, providing the illusion of parallelism to users. This capability is especially significant in time-sharing systems, where multiple users can interact with the computer simultaneously, fostering a more interactive and responsive computing experience. The seamless coordination of these tasks is emblematic of the advanced capabilities of modern operating systems.

User interface provision is another paramount function of operating systems, contributing directly to the accessibility and usability of computing devices. Over the years, the evolution of user interfaces has transformed from command-line interactions to graphical user interfaces (GUIs), drastically enhancing the interaction between users and machines. The interface acts as a conduit through which users issue commands, launch applications, and manage files, serving as a crucial point of interaction with the digital realm. A well-designed user interface not only simplifies the user experience but also influences the adoption and acceptance of computing technologies.

File and data management represent an integral aspect of the operating system's purpose, organizing and overseeing the storage and retrieval of data. Operating systems implement file systems that structure data into files and directories, providing a systematic approach to data organization. This functionality facilitates efficient data manipulation for both users and applications, contributing to the seamless functioning of computing systems. The significance of this organizational capability becomes apparent in scenarios where vast amounts of data need to be stored, accessed, and managed.

Security, in the context of operating systems, assumes paramount importance in the contemporary digital landscape. Operating systems implement a myriad of security features, ranging from user authentication and access controls to encryption mechanisms. These measures are designed to safeguard the system against unauthorized access, malicious activities, and data breaches. As computing devices become increasingly interconnected, the role of operating systems in ensuring the confidentiality, integrity, and availability of data becomes more critical than ever. Security considerations permeate all levels of the operating system, reflecting its foundational role in maintaining the trustworthiness of digital interactions.

The bootstrapping process, a seemingly mundane but essential function of operating systems, initiates the system's operation. When a computer is powered on, the operating system is loaded into memory, configuring hardware components and preparing the system for user interaction. This seamless transition from hardware initialization to the execution of user applications is a testament to the operating system's role in orchestrating the startup sequence. While often overlooked, the bootstrapping process underscores the foundational significance of operating systems in bringing computing devices to life.

The adaptability of operating systems to diverse hardware architectures is a testament to their resilience and flexibility. From the early days of mainframes to the era of personal computers and the current landscape of mobile and embedded devices, operating systems have evolved to accommodate a wide range of computing environments. This adaptability is a key factor in their significance, providing a consistent and standardized platform that allows software developers to create applications capable of running on various hardware configurations. Operating systems thus serve as a unifying force in the ever-expanding landscape of computing technologies.

Beyond traditional computing devices, the significance of operating systems extends to embedded systems, which power an extensive array of electronic devices. These specialized operating systems cater to the specific requirements of devices ranging from smart appliances to industrial machinery. Embedded systems illustrate the versatility of operating systems, adapting to diverse application domains and playing a crucial role in the seamless functioning of myriad electronic devices.

In the realm of servers and data centers, operating systems are foundational to the delivery of services and the efficient utilization of resources. Server operating systems, such as Linux variants and Windows Server, provide the underlying infrastructure for hosting websites, running applications, and managing networked environments. The reliability, scalability, and performance of these server operating systems directly impact the success of businesses and organizations relying on these infrastructures for their digital operations.

The educational and research significance of operating systems is underscored by their role as learning tools. Studying operating systems provides valuable insights into computer architecture, system design, and software development. It serves as a foundational learning ground, offering students and researchers the opportunity to understand the intricacies of managing hardware resources, implementing security measures, and optimizing system performance. The educational significance lies in the transferable knowledge gained, applicable to various fields within the broader domain of computer science.

The advent of virtualization and containerization technologies has brought new dimensions to the role of operating systems. Virtualization enables multiple operating systems to run concurrently on a single physical machine, fostering resource isolation and efficient utilization. Containerization, exemplified by technologies like Docker, encapsulates applications and their dependencies, facilitating consistent deployment across different environments. These advancements contribute to the flexibility, scalability, and portability of computing infrastructures, expanding the horizons of what operating systems can achieve.

Looking ahead, the integration of artificial intelligence (AI) into operating systems heralds a new era. AI-driven features, such as predictive analysis, automated system maintenance, and adaptive resource allocation, promise to enhance the efficiency and user experience of operating systems. The evolving landscape of technology, marked by trends like edge computing, quantum computing, and sustainability initiatives, will undoubtedly shape the future trajectory of operating systems, driving further innovation and adaptation.

In conclusion, the purpose and significance of operating systems extend far beyond their seemingly technical role. They are the unsung heroes that mediate between users and hardware, ensuring a seamless and secure computing experience. From resource management to user interface provision, from security enforcement to adaptability across diverse environments, operating systems are the linchpin that weaves together the intricate tapestry of modern digital interactions. Their historical evolution mirrors the trajectory of technological advancements, and their continued relevance underscores their indispensable role in shaping the past, present, and future of computing environments.

Relationship between hardware and software

The relationship between hardware and software is the cornerstone of modern computing, representing the intricate interplay between the tangible, physical components of a computer system and the intangible, logical instructions that govern its operation. Hardware constitutes the physical machinery, encompassing the central processing unit (CPU), memory modules, storage devices, input/output peripherals, and the various interconnected components that collectively form a computer system. On the other hand, software represents the set of programs, applications, and instructions that enable the hardware to perform specific tasks, ranging from basic operations to complex computations and user interactions.

At its core, hardware provides the foundation upon which software operates. The CPU, often referred to as the brain of the computer, executes instructions fetched from memory, performing arithmetic and logical operations at a rapid pace. Memory modules, such as RAM (Random Access Memory), temporarily store data and instructions for quick access by the CPU. Storage devices, like hard drives or solid-state drives, house the operating system, applications, and user data persistently. Input devices, such as keyboards and mice, enable users to interact with the system, while output devices, including displays and printers, present information to users in a comprehensible manner.

The symbiotic relationship between hardware and software is evident in the bootstrapping process, where the computer is powered on, and the operating system is loaded into memory. During this initialization phase, hardware components are configured, and the system prepares to execute the first set of instructions. The operating system, a critical piece of software, serves as the intermediary that manages hardware resources, facilitates user interactions, and provides a platform for other software applications to run.

The hardware-software relationship becomes even more apparent when considering the layers of abstraction provided by operating systems. Operating systems abstract the complexities of hardware, presenting a uniform interface for software developers and users. This abstraction allows software to be written independently of the specific hardware details, enhancing portability and ease of development. Software applications interact with the operating system through defined interfaces, requesting resources and services without needing to understand the intricacies of underlying hardware components.

Programs and applications, collectively referred to as software, are written in high-level programming languages, providing an abstraction layer that shields developers from the low-level details of hardware architecture. The compiler or interpreter, another layer of software, translates these high-level instructions into machine code that the CPU can execute. This process of abstraction enables software developers to focus on creating functional and efficient applications without delving into the intricacies of hardware design.

The execution of software on hardware involves a dynamic interplay of various components. As a program runs, the CPU fetches instructions from memory, decodes them, and executes the corresponding operations. Data is manipulated and stored in memory locations, and input/output operations facilitate communication with external devices. This seamless interaction between hardware and software is orchestrated by the operating system, which manages the flow of instructions and data between different components.

One of the critical aspects of the hardware-software relationship is the concept of drivers. Drivers are software components that act as intermediaries between the operating system and specific hardware devices. They provide a standardized interface for the operating system to communicate with diverse hardware components, ensuring compatibility and enabling the seamless integration of new devices into a system. Drivers exemplify how software bridges the gap between the generalized instructions of an operating system and the specialized functionalities of individual hardware peripherals.

The versatility of modern computing is a testament to the adaptability of software to different hardware configurations. Software applications, whether they are word processors, graphics editors, or web browsers, can run on a variety of hardware platforms with minimal modifications. This cross-platform compatibility is achieved through standardization and the abstraction provided by operating systems, allowing software to be agnostic to the underlying hardware details. As a result, users can run the same software on different devices, from personal computers to smartphones and embedded systems.

The relationship between hardware and software is particularly evident in the context of embedded systems. Embedded systems are specialized computing devices embedded within larger systems, such as those found in automobiles, household appliances, and industrial machinery. The software running on these embedded systems is tailored to the specific functionalities of the hardware, emphasizing efficiency and reliability. The close integration of hardware and software in embedded systems highlights the need for a seamless collaboration between the two components to achieve optimal performance.

The concept of firmware further emphasizes the intersection of hardware and software. Firmware is a type of software that is embedded in hardware components, providing low-level control and functionality. It acts as a bridge between hardware and higher-level software, enabling the customization of specific hardware behaviors. Firmware is commonly found in devices like routers, printers, and graphics cards, where it plays a crucial role in ensuring the proper functioning and compatibility of hardware components.

The evolution of computing architectures, from mainframes to personal computers and now to cloud-based infrastructures, underscores the evolving nature of the hardware-software relationship. Cloud computing, characterized by the provisioning of computing resources over the internet, introduces new dynamics to this relationship. Users can access and deploy software applications without the need to own and maintain dedicated hardware. Cloud service providers manage the underlying hardware infrastructure, while users focus on developing and utilizing software solutions. This shift towards cloud-based computing exemplifies how the relationship between hardware and software continues to adapt to emerging paradigms in the digital landscape.

Security considerations are integral to the hardware-software relationship. Both hardware and software components play crucial roles in ensuring the security of a computing system. Hardware-based security features, such as Trusted Platform Modules (TPMs) and hardware encryption, provide a foundation for secure computing environments. Software-based security measures, implemented through operating systems and applications, include user authentication, access controls, and encryption algorithms. The collaboration between hardware and software is essential in creating robust security architectures that protect against threats and vulnerabilities.

Looking ahead, the future of computing will likely witness further integration of hardware and software to meet the demands of emerging technologies. The advent of quantum computing, for example, introduces a paradigm shift where hardware components operate based on the principles of quantum mechanics. Quantum software, designed to harness the unique capabilities of quantum hardware, will be pivotal in realizing the full potential of quantum computing. Similarly, advancements in artificial intelligence (AI) and machine learning are reshaping the hardware-software relationship, with specialized hardware accelerators designed to optimize the execution of AI algorithms.

In conclusion, the relationship between hardware and software is intrinsic to the functionality and versatility of modern computing systems. It is a dynamic interplay where hardware provides the physical foundation, and software provides the logical instructions that bring the system to life. From the bootstrapping process to the execution of complex software applications, the collaboration between hardware and software is evident at every level. This symbiotic relationship enables the seamless operation of diverse computing devices, from personal computers to embedded systems and cloud-based infrastructures. As technology continues to advance, the intricate dance between hardware and software will evolve, shaping the future landscape of computing innovations and experiences.

Processes, threads, and multitasking

Processes, threads, and multitasking constitute fundamental concepts in the realm of operating systems, embodying the mechanisms through which a computer system efficiently manages and executes tasks. At its core, a process represents the execution of a program, encapsulating the program's code, data, and system resources during its runtime. Processes provide isolation, ensuring that one process does not interfere with the memory or operations of another. The operating system, acting as the orchestrator, oversees the creation, scheduling, and termination of processes, maintaining system stability and responsiveness.

Within the context of a process, threads emerge as the next level of granularity. A thread, often referred to as a lightweight process, represents the smallest unit of execution within a process. Threads within the same process share the same code and data space but maintain separate execution contexts, including their own program counter and registers. Threads enable concurrent execution of tasks within a process, allowing for parallelism and efficient utilization of multi-core processors. The coordination and synchronization of threads are vital aspects, as they share resources and need mechanisms, such as locks and semaphores, to prevent conflicts and ensure data consistency.

Multitasking, a pivotal concept in operating systems, embodies the concurrent execution of multiple tasks or processes. This capability allows a computer system to appear as if it is performing several tasks simultaneously, enhancing user experience and system efficiency. In a multitasking environment, processes or threads share the CPU's execution time, interleaving their execution to give the illusion of simultaneous operation. Operating systems employ various scheduling algorithms to determine the order in which processes or threads are executed, optimizing for factors such as fairness, responsiveness, and overall system throughput.

The concept of processes, threads, and multitasking becomes more tangible when considering the evolution of computing paradigms. In the early days of computing, the concept of batch processing prevailed, where a sequence of jobs were executed sequentially without user interaction. The transition to time-sharing systems marked a paradigm shift, introducing the idea of multiple users interacting with the computer simultaneously. Processes were created for each user, and the operating system scheduled their execution, providing a more interactive and shared computing environment.

The advent of multitasking operating systems further refined the execution model, allowing a single user to run multiple applications concurrently. Each application, treated as a separate process, could execute independently, providing users with the ability to switch between tasks seamlessly. This evolution represented a leap in user experience, making computing more dynamic and responsive.

Threads emerged as a response to the growing need for more fine-grained control over concurrent execution within a process. Unlike processes, threads within the same process share the same resources, allowing for more efficient communication and coordination. This finer level of granularity became essential as applications became more complex, and the demand for parallelism increased.

The coordination and synchronization of threads within a process are critical for maintaining data integrity and preventing race conditions. Mutexes, semaphores, and other synchronization mechanisms became integral components in the development of concurrent and parallel applications. This shift towards multithreading reflected the industry's acknowledgment of the benefits of parallel execution in improving performance and responsiveness.

As computing systems evolved, the concept of multitasking expanded beyond personal computers to encompass servers, embedded systems, and mobile devices. Server operating systems embraced multitasking to efficiently handle diverse workloads, ranging from serving web pages to processing database queries concurrently. Embedded systems, found in devices like smartphones and IoT devices, leveraged multitasking to manage multiple tasks simultaneously, enhancing the overall user experience.

The significance of processes, threads, and multitasking is evident in contemporary computing scenarios. In desktop environments, users routinely run multiple applications concurrently, switching between them effortlessly. Operating systems employ sophisticated scheduling algorithms to allocate CPU time to processes or threads, ensuring a responsive and equitable user experience. The advent of virtualization technologies introduced another layer of multitasking, allowing multiple operating systems to run on the same physical hardware concurrently.

In the realm of server environments, multitasking is paramount for handling numerous requests simultaneously. Web servers, for example, must efficiently manage concurrent connections, serving web pages and processing user requests concurrently. The ability to handle multitasking efficiently is crucial for the scalability and responsiveness of server applications, especially in the context of cloud computing where the demand for resources fluctuates dynamically.

Multitasking plays a pivotal role in real-time operating systems (RTOS), where tasks must meet strict timing constraints. RTOSs prioritize tasks based on their urgency, ensuring that critical tasks are executed promptly. This level of determinism is crucial in applications such as industrial automation, aerospace systems, and medical devices where timing accuracy is paramount.

The impact of processes, threads, and multitasking is also evident in the field of parallel computing. High-performance computing clusters and supercomputers leverage parallelism to solve complex problems by breaking them down into smaller tasks that can be executed concurrently. Parallel programming models, such as MPI (Message Passing Interface) and OpenMP, enable developers to harness the power of multiple processors or cores, emphasizing the importance of concurrent execution.

Multitasking's role in the evolution of user interfaces is noteworthy. Graphical user interfaces (GUIs) in modern operating systems enable users to interact with multiple applications concurrently, fostering a seamless and intuitive user experience. Task-switching and window management functionalities allow users to navigate effortlessly through running applications, emphasizing the role of multitasking in shaping the way users interact with computers.

The relationship between processes, threads, and multitasking extends into the domain of mobile computing. Smartphones and tablets, powered by multitasking operating systems like iOS and Android, enable users to run diverse applications concurrently. The management of background processes and efficient task-switching contribute to the fluidity of user interactions, reflecting the significance of multitasking in the mobile computing landscape.

Challenges associated with multitasking include resource contention, where processes or threads compete for limited resources such as CPU time and memory. Operating systems must implement effective scheduling algorithms and resource management strategies to mitigate contention and ensure fair access. Additionally, the complexity of coordinating concurrent execution, especially in multi-threaded applications, introduces potential issues such as deadlocks and race conditions. Software developers must employ synchronization mechanisms judiciously to prevent these issues.

Looking to the future, the importance of processes, threads, and multitasking remains paramount as computing systems continue to evolve. Emerging technologies, including edge computing, quantum computing, and the integration of artificial intelligence, will undoubtedly influence the way multitasking is approached. Edge computing, with its emphasis on processing data closer to the source, demands efficient multitasking capabilities for handling diverse tasks across distributed environments. Quantum computing introduces a paradigm shift where traditional notions of multitasking may be redefined, opening new possibilities for parallelism at the quantum level.

In conclusion, processes, threads, and multitasking represent foundational concepts that have shaped the evolution of operating systems and computing paradigms. Processes encapsulate the execution of programs, threads provide a finer level of granularity for concurrent execution within a process, and multitasking enables the concurrent execution of multiple tasks. This dynamic interplay between hardware and software has propelled computing systems from batch processing to interactive and parallel computing environments. The ongoing significance of these concepts is evident in diverse computing scenarios, ranging from personal computers to servers, embedded systems, and emerging technologies. As we navigate the ever-evolving landscape of computing, the principles of processes, threads, and multitasking will continue to play a central role in shaping the efficiency, responsiveness, and scalability of computing systems.

Memory management and file systems

Memory management and file systems stand as integral components in the architecture of operating systems, collectively orchestrating the efficient utilization of resources and the organized storage and retrieval of data. Memory management is a foundational aspect, encompassing the allocation and deallocation of a computer's memory to ensure optimal performance and stability. In a computer system, memory is a finite resource, and effective memory management is essential for enabling processes and applications to run seamlessly without contention. The operating system plays a central role in overseeing memory management, employing techniques such as segmentation and paging to allocate memory space, manage the sharing of resources, and prevent conflicts among concurrently executing processes.

At its core, memory management involves the allocation of memory to processes, the tracking of utilized and free memory regions, and the release of memory once a process completes its execution. The operating system employs data structures like page tables to map logical addresses to physical addresses, facilitating the translation between virtual memory and actual RAM (Random Access Memory). Virtual memory allows processes to access a larger address space than the physical RAM available, mitigating the limitations of physical memory size and enhancing the overall system's flexibility. This dynamic allocation of memory ensures efficient use of resources and enables the execution of multiple processes concurrently.

Concurrency in memory management becomes a critical consideration in modern operating systems, as multiple processes share the same physical memory. Operating systems implement mechanisms such as memory protection and address space isolation to prevent one process from accessing or modifying the memory space of another. Memory protection features include read-only memory pages, preventing unintentional data modification, and executable code pages, safeguarding against unauthorized alterations to program instructions. These measures contribute to the security and stability of the system, ensuring that processes operate independently without interfering with each other.

Furthermore, the concept of virtual memory introduces the idea of swapping, where portions of a process's memory are temporarily moved to disk storage to free up physical RAM. This mechanism, known as paging, allows the operating system to handle more processes than the physical memory would otherwise accommodate. When a process needs data from a swapped-out page, it is brought back into physical memory, maintaining the illusion of a larger memory space for each process. Efficient algorithms for page replacement, such as Least Recently Used (LRU) or First-In-First-Out (FIFO), optimize the swapping process, minimizing the impact on system performance.

In the realm of file systems, the focus shifts to the organization, storage, and retrieval of data on persistent storage devices, such as hard drives or solid-state drives. File systems provide a structured and hierarchical approach to storing data, allowing users and applications to organize information into files and directories. The file system abstracts the complexities of underlying storage devices, presenting a unified interface for interacting with data. The operating system's file system components manage file creation, modification, deletion, and access permissions, ensuring data integrity and security.

One of the fundamental concepts in file systems is the directory structure, a hierarchical arrangement that organizes files into directories or folders. Directories provide a logical organization of files, making it easier for users to navigate and manage their data. The operating system maintains a file allocation table or an inode table, depending on the file system type, to keep track of the storage locations of files and their associated metadata. This organizational structure enhances the efficiency of data retrieval and storage, contributing to a more user-friendly and organized computing experience.

File systems employ various strategies for storing and retrieving data, such as block-level allocation and cluster allocation. These methods determine how data is organized into units, optimizing storage space and access speed. Additionally, file systems implement techniques like caching to enhance performance by storing frequently accessed data in memory for quicker retrieval. Caching reduces the need to access slower persistent storage devices, contributing to overall system responsiveness.

Security considerations play a crucial role in file systems, as they store sensitive user and system data. Access control mechanisms, including file permissions and ownership, ensure that only authorized users can read, write, or execute specific files. Encryption is another layer of security applied to file systems, protecting data from unauthorized access even if physical storage devices are compromised. File system journaling, a technique employed in modern file systems like ext4, enhances data integrity by recording changes before they are applied, reducing the risk of data corruption in the event of a system crash or power failure.

The concept of file systems extends beyond traditional desktop and server environments to encompass a diverse range of devices and platforms. Mobile operating systems, such as iOS and Android, incorporate file systems tailored to the unique requirements of smartphones and tablets. The design considerations for these file systems prioritize efficient storage utilization, quick data access, and seamless integration with mobile applications. Similarly, embedded systems employ specialized file systems optimized for specific use cases, such as those found in automotive systems, IoT devices, or industrial control systems.

In networked environments, file systems facilitate the sharing and collaboration of data across multiple computers. Network File Systems (NFS) and Common Internet File System (CIFS) enable users to access files remotely as if they were stored locally. These networked file systems contribute to the seamless exchange of data in distributed computing environments, supporting collaborative work and data sharing across geographically dispersed locations.

The evolution of file systems is closely tied to advancements in storage technology. Traditional file systems designed for hard disk drives (HDDs) face challenges when adapting to the characteristics of solid-state drives (SSDs). File systems optimized for SSDs leverage techniques like wear leveling and trim commands to enhance performance and longevity. As storage technologies continue to evolve, file systems will adapt to meet the demands of emerging storage devices, such as non-volatile memory (NVM) and future innovations.

The relationship between memory management and file systems becomes evident in scenarios where data must be efficiently moved between the volatile memory and persistent storage. Demand paging, a technique used in virtual memory systems, retrieves data from storage to memory only when it is needed, minimizing the initial loading time of programs. Caching mechanisms, employed by both memory management and file systems, contribute to optimized data access by storing frequently used data in memory. The collaboration between memory and file systems is essential for balancing the trade-offs between speed, capacity, and data consistency in computing environments.

Challenges in memory management and file systems include the need for balancing conflicting requirements, such as maximizing data access speed while minimizing storage space usage. Fragmentation, both in memory and on storage devices, poses challenges for efficient resource utilization. Operating systems must implement strategies to address fragmentation, whether through memory compaction or storage defragmentation techniques. Additionally, as the volume of data generated and processed continues to grow, scalability becomes a crucial consideration in both memory management and file systems, necessitating innovative solutions for handling massive datasets.

Looking forward, the future of memory management and file systems will likely be shaped by emerging technologies and paradigms. The advent of persistent memory technologies, blurring the distinction between volatile memory and storage, will influence how operating systems manage data. In-memory databases, which keep data primarily in RAM for faster access, represent a shift towards maximizing the utilization of volatile memory. Additionally, advancements in non-volatile memory technologies may lead to new approaches in file system design, enabling faster and more durable storage solutions.

In conclusion, memory management and file systems serve as cornerstones in the architecture of operating systems, providing the infrastructure for efficient resource utilization and organized data storage. Memory management orchestrates the allocation and deallocation of memory, ensuring optimal performance and preventing conflicts among concurrently executing processes. File systems organize and manage data on persistent storage devices, offering a structured approach to file and directory organization while addressing security and access control considerations. The collaboration between memory management and file systems contributes to the seamless functioning of modern computing environments, with implications for diverse applications ranging from traditional desktop computing to mobile devices, embedded systems, and networked environments. As technology continues to advance, memory management and file systems will adapt to meet the evolving demands of computing, storage, and data management.

Overview of various OS types (e.g., real-time, distributed)

The landscape of operating systems is diverse, reflecting the varied requirements and contexts in which computing systems operate. One categorization of operating systems revolves around their functionalities and purposes. Real-time operating systems (RTOS) stand as a specialized category designed to meet stringent timing constraints, ensuring timely and predictable responses to external events. In applications such as industrial automation, aerospace systems, and medical devices, where precise timing is crucial, real-time operating systems prioritize the execution of critical tasks within predetermined deadlines. These systems employ deterministic scheduling algorithms, ensuring that high-priority tasks receive immediate attention, making them well-suited for environments where the consequences of delays can be critical.

Distributed operating systems, on the other hand, focus on the coordination and management of multiple interconnected computing nodes. In distributed systems, computing resources are distributed across different machines that communicate and collaborate to achieve a common goal. This model is prevalent in cloud computing infrastructures, where data centers consist of a network of interconnected servers. Distributed operating systems facilitate resource sharing, load balancing, and fault tolerance, ensuring that tasks can seamlessly transition between nodes without disrupting overall system functionality. The emphasis on scalability and reliability makes distributed operating systems suitable for the dynamic and interconnected nature of modern computing environments.

Network operating systems form another category, emphasizing communication and coordination in networked environments. These systems facilitate the sharing of resources and data among interconnected computers. Network operating systems often include file sharing, printer sharing, and user authentication mechanisms, enabling users to access resources across the network as if they were local. In business and enterprise settings, network operating systems play a crucial role in managing shared resources, supporting collaborative work, and providing centralized control over networked assets.

Mobile operating systems cater specifically to the unique requirements of mobile devices such as smartphones and tablets. These systems prioritize energy efficiency, responsiveness, and support for a diverse range of applications tailored for mobile use. Prominent examples include iOS and Android, which dominate the mobile operating system market. Mobile operating systems incorporate features like touch-based interfaces, location-based services, and app ecosystems to enhance user experiences in a mobile context. The emphasis on portability and user interaction distinguishes mobile operating systems from their desktop counterparts.

Embedded operating systems find application in a myriad of devices beyond traditional computers, ranging from household appliances and automotive systems to industrial machinery and medical devices. These specialized operating systems are designed to meet the specific requirements of embedded systems, often characterized by resource constraints and real-time demands. Embedded operating systems prioritize reliability, stability, and efficiency, tailoring their functionalities to the unique needs of the devices they power. The prevalence of embedded systems in various aspects of daily life underscores the significance of these operating systems in enabling the functionality of electronic devices.

General-purpose operating systems, such as Windows, macOS, and various Linux distributions, serve as versatile platforms that cater to a wide range of computing needs. These operating systems are designed to support a diverse array of applications and hardware configurations, providing a comprehensive set of features for both personal and professional use. General-purpose operating systems offer graphical user interfaces, support for multitasking, and extensive driver compatibility, making them suitable for desktops, laptops, and servers. The widespread adoption of general-purpose operating systems has contributed to the democratization of computing, enabling users to perform a myriad of tasks with ease.

Time-sharing operating systems represent a paradigm where multiple users share access to a single computing system concurrently. This model, rooted in the early days of computing, evolved to support interactive and shared computing experiences. Time-sharing systems divide the CPU's processing time among multiple users, allowing them to interact with the system in a seemingly simultaneous manner. This approach fosters efficient resource utilization and user interactivity, forming the basis for the development of modern multitasking operating systems. The principles of time-sharing continue to influence contemporary operating systems, contributing to the dynamic and interactive nature of computing environments.

Real-time, distributed, network, mobile, embedded, and general-purpose operating systems collectively form a spectrum of functionalities, each tailored to specific computing contexts and requirements. The evolution of these operating systems has been shaped by technological advancements, changing user needs, and the expanding landscape of computing applications. As computing continues to evolve, operating systems will likely adapt to meet the demands of emerging technologies, ensuring that they remain at the forefront of enabling efficient, secure, and user-friendly computing experiences across diverse domains.

Pros and cons of different systems

Various operating systems have distinct strengths and weaknesses, and understanding the pros and cons of each can aid in selecting the most suitable system for specific use cases. Beginning with Windows, Microsoft's operating system, it stands out for its widespread adoption, user-friendly interface, and extensive compatibility with software and hardware. The graphical user interface (GUI) is intuitive, making it accessible for users with varying levels of technical expertise. However, Windows has faced criticism for its susceptibility to malware and viruses, requiring users to invest in additional security measures. Additionally, the licensing cost associated with Windows can be a deterrent, particularly for budget-conscious users and organizations.

In the realm of macOS, Apple's operating system, the seamless integration with Apple hardware and emphasis on design and user experience are noteworthy advantages. macOS offers a Unix-based foundation, appealing to developers, and the operating system is known for its stability and reliability. However, the proprietary nature of macOS limits hardware choices to Apple products, and the cost of these devices tends to be higher than that of their Windows counterparts. Software compatibility can also be a consideration, as some applications may be exclusive to Windows or have limited support on macOS.

Linux, with its diverse range of distributions (distros), is celebrated for its open-source nature, robust security features, and flexibility. Linux is commonly used in server environments, owing to its stability and efficiency, and it powers many of the world's supercomputers. The vast array of available distros allows users to choose an operating system tailored to their preferences and requirements. However, Linux can pose challenges for those accustomed to graphical interfaces, as certain distributions rely heavily on the command line. Software compatibility, particularly for proprietary applications, can also be a concern in the Linux ecosystem.

Real-time operating systems (RTOS) excel in applications where precise timing is critical, such as industrial automation and medical devices. RTOS offers deterministic response times, ensuring that tasks are executed within predefined deadlines. The ability to handle tasks with high precision makes RTOS indispensable in scenarios where the consequences of delays can be severe. However, the specialized nature of RTOS limits its applicability to specific domains, and the complexity of real-time systems may require specialized knowledge for development and maintenance.

Distributed operating systems, designed for environments with multiple interconnected computers, offer advantages in terms of scalability, fault tolerance, and resource sharing. These systems enable efficient load balancing and can continue to operate even if some nodes fail. However, the complexity of managing distributed resources and ensuring consistency across multiple nodes poses challenges. Communication latency and potential network failures are additional concerns that must be addressed in distributed operating systems.

Network operating systems, emphasizing resource sharing and collaboration in networked environments, simplify the management of shared resources such as files and printers. These systems facilitate centralized control and user authentication, enhancing security and access control in networked settings. Nevertheless, network operating systems may face challenges related to scalability and can be dependent on network stability for optimal performance.

Mobile operating systems, exemplified by iOS and Android, are tailored for smartphones and tablets, offering intuitive touch-based interfaces, app ecosystems, and energy-efficient design. These systems prioritize responsiveness and portability, contributing to the widespread adoption of mobile devices. However, the closed ecosystems of iOS and Android can limit customization options for users, and app availability may vary between platforms. Security concerns, particularly in the Android ecosystem, have also been a point of discussion.

Embedded operating systems play a crucial role in devices beyond traditional computers, such as household appliances, automotive systems, and medical devices. These systems are designed to operate with minimal resources, ensuring efficiency and reliability in resource-constrained environments. The challenges lie in the diversity of embedded systems, each with unique requirements, and the need for specialized knowledge in developing and maintaining embedded operating systems.

General-purpose operating systems, like Windows, macOS, and various Linux distributions, offer versatility and widespread applicability. They cater to a broad range of computing needs, providing support for a diverse array of applications and hardware configurations. The user-friendly interfaces and extensive software compatibility contribute to their popularity. However, the generality of these operating systems can result in resource inefficiencies, as they may include features that are not relevant to specific use cases.

Time-sharing operating systems, rooted in the concept of allowing multiple users to share access to a single computing system concurrently, contribute to efficient resource utilization and user interactivity. These systems, which divide CPU processing time among multiple users, have evolved to form the basis for modern multitasking operating systems. The advantages include improved user interactivity and dynamic resource allocation. However, the potential for contention over shared resources and challenges in maintaining fairness and responsiveness are considerations in time-sharing systems.

In conclusion, the diverse landscape of operating systems presents a multitude of choices, each with its own set of advantages and drawbacks. Selecting the most suitable operating system depends on factors such as the intended use case, user preferences, hardware requirements, and considerations for security and stability. The ongoing evolution of technology ensures that operating systems will continue to adapt and innovate, addressing emerging challenges and catering to the ever-changing landscape of computing needs.

Analysis of successful operating systems (e.g., UNIX, Windows, Linux)

Operating systems serve as the backbone of computing, and the success of certain systems, such as UNIX, Windows, and Linux, can be attributed to a combination of historical context, design principles, adaptability, and community support. UNIX, born out of Bell Labs in the late 1960s, set the stage for many modern operating systems. Its design philosophy, emphasizing simplicity, modularity, and the notion that "everything is a file," has influenced a wide array of subsequent operating systems. UNIX introduced the concept of a multi-user, multi-tasking environment, enabling concurrent execution of processes and efficient resource utilization. The portability of UNIX across different hardware architectures played a crucial role in its widespread adoption, making it a foundational operating system for servers and workstations.

Windows, developed by Microsoft, rose to prominence with the advent of personal computing in the 1980s. The success of Windows can be attributed to its user-friendly graphical interface, making computing accessible to a broader audience. The Windows operating system became synonymous with desktop computing, powering a vast majority of personal computers globally. Microsoft's focus on software compatibility and a comprehensive suite of applications, along with strategic partnerships with hardware manufacturers, contributed to Windows becoming the dominant force in the desktop operating system market. The iterative development approach and regular release cycles have kept Windows relevant and adaptable to evolving technological landscapes.

Linux, emerging in the early 1990s as an open-source Unix-like operating system kernel, represents a paradigm of collaborative development and community-driven innovation. The success of Linux can be traced to its inherent openness, flexibility, and the contributions of a global community of developers. The Linux kernel serves as the foundation for numerous distributions (distros), each catering to specific use cases and user preferences. The adoption of Linux in diverse environments, from servers to embedded systems and mobile devices, showcases its versatility. The strong emphasis on security, stability, and the ability to customize every aspect of the system has made Linux a preferred choice for developers, enterprises, and enthusiasts alike.

The success of these operating systems can be analyzed through various lenses. In terms of architecture and design, UNIX's pioneering concepts, such as a hierarchical file system, shell scripting, and the client-server model, have become integral parts of modern computing. UNIX's influence extends to the development of POSIX standards, fostering compatibility across various Unix-like systems. On the other hand, Windows introduced innovations like the Windows Registry, a centralized configuration database, and the Windows API, providing developers with a standardized way to create software for the platform. The familiarity of the Windows graphical user interface (GUI) and the integration of multimedia capabilities further contributed to its popularity.

Linux, rooted in the principles of open source and collaborative development, embodies a different model. The transparent nature of its source code allows users and developers to inspect, modify, and distribute the code freely. The adoption of the General Public License (GPL) ensures that derivative works remain open source, fostering a culture of collaboration and sharing. The Linux development model relies on a decentralized network of contributors, with Linus Torvalds leading the kernel development. This distributed approach has proven effective in rapidly responding to emerging technologies and ensuring the continuous improvement of the Linux kernel.

In terms of user experience, Windows has consistently prioritized ease of use. The evolution from the command-line interfaces of early versions to the visually intuitive Windows GUI marked a significant shift in user interaction. The Windows Start menu, taskbar, and the point-and-click paradigm made computing more accessible to a wider audience. The seamless integration of hardware drivers and the Plug and Play (PnP) system simplified the installation of peripherals. Microsoft's commitment to backward compatibility, allowing older software to run on newer versions of Windows, has contributed to the platform's longevity.

UNIX, with its command-line interface and focus on scripting, initially targeted a more technical user base. However, this has evolved with the development of user-friendly Unix-like operating systems, such as macOS, which incorporates a Unix-based foundation beneath its graphical interface. The macOS GUI, inspired by the principles of simplicity and aesthetics, caters to both technical and non-technical users. The success of macOS lies in its ability to offer Unix power alongside a polished user experience, appealing to creative professionals and developers.

Linux, known for its versatility, can be tailored to a broad spectrum of user preferences. Linux desktop environments, such as GNOME, KDE, and XFCE, offer diverse user interfaces, catering to both traditional desktop users and those seeking a more minimalistic experience. The plethora of Linux distributions allows users to choose a system aligned with their specific needs, whether it be for desktop use, server deployment, or embedded systems. The command-line interface in Linux remains powerful for advanced users and administrators, providing granular control over system configurations.

From a deployment perspective, UNIX has entrenched itself in server environments, particularly in the form of various Linux distributions. The stability, security features, and robust networking capabilities make Linux a preferred choice for server deployments across the globe. The concept of virtualization, containerization, and cloud computing align well with the modular and scalable nature of Unix-like operating systems. Linux powers a significant portion of web servers, data centers, and cloud infrastructure, attesting to its reliability in demanding server environments.

Windows, synonymous with desktop computing, has also established a strong presence in enterprise server environments. Microsoft's Windows Server operating system provides a suite of tools and services for managing network infrastructure, directory services, and application deployment. The integration of Windows Server with Active Directory has been instrumental in simplifying user authentication, access control, and group policy management in enterprise settings. The Windows ecosystem extends to cloud services, with Azure offering a comprehensive platform for hosting applications and services.

Linux, in addition to dominating server deployments, has made significant inroads into embedded systems, networking devices, and mobile devices. The lightweight nature of Linux and its adaptability to diverse architectures make it suitable for resource-constrained environments. Android, based on the Linux kernel, has become the dominant operating system for mobile devices, powering the majority of smartphones globally. The embedded Linux ecosystem supports a myriad of devices, from smart appliances to IoT devices, showcasing its flexibility in catering to the evolving landscape of connected devices.

The community aspect plays a pivotal role in the success of these operating systems. UNIX, with its roots in academic and research institutions, fostered a collaborative culture that transcended organizational boundaries. This culture influenced subsequent Unix-like systems, including Linux. The Linux community, comprised of developers, enthusiasts, and organizations, actively contributes to the development and support of the kernel and associated software. This decentralized, global collaboration ensures a continuous cycle of innovation, security updates, and improvements.

Windows, being a proprietary system, relies on a different model of community engagement. Microsoft maintains tight control over the development of Windows, but user feedback and beta testing play roles in shaping the direction of the operating system. The Windows Insider Program allows users to preview upcoming features and provide feedback, creating a degree of community involvement. Additionally, Microsoft collaborates with third-party developers to ensure software compatibility and foster a thriving ecosystem of applications.

In conclusion, the success of UNIX, Windows, and Linux can be attributed to a combination of historical significance, design principles, adaptability, and community support. UNIX, with its pioneering concepts and influence on subsequent systems, laid the groundwork for modern computing. Windows, with its emphasis on user-friendly interfaces and broad software compatibility, became synonymous with desktop computing. Linux, driven by the principles of open source and collaboration, emerged as a versatile and widely adopted platform. Each operating system has carved its niche in the computing landscape, addressing different needs and preferences. As technology continues to evolve, these operating systems will undoubtedly adapt to meet the challenges and opportunities of the ever-changing digital ecosystem.

Lessons learned from historical developments

Historical developments in various domains, whether technological, social, or political, offer valuable lessons that shape our understanding of the present and guide us into the future. In the realm of technology, the evolution of computing provides insights into the transformative power of innovation. The transition from mainframes to personal computers marked a shift in accessibility and empowerment, highlighting the importance of democratizing technology. Lessons from this development emphasize the significance of user-centric design and the potential for small, accessible devices to revolutionize industries and empower individuals.

The advent of the internet and the subsequent rise of the World Wide Web exemplify the transformative impact of interconnected networks. The lessons learned from this historical development underscore the importance of connectivity, information sharing, and collaboration. The internet has become a global infrastructure, transcending geographical boundaries and fostering a digital ecosystem where information flows freely. However, challenges related to privacy, security, and digital divides remind us to approach connectivity with a mindful and inclusive perspective, ensuring that the benefits are equitably distributed.

The history of telecommunications, from the invention of the telegraph to the proliferation of smartphones, teaches us about the relentless pursuit of faster and more efficient communication. The lessons learned include the importance of interoperability, standards, and the continual quest for technological advancements to meet growing demands. Additionally, the convergence of communication technologies highlights the need for holistic approaches that integrate diverse forms of communication into unified and seamless experiences.

The development of transportation systems throughout history provides lessons in the interconnectedness of societies and economies. From the construction of railways to the invention of automobiles and airplanes, the lessons learned emphasize the role of transportation in shaping landscapes, economies, and cultural exchanges. However, the environmental impact of certain transportation technologies serves as a reminder of the need for sustainable and eco-friendly solutions in future developments.

In the field of medicine, the historical development of vaccines and antibiotics underscores the transformative power of scientific innovation in combating diseases. Lessons learned from breakthroughs like the eradication of smallpox and the discovery of penicillin highlight the importance of research, collaboration, and public health initiatives. However, challenges such as antibiotic resistance and global health disparities necessitate ongoing efforts to address emerging health threats and ensure equitable access to healthcare solutions.

Historical lessons from political developments, including revolutions, wars, and the struggle for civil rights, emphasize the enduring quest for justice, equality, and human rights. The struggles against colonialism, apartheid, and totalitarian regimes highlight the resilience of human spirit and the potential for collective action to bring about positive change. However, these lessons also underscore the ongoing challenges in achieving lasting social justice, as systemic inequalities persist in various forms across the globe.

Environmental history teaches us about the intricate relationship between human activities and the natural world. From industrial revolutions to environmental conservation movements, historical developments underscore the consequences of unsustainable practices and the imperative for ecological stewardship. Lessons learned include the importance of balancing human needs with environmental preservation, adopting sustainable technologies, and fostering a global commitment to address climate change.

The evolution of space exploration provides profound lessons in human ambition, scientific curiosity, and international collaboration. The historical achievements of reaching the moon, launching space probes, and establishing space stations highlight the boundless potential of human ingenuity. Lessons learned from space exploration include the need for international cooperation in addressing shared challenges, pushing the boundaries of knowledge, and inspiring future generations to explore new frontiers.

Economic history, shaped by industrial revolutions, market dynamics, and globalization, provides lessons on the interconnectedness of economies and the transformative power of technological advancements. The lessons learned include the importance of adaptability, innovation, and ethical considerations in economic development. The challenges of income inequality, economic recessions, and financial crises underscore the need for responsible economic policies that prioritize inclusivity and long-term sustainability.

The history of social movements, from the fight for women's suffrage to the civil rights movement and LGBTQ+ rights activism, offers lessons in resilience, solidarity, and the power of grassroots organizing. These historical developments highlight the impact of collective voices in challenging oppressive systems and advancing social progress. Lessons learned include the ongoing need for advocacy, education, and intersectional approaches to address systemic injustices and promote inclusivity.

The lessons from historical developments in education underscore the transformative power of knowledge dissemination and the evolution of teaching methodologies. From the establishment of formal educational institutions to the advent of online learning, historical developments emphasize the importance of adapting educational systems to the changing needs of societies. Lessons include the role of education in fostering critical thinking, cultural awareness, and lifelong learning, as well as addressing disparities in access to quality education.

The history of technological revolutions, from the industrial age to the digital era, teaches us about the inevitability of change and the need for adaptability. Lessons learned include the importance of embracing technological advancements while mitigating potential negative impacts on employment, privacy, and social dynamics. The ethical considerations in the development and deployment of technologies, such as artificial intelligence and biotechnology, underscore the need for responsible innovation that prioritizes ethical frameworks and human well-being.

In conclusion, the lessons learned from historical developments span a diverse array of domains, providing insights into the complexities of human progress and the challenges that accompany it. These lessons underscore the importance of adaptability, ethical considerations, collaboration, and a holistic understanding of the interconnectedness of various facets of human existence. As we navigate the present and shape the future, drawing upon the wisdom embedded in historical narratives becomes essential for informed decision-making and building a more equitable, sustainable, and inclusive world.

Chapter 2: Blueprinting Brilliance: Design Principles and Strategies

Overview of key design considerations

Key design considerations span a multitude of disciplines, encompassing fields such as architecture, product design, software development, and user experience. In architecture, one of the pivotal considerations is functionality, ensuring that the designed space or structure serves its intended purpose efficiently. Beyond functionality, aesthetics play a crucial role, as the design should harmonize with its surroundings and evoke a sense of beauty. Sustainability is increasingly becoming a paramount consideration, pushing designers to integrate eco-friendly materials and energy-efficient solutions. Accessibility is another fundamental aspect, emphasizing inclusivity and ensuring that spaces and structures are usable by people of diverse abilities.

In product design, considerations begin with defining the purpose and target audience of the product. The user-centered design approach prioritizes understanding user needs, behaviors, and preferences to create products that seamlessly integrate into users' lives. Ergonomics, or the study of how humans interact with products, guides the design of products that are comfortable, efficient, and safe to use. Material selection is a critical consideration, influencing both the product's functionality and its environmental impact. The product life cycle, from manufacturing to disposal, prompts designers to adopt sustainable practices and consider the end-of-life implications of their creations.

Software development involves a unique set of design considerations, starting with defining clear and achievable goals for the software application. User experience (UX) design focuses on creating interfaces and interactions that are intuitive, enjoyable, and efficient for users. Accessibility in software design extends the usability of applications to individuals with diverse abilities. Scalability is a crucial consideration, ensuring that software systems can handle increased loads and adapt to growing user bases. Security is another paramount concern, necessitating the implementation of measures to protect user data and the integrity of the software.

In the realm of user experience (UX) and user interface (UI) design, considerations revolve around creating seamless and meaningful interactions between users and digital interfaces. Usability is foundational, ensuring that users can easily navigate and accomplish tasks within the interface. Visual design principles, including color schemes, typography, and layout, contribute to the overall aesthetic appeal and brand identity. Consistency across the user interface enhances user familiarity and contributes to a cohesive user experience. Responsiveness, or the adaptability of the interface across different devices and screen sizes, is a key consideration in a multi-platform digital landscape.

Environmental design, encompassing landscapes, urban planning, and interior spaces, involves considerations that shape the human experience within built environments. Biophilic design integrates natural elements into spaces, fostering a connection with nature and promoting well-being. Wayfinding design focuses on creating intuitive navigation systems within spaces, ensuring that individuals can easily orient themselves and navigate the environment. Sustainability is a pervasive consideration, guiding designers to minimize environmental impact, utilize renewable resources, and design spaces that promote energy efficiency.

In the field of graphic design, considerations extend beyond aesthetics to effective communication. Typography plays a vital role in conveying information, evoking emotions, and establishing visual hierarchy. Color theory guides designers in selecting colors that align with the intended message and resonate with the target audience. Composition and layout considerations influence the visual flow of design elements, ensuring clarity and balance in the overall design. Branding considerations emphasize the creation of visual identities that reflect the essence and values of organizations or products.

In the context of industrial design, considerations encompass the entire lifecycle of a product, from conceptualization to production and eventual disposal. Form and function must be in harmony, with the aesthetic design complementing the product's intended use. Materials and manufacturing processes play a critical role, influencing not only the product's quality and durability but also its environmental footprint. Ergonomics is integral, ensuring that the product is comfortable, safe, and efficient for users. Prototyping and testing contribute to refining designs and addressing potential issues before mass production.

In fashion design, considerations start with conceptualizing collections that resonate with target demographics and align with brand identities. Textile selection influences not only the aesthetic appeal but also the comfort and sustainability of garments. Pattern making and garment construction considerations are essential for creating clothing that fits well and moves with the body. Sustainability in fashion design is gaining prominence, prompting designers to explore eco-friendly materials, ethical production practices, and circular fashion concepts that minimize waste.

In web design, considerations revolve around creating digital experiences that are both visually appealing and highly functional. Responsive design ensures that websites adapt seamlessly to different screen sizes and devices. Navigation design guides users through the website intuitively, while information architecture organizes content for easy access. Performance optimization is crucial for quick loading times, enhancing user satisfaction. Accessibility considerations ensure that websites are usable by individuals with diverse abilities, promoting inclusivity in the digital space.

Considerations in the field of vehicle design encompass a wide range of factors, starting with defining the vehicle's purpose and target market. Ergonomics play a pivotal role in designing comfortable and safe interiors that cater to the needs of drivers and passengers. Aerodynamics and fuel efficiency considerations influence the overall vehicle design to enhance performance and reduce environmental impact. Materials selection and manufacturing processes impact both the vehicle's safety and its ecological footprint. Human-machine interface (HMI) considerations guide the design of intuitive and distraction-free controls for a seamless driving experience.

In conclusion, key design considerations are integral to the success of creations across diverse disciplines. Whether in architecture, product design, software development, user experience, environmental design, graphic design, industrial design, fashion design, or web design, these considerations shape the form, function, and impact of the designed outcome. From user-centric principles and sustainability to aesthetics, accessibility, and beyond, the lessons learned from historical and contemporary design efforts underscore the need for a holistic and thoughtful approach that prioritizes the well-being of users, the environment, and society at large.

Balancing flexibility and efficiency

Balancing flexibility and efficiency represents a nuanced challenge across various domains, requiring a thoughtful approach to optimize outcomes while adapting to dynamic circumstances. In organizational management, achieving an equilibrium between flexibility and efficiency is crucial for navigating unpredictable business environments. A highly efficient organization may prioritize streamlined processes and rigid structures, aiming for consistency and cost-effectiveness. However, in rapidly changing markets or industries, an excessive focus on efficiency may lead to inflexibility, hindering the organization's ability to adapt to new opportunities or challenges. Striking the right balance involves fostering a culture that values adaptability, encourages innovation, and embraces change, allowing the organization to remain efficient while remaining responsive to evolving conditions.

In manufacturing and production, the tension between flexibility and efficiency manifests in the choice of production systems. Traditional mass production lines emphasize efficiency through standardized processes, economies of scale, and specialized machinery. However, such systems may lack the agility needed to accommodate frequent product changes or customization. Flexible manufacturing systems, on the other hand, prioritize adaptability by allowing rapid reconfiguration of production lines to accommodate diverse products. Balancing flexibility and efficiency in manufacturing entails selecting the most suitable production model based on factors like market demand, product variability, and the need for quick adaptation to changes in consumer preferences.

In technology development, particularly in software engineering, the dichotomy between flexibility and efficiency plays a central role. Efficient coding practices often prioritize optimized performance, reduced resource usage, and streamlined execution. However, an overly rigid, highly efficient codebase may struggle to accommodate future updates, changes in requirements, or emerging technologies. Agile development methodologies, emphasizing flexibility, iterative cycles, and collaboration, offer an alternative by fostering adaptability to evolving project needs. Striking a balance involves adopting practices like modular design and code refactoring to maintain efficiency while ensuring the flexibility to respond to changing project dynamics.

Within the context of project management, the challenge lies in optimizing project timelines, resource utilization, and adaptability. A rigid, highly efficient project management approach may prioritize strict adherence to timelines and resource budgets but could struggle to accommodate unforeseen changes or shifts in project priorities. Agile project management methodologies, with their focus on flexibility, iterative development, and customer feedback, offer a more adaptive approach. Achieving a balance involves integrating agile principles with structured project planning, ensuring that efficiency goals are not compromised while allowing for necessary adjustments in response to changing project requirements.

In educational systems, the interplay between flexibility and efficiency is evident in curriculum design and teaching methodologies. A highly efficient educational system might prioritize standardized curricula, assessments, and teaching methods to optimize resource allocation and ensure consistent learning outcomes. However, such systems may struggle to accommodate diverse learning styles, individual needs, or emerging educational trends. Flexible educational approaches, such as personalized learning, project-based learning, and adaptive curriculum design, aim to cater to individual student needs and foster critical thinking. Achieving a balance involves integrating flexible teaching methods within a framework that ensures efficiency in delivering quality education to a diverse student population.

In healthcare systems, the challenge is to deliver efficient and effective care while remaining adaptable to evolving medical knowledge, patient needs, and technological advancements. Traditional healthcare models may emphasize efficiency through standardized procedures and protocols, aiming to maximize patient throughput and minimize costs. However, such models may face challenges in addressing the diverse and evolving health needs of individuals. Patient-centered and flexible healthcare models, such as telemedicine, personalized medicine, and collaborative care, seek to enhance adaptability and responsiveness to individual patient requirements. Striking a balance involves integrating flexible approaches within healthcare systems to ensure efficient and patient-centric care delivery.

The dichotomy between flexibility and efficiency is particularly pronounced in supply chain management. Efficient supply chain models prioritize cost reduction, timely delivery, and inventory optimization through standardized processes. However, rigid supply chains may struggle to adapt to sudden changes in demand, supply disruptions, or shifts in market dynamics. Flexible supply chain strategies, such as just-in-time inventory management and agile supply chain networks, aim to enhance responsiveness and adaptability. Achieving a balance involves designing supply chain frameworks that maintain efficiency while incorporating flexibility to anticipate and navigate unforeseen disruptions.

In urban planning and infrastructure development, balancing flexibility and efficiency is critical for creating sustainable, resilient, and livable cities. Efficient urban planning may focus on standardized zoning, transportation networks, and resource allocation for optimized functionality. However, overly rigid urban designs may hinder adaptation to evolving population dynamics, technological advancements, or changing environmental conditions. Flexible urban planning approaches, embracing concepts like mixed-use development, smart infrastructure, and adaptable public spaces, aim to create resilient cities that can evolve with the needs of their inhabitants. Achieving a balance involves integrating efficiency principles within urban planning frameworks that prioritize adaptability and sustainability.

In the context of personal and professional development, individuals often grapple with finding the right balance between a structured, efficient approach and the need for flexibility to navigate unexpected opportunities or challenges. A highly regimented, efficient daily routine may lead to productivity but could stifle creativity or limit the ability to seize unforeseen opportunities. On the other hand, a purely flexible approach without structure may result in inefficiency and a lack of progress toward long-term goals. Achieving a balance involves creating a personalized approach that incorporates efficient habits and routines while remaining open to adapting plans based on changing circumstances and personal growth aspirations.

Environmental conservation presents a unique arena where balancing flexibility and efficiency is essential for addressing complex ecological challenges. Highly efficient industrial processes may prioritize resource extraction and production optimization but could lead to environmental degradation and depletion. Flexible and sustainable practices, such as circular economy models, conservation-focused policies, and renewable energy initiatives, aim to mitigate environmental impact and adapt to changing ecological conditions. Striking a balance involves transitioning towards efficient, eco-friendly practices while maintaining the flexibility to adjust strategies based on emerging environmental concerns and scientific insights.

In the context of international relations and diplomacy, achieving a balance between flexibility and efficiency is essential for addressing global challenges, fostering cooperation, and responding to geopolitical shifts. Rigid, highly efficient diplomatic approaches may struggle to adapt to evolving international dynamics or emerging issues that demand nimble responses. Flexible diplomatic strategies, such as multilateral cooperation, diplomatic dialogue, and adaptive alliances, aim to enhance responsiveness and collaboration on global issues. Balancing flexibility and efficiency in international relations involves navigating the complexities of geopolitical landscapes while ensuring effective and adaptable diplomatic engagements.

In conclusion, the interplay between flexibility and efficiency is a multifaceted consideration that permeates diverse aspects of human endeavors. Whether in organizational management, manufacturing, technology development, project management, education, healthcare, supply chain management, urban planning, personal development, environmental conservation, or international relations, finding the right equilibrium is pivotal for success. The dynamic nature of contemporary challenges demands an integrative approach that harnesses the benefits of efficiency while embracing the adaptability offered by flexibility. Striking this balance requires a nuanced understanding of the specific contexts, goals, and stakeholders involved, ensuring that the outcomes are not only optimized for efficiency but also resilient in the face of change and uncertainty.

Graphical vs. command-line interfaces

The choice between graphical user interfaces (GUIs) and command-line interfaces (CLIs) represents a fundamental decision in the design and user experience of computer systems, each offering distinct advantages and trade-offs. Graphical user interfaces, characterized by visual elements such as icons, windows, and buttons, provide an intuitive and user-friendly way for individuals to interact with computers. GUIs simplify complex tasks by offering a visual representation of system functions and applications, making computing accessible to a broader audience. The graphical nature of these interfaces enables users to perform tasks through direct manipulation, reducing the need to memorize command syntax and facilitating a more visually guided interaction. Icons and images serve as recognizable representations of actions, enhancing usability for individuals less familiar with command-line syntax or those seeking a more visually intuitive experience.

Command-line interfaces, in contrast, rely on text-based input and output, requiring users to input commands through a keyboard. This approach, rooted in the early days of computing, provides a powerful and efficient means of interacting with a system, especially for users with technical expertise. CLIs allow for precise control and scripting, enabling automation of repetitive tasks and complex operations. The lack of graphical overhead in a CLI often results in faster execution of commands and reduced system resource usage. Furthermore, CLIs are inherently scriptable, fostering the development of scripts and batch files that can execute sequences of commands, enhancing efficiency for experienced users who are comfortable with text-based interactions.

The choice between GUIs and CLIs often hinges on the target audience and the nature of the tasks involved. GUIs excel in scenarios where visual representation aids understanding and where users may not possess technical expertise. Operating systems like Windows and macOS prominently feature GUIs, providing users with a familiar environment characterized by desktop icons, taskbars, and visually intuitive applications. GUIs are prevalent in applications such as word processors, graphic design tools, and web browsers, where visual elements enhance user interaction and simplify complex operations.

On the other hand, CLIs find a natural home in environments where precision, automation, and resource efficiency are paramount. Many server environments, particularly those running Unix-like operating systems such as Linux, rely heavily on command-line interactions. System administrators and developers often leverage the power of CLIs to perform tasks ranging from file manipulation and software installation to network configuration and debugging. The command-line environment provides a direct and concise way to interact with the system, allowing users to execute commands with specific parameters and options to achieve desired outcomes.

Despite their distinctive strengths, the debate between GUIs and CLIs is not a binary choice; instead, it often revolves around finding a balance that optimally serves the needs of users. In some cases, systems integrate both interfaces, offering a hybrid approach that caters to a broader spectrum of users and use cases. For instance, many modern operating systems incorporate a graphical desktop environment alongside a command-line terminal, providing users with the flexibility to choose the interface that best suits their preferences and tasks. This hybrid approach combines the visual simplicity of GUIs with the precision and efficiency of CLIs, offering users the best of both worlds.

The effectiveness of GUIs and CLIs also extends to the realm of software development. Integrated Development Environments (IDEs) often provide a GUI-driven interface for coding, debugging, and testing, offering features like code completion, visual debugging tools, and project management. IDEs aim to enhance the development experience, particularly for those who may not be proficient in writing code using only a command-line interface. On the other hand, many developers, especially in fields like web development and scripting, still prefer command-line tools and text editors for their simplicity, speed, and the ability to integrate seamlessly with version control systems and build processes.

Accessibility considerations play a significant role in the GUI vs. CLI debate. GUIs, with their visual representations, tend to be more accessible to users with diverse abilities, including those with limited technical expertise or physical impairments. Features such as clickable buttons, drag-and-drop functionality, and visual feedback enhance the user experience for individuals who may face challenges with textual interfaces. However, accessibility tools and advancements in screen reader technology have made CLIs more navigable for users with visual impairments, ensuring that both interfaces can be designed and adapted to accommodate a wide range of users.

Security considerations also influence the choice between GUIs and CLIs, particularly in server environments. The reduced attack surface of CLIs, stemming from their text-based nature and minimal visual components, often makes them less vulnerable to certain types of attacks compared to GUIs. Server administrators often prefer CLIs for tasks involving security configurations, as the lack of graphical elements reduces the potential points of exploitation. However, GUIs can provide visual indicators and alerts that enhance security awareness for less experienced users, aiding in the prevention of inadvertent security breaches.

The evolution of technology has seen attempts to bridge the gap between GUIs and CLIs, aiming to offer users the benefits of both interfaces seamlessly. Command-line tools with graphical front-ends, often referred to as "command-line interfaces with graphical capabilities" or "graphical shells," provide users with a visual representation of command-line operations. These tools offer a middle ground, allowing users to leverage the power of command-line syntax while benefiting from a graphical environment that aids in discovery and understanding. Such tools find applications in fields like data science, where users may transition from graphical data visualization tools to command-line operations for advanced analysis and scripting.

In conclusion, the choice between graphical user interfaces and command-line interfaces is a nuanced decision influenced by factors such as user proficiency, task complexity, system requirements, and accessibility considerations. GUIs, with their visual intuitiveness and broad accessibility, cater to a wide audience and excel in scenarios where ease of use and visual representation are paramount. CLIs, on the other hand, offer precision, automation capabilities, and resource efficiency, making them well-suited for technical tasks, server environments, and scripting.

The ongoing evolution of computing environments continues to blur the lines between GUIs and CLIs, with hybrid approaches and tools that attempt to offer users the best of both worlds. Ultimately, the choice between GUIs and CLIs often boils down to user preferences, the nature of the tasks at hand, and the specific requirements of the system or application. In a computing landscape that embraces diversity and user-centric design, the coexistence of graphical and command-line interfaces ensures that users can select the interface that aligns with their skills, preferences, and the demands of their computing tasks.

Human-computer interaction principles

Human-Computer Interaction (HCI) principles form the foundation for designing systems that facilitate seamless interaction between humans and computers, emphasizing user-centered design to optimize usability, accessibility, and overall user satisfaction. One fundamental principle is usability, emphasizing the importance of designing systems that are easy to learn, efficient to use, and error-tolerant. This involves considering factors such as simplicity, clarity, and consistency in user interfaces, ensuring that users can quickly grasp how to operate a system without unnecessary complexity or ambiguity.

Another critical HCI principle is learnability, recognizing that users should be able to acquire new skills and knowledge to interact with a system over time. Systems should provide a gradual learning curve, enabling users to become proficient with increased use and practice. Intuitive design, where the system's interface aligns with users' mental models and expectations, contributes to learnability by reducing the cognitive load associated with understanding and using the interface.

Feedback is a key HCI principle that emphasizes providing users with timely and informative responses to their actions. Effective feedback mechanisms, such as visual cues, sound notifications, or haptic responses, inform users about the system's state, confirming that their input has been received and processed. Feedback enhances user confidence, reduces uncertainty, and contributes to a more responsive and user-friendly interaction.

The principle of affordance refers to the perceptible properties of an object or system that suggest how it can be used. Designing interfaces with clear affordances ensures that users can easily understand the functionality and potential interactions with different elements. Buttons, icons, and menus, for example, should visually convey their intended purpose, guiding users on how to navigate and interact with the system.

Another key HCI principle is consistency, emphasizing the need for uniformity and predictability across the system's interface. Consistent design elements, such as similar layouts, color schemes, and interaction patterns, contribute to a coherent user experience. Consistency fosters familiarity, reducing the likelihood of user confusion and enhancing the efficiency of interaction across different parts of the system.

The principle of flexibility acknowledges that users have diverse needs and preferences, requiring systems to accommodate a range of user characteristics. Customization options, adaptive interfaces, and adjustable settings empower users to tailor the system to their individual preferences, contributing to a more inclusive and user-centric design.

Accessibility is a fundamental HCI principle focused on ensuring that computer systems are usable by individuals with diverse abilities. Designing for accessibility involves considering factors such as screen readers for users with visual impairments, alternative input methods for those with motor disabilities, and captioning for users with hearing impairments. An accessible design not only complies with ethical standards but also broadens the reach of the system to a more diverse user base.

The principle of efficiency underscores the importance of designing systems that allow users to accomplish their tasks with minimal time and effort. Streamlining workflows, optimizing navigation paths, and providing shortcuts contribute to the overall efficiency of the user interaction. Efficiency is particularly crucial in domains where users aim to complete tasks quickly and with precision.

Error prevention and recovery are essential HCI principles that recognize the inevitability of user errors. Designing systems with clear error messages, undo functionalities, and user-friendly error recovery processes minimizes the impact of mistakes and fosters a forgiving user interface. The goal is to create a system that guides users towards correct actions and helps them recover gracefully from errors.

The principle of memorability emphasizes designing interfaces that enable users to remember how to use the system after an initial learning phase. Creating memorable interfaces involves clear labeling, consistent iconography, and intuitive navigation structures. The aim is to reduce the cognitive load associated with relearning the system each time a user interacts with it, promoting long-term usability and user confidence.

In the context of HCI, the principle of user satisfaction recognizes that a positive emotional experience is integral to the overall success of a system. Beyond functional aspects, user satisfaction is influenced by aesthetics, engagement, and the overall enjoyment of the interaction. Designing interfaces that evoke positive emotions contributes to user loyalty, increased adoption, and a more positive perception of the system.

Collaboration and communication are essential HCI principles in contexts where users interact with each other through computer-mediated communication systems. Designing interfaces that facilitate effective collaboration, whether through messaging platforms, collaborative editing tools, or virtual environments, involves considering factors such as real-time feedback, clear communication channels, and intuitive collaboration features.

The principle of scalability acknowledges the importance of designing systems that can adapt to varying levels of complexity and user demands. Scalable interfaces should accommodate both novice users and advanced users, providing features and functionalities that scale seamlessly as users gain expertise and as the system evolves. Scalability is particularly crucial in dynamic environments where user requirements may change over time.

Ethical considerations form an integral part of HCI principles, emphasizing the responsible and ethical use of technology. Designers must consider the potential impact of their designs on user privacy, security, and well-being. Ethical HCI principles promote transparency in data collection, informed consent, and the protection of user rights, aligning design practices with ethical standards and societal values.

Context awareness is a modern HCI principle that recognizes the importance of designing systems that are aware of and responsive to the user's context, including their location, preferences, and situational needs. Context-aware interfaces can adapt their behavior based on environmental factors, enhancing user experience by providing relevant information and functionalities in real-time.

The principle of adaptability underscores the need for systems to adjust their behavior based on changing conditions, user preferences, or emerging technologies. Designing adaptable interfaces involves incorporating features such as automatic updates, flexible configurations, and compatibility with evolving technologies, ensuring that the system remains relevant and effective over time.

In conclusion, Human-Computer Interaction principles encompass a comprehensive set of guidelines and considerations aimed at creating systems that prioritize user needs, preferences, and overall satisfaction. These principles evolve with advancements in technology, encompassing both traditional aspects of usability and emerging trends such as context awareness and adaptability. A successful application of HCI principles results in interfaces that are not only functional and efficient but also enjoyable, accessible, and ethically designed to enhance the overall human experience with technology.

Designing for growth and adaptability

Designing for growth and adaptability is a multifaceted endeavor that involves creating systems, products, and strategies capable of evolving seamlessly in response to changing circumstances, user needs, and technological advancements. The concept of growth encompasses both scalability and expansiveness, ensuring that a design can accommodate an increasing volume of users, data, or functionalities without compromising performance or user experience. Scalability is fundamental in systems that anticipate growth, allowing them to handle larger workloads, user bases, or data sets while maintaining efficiency. This involves designing robust architectures, employing flexible frameworks, and optimizing resource allocation to prevent bottlenecks and performance degradation as the system scales.

Adaptability, on the other hand, is about creating designs that can flexibly respond to dynamic conditions, whether they be shifting user behaviors, emerging technologies, or evolving market demands. An adaptable design anticipates change and provides mechanisms to incorporate new features, update existing functionalities, and pivot in response to unforeseen challenges. This requires a forward-thinking approach to design, incorporating modular structures, open-ended frameworks, and user-friendly customization options. By fostering adaptability, designs can endure the test of time, remaining relevant and effective in the face of evolving landscapes.

In the realm of software and application development, designing for growth involves architecting systems that can effortlessly handle an increasing number of users, transactions, or data points. Scalability considerations start at the foundational level, with the selection of appropriate databases, servers, and frameworks that can scale horizontally or vertically as needed. Cloud computing, with its on-demand resources and elastic scalability, has become integral to designing applications that can dynamically adjust to varying workloads. Consideration for growth also extends to the user interface and experience, ensuring that interfaces remain responsive and intuitive even as user bases expand.

Adaptability in software design involves anticipating changes in user preferences, technological standards, and market trends. Agile development methodologies, emphasizing iterative development and continuous feedback, contribute to the adaptability of software by allowing for quick adjustments in response to evolving requirements. APIs (Application Programming Interfaces) provide a means for systems to communicate and integrate with external services, facilitating the seamless addition of new features or functionalities. Future-proofing software through modular design and backward compatibility enables easier adaptation to emerging technologies without compromising existing user experiences.

In the context of product design, creating adaptable solutions requires a deep understanding of user needs, behaviors, and the evolving context in which the product operates. Designing for growth involves crafting products that can scale to meet increased demand, whether in terms of production volume, user adoption, or market reach. Modular design principles allow for the integration of new features or modifications without requiring a complete overhaul, ensuring that products can evolve over time. Adaptable product designs also consider the environmental impact, emphasizing sustainable materials and manufacturing processes that align with changing consumer expectations and regulatory standards.

The concept of growth and adaptability is particularly pertinent in the field of user interface (UI) and user experience (UX) design. Interfaces must be designed to accommodate the diverse needs and preferences of users, ensuring inclusivity and accessibility. Scalable UI/UX design considers the potential growth of user demographics, device types, and usage scenarios. Responsive design techniques, allowing interfaces to adapt seamlessly across different screen sizes and devices, contribute to scalability. On the adaptability front, user-centric design involves continuous user research, usability testing, and feedback loops to incorporate user insights and refine the design based on changing user expectations and behaviors.

In e-commerce and digital platforms, growth and adaptability are paramount for staying competitive in dynamic markets. Scalability in these contexts involves designing systems that can handle surges in traffic, diverse product catalogs, and complex transactional processes. Cloud-based solutions provide the flexibility to scale server infrastructure on-demand. Adaptable e-commerce platforms anticipate changing consumer behaviors and technological trends, integrating features like personalized recommendations, flexible payment options, and responsive interfaces that align with the evolving expectations of online shoppers.

In the realm of organizational management and business strategies, designing for growth and adaptability involves cultivating a corporate culture that embraces innovation, flexibility, and continuous learning. Scalable business models anticipate expansion into new markets, diversification of product or service offerings, and scalability of operations. Entrepreneurial organizations often emphasize adaptable structures, encouraging employees to experiment, iterate, and pivot based on market feedback. Adopting agile methodologies at the organizational level contributes to adaptability by fostering a nimble and responsive approach to changing market dynamics.

Infrastructure design, particularly in the context of urban planning and architecture, requires a thoughtful consideration of growth and adaptability. Scalable urban planning involves designing infrastructure that can accommodate population growth, technological advancements, and shifts in transportation needs. Adaptable architectural designs consider flexible usage of spaces, accommodating changes in functionalities over time. Sustainable and resilient infrastructure designs anticipate environmental changes, ensuring that urban spaces can withstand and recover from unforeseen challenges such as climate events.

In the educational domain, designing for growth and adaptability involves creating learning environments that can scale to accommodate diverse student populations and evolving pedagogical approaches. Scalable educational systems consider the potential increase in student enrollment, technological integration, and the expansion of course offerings. Adaptable curricula respond to changes in educational methodologies, emerging fields of study, and advancements in technology, ensuring that students are prepared for the demands of a rapidly evolving job market.

The principles of growth and adaptability are integral in the field of artificial intelligence (AI) and machine learning. Scalability in AI models involves designing algorithms that can handle larger datasets, increasing computational demands, and diverse use cases. The adaptability of AI models is crucial for continuous learning and improvement, allowing systems to update their knowledge based on new data and changing patterns. Human-AI interaction design focuses on creating interfaces that facilitate user understanding and control over AI systems, emphasizing transparency and adaptability to user preferences.

Environmental sustainability initiatives embody the principles of growth and adaptability, aiming to create systems that can endure and evolve in harmony with ecological systems. Scalable sustainability strategies consider the potential increase in resource demands, population growth, and the expansion of urban areas. Adaptable environmental designs incorporate technologies and practices that respond to changing climate conditions, resource availability, and environmental conservation priorities.

In conclusion, designing for growth and adaptability is a holistic and dynamic approach that spans various domains, from software development and product design to organizational management, urban planning, education, and environmental sustainability. The principles of scalability and adaptability are interwoven, ensuring that designs can accommodate expansion, evolving requirements, and unforeseen changes. The continuous pursuit of innovation, user-centricity, and a forward-thinking mindset are essential elements in creating designs that can withstand the test of time, respond to dynamic conditions, and provide enduring value in a rapidly changing world.

Handling increased system complexity

Handling increased system complexity is a multifaceted challenge that permeates various domains, including software development, engineering, organizational management, and infrastructure design. As systems evolve to meet expanding functionalities, user demands, and technological advancements, managing complexity becomes pivotal to ensure efficiency, maintainability, and overall system performance. In software development, the proliferation of features, integrations, and dependencies contributes to system complexity. Managing this complexity involves adopting modular design principles, breaking down large systems into smaller, more manageable components or modules. Modularization enhances maintainability, facilitates collaborative development, and allows for the isolation of changes, minimizing the ripple effects of modifications on the entire system.

Engineering systems, particularly those in fields like aerospace, automotive, or telecommunications, often grapple with increased complexity as technological advancements introduce intricate components, interconnected subsystems, and diverse functionalities. Adopting systems engineering approaches becomes imperative, emphasizing a holistic perspective that considers the entire system lifecycle. System architecture frameworks, such as Model-Based Systems Engineering (MBSE), assist in visualizing and managing complex systems through detailed models, facilitating communication among multidisciplinary teams and stakeholders. Effective management of increased complexity in engineering systems involves rigorous requirements engineering, traceability, and validation processes to ensure that system components align with overarching objectives.

Organizational management encounters heightened complexity as businesses expand, diversify, and adapt to changing market dynamics. In such contexts, embracing scalable and agile organizational structures becomes crucial. Scalability allows organizations to grow without sacrificing operational efficiency, while agile methodologies promote adaptability by fostering iterative, collaborative approaches to decision-making and project execution. Developing a culture of cross-functional collaboration, communication, and knowledge sharing is pivotal in managing increased organizational complexity. Strategic frameworks such as the Cynefin framework, which categorizes problem domains to guide decision-making, can aid organizations in navigating complex challenges and making informed choices.

Infrastructure design, whether in urban planning or information technology, faces escalating complexity due to factors like population growth, technological advancements, and changing environmental considerations. In urban planning, managing increased complexity involves adopting smart city concepts that leverage data-driven technologies for efficient resource allocation, traffic management, and environmental sustainability. In information technology infrastructure, the rise of cloud computing introduces dynamic, distributed systems that demand sophisticated management. Tools like Infrastructure as Code (IaC) automate infrastructure provisioning and configuration, offering a systematic approach to handle the intricacies of modern, scalable IT environments.

Navigating increased complexity in educational systems requires innovative approaches to curriculum design, pedagogy, and administrative processes. As educational institutions adapt to technological advancements, changing student demographics, and evolving teaching methodologies, managing complexity involves incorporating flexible curriculum structures, embracing digital learning platforms, and fostering adaptability among educators. Implementing Learning Management Systems (LMS) provides a centralized platform for curriculum delivery, assessment, and communication, streamlining administrative processes and offering a scalable solution to accommodate growing student populations.

In the context of artificial intelligence (AI) and machine learning (ML) systems, managing heightened complexity arises from the intricate algorithms, massive datasets, and evolving model architectures. Adopting robust model development practices, such as version control, documentation, and rigorous testing, helps in managing the complexity of AI and ML systems. Furthermore, implementing explainability and interpretability measures becomes crucial to enhance the transparency of complex models, ensuring that stakeholders, including end-users, can comprehend and trust the system's decisions.

Addressing the challenges posed by increased system complexity requires a strategic and interdisciplinary approach that incorporates principles of systems thinking, modularity, and scalability. In software engineering, embracing microservices architecture contributes to the modularization of applications, allowing developers to focus on smaller, manageable components with defined responsibilities. Containerization technologies like Docker enable the encapsulation of applications and their dependencies, promoting consistency across various environments and easing deployment complexities.

The increased complexity of interconnected systems introduces challenges related to security, privacy, and compliance. In cybersecurity, managing the complexities of evolving threat landscapes necessitates implementing robust security measures, such as encryption, access controls, and continuous monitoring. Privacy considerations require adherence to regulatory frameworks and the implementation of privacy-by-design principles, ensuring that systems are designed with privacy considerations integrated from the outset.

The rise of Internet of Things (IoT) technologies adds another layer of complexity to system design, as interconnected devices generate vast amounts of data and introduce new dimensions of interoperability challenges. Implementing standardized communication protocols, security measures, and scalable data processing architectures becomes essential in managing the intricacies of IoT ecosystems. Edge computing, which involves processing data closer to the source rather than relying solely on centralized cloud infrastructure, emerges as a solution to address latency and bandwidth challenges in complex IoT environments.

In the financial sector, managing increased system complexity is paramount as institutions grapple with diverse financial products, global regulatory frameworks, and intricate market dynamics. Adopting robust risk management practices, such as stress testing and scenario analysis, becomes crucial in navigating complex financial systems. Advanced analytics and machine learning algorithms offer tools for analyzing complex market trends, customer behaviors, and risk factors, enhancing decision-making capabilities in the face of heightened financial complexities.

The healthcare industry contends with increased complexity due to factors such as medical advancements, interoperability requirements, and the integration of digital health technologies. Managing complexity in healthcare systems involves implementing electronic health record (EHR) systems that facilitate seamless information exchange among healthcare providers. Interoperability standards, such as Health Level Seven International (HL7) and Fast Healthcare Interoperability Resources (FHIR), contribute to the integration of diverse health information systems, fostering a comprehensive and accessible patient record.

In conclusion, handling increased system complexity demands a strategic and adaptive approach across various domains. Whether in software development, engineering, organizational management, infrastructure design, education, artificial intelligence, cybersecurity, finance, or healthcare, the principles of modularity, scalability, and systems thinking emerge as essential strategies. Embracing technologies, methodologies, and frameworks that facilitate modular design, scalability, and adaptability ensures that systems can evolve, thrive, and deliver enduring value in the face of growing intricacies and dynamic challenges. The pursuit of simplicity within complexity becomes a guiding principle, emphasizing the need for thoughtful design, interdisciplinary collaboration, and strategic planning to navigate the complexities inherent in modern systems.

Strategies for minimizing system failures

Minimizing system failures is a critical aspect of maintaining the reliability, performance, and user satisfaction of complex systems across various domains, including software development, engineering, organizational management, and infrastructure design. One strategy involves implementing rigorous testing methodologies throughout the development life cycle of software systems. Adopting practices such as unit testing, integration testing, and end-to-end testing helps identify and rectify potential issues before they propagate into production environments. Automated testing frameworks and continuous integration pipelines contribute to a proactive approach, allowing developers to detect and address failures early in the development process, minimizing the likelihood of issues reaching end-users.

In engineering systems, reliability-centered maintenance (RCM) is a strategic approach to minimize failures by prioritizing maintenance activities based on their impact on system performance. RCM involves analyzing the failure modes and consequences of components within a system, determining the most effective maintenance strategies, and optimizing resources to prevent critical failures. Predictive maintenance techniques, leveraging sensor data and analytics, enable engineers to anticipate equipment failures and perform interventions before issues escalate, ensuring optimal system reliability.

Organizational management plays a crucial role in minimizing system failures by fostering a culture of accountability, transparency, and continuous improvement. Implementing robust change management processes helps organizations assess the potential impact of system changes and implement them in a controlled manner. Encouraging open communication channels and feedback loops ensures that employees can report issues promptly, facilitating swift resolution. Furthermore, investing in employee training and skill development enhances the competence of teams, reducing the likelihood of human errors that may contribute to system failures.

In infrastructure design, redundancy and fault tolerance are pivotal strategies for minimizing system failures. Building systems with redundant components ensures that if one component fails, another can seamlessly take over, preventing disruptions. Redundancy is often employed in critical infrastructure such as data centers, where multiple servers, power supplies, and network connections are deployed to ensure continuous operation. Fault-tolerant design principles involve anticipating potential failure points and implementing mechanisms to gracefully handle and recover from failures without compromising overall system functionality.

In software development, adopting robust error handling and logging practices is essential to minimize system failures. Well-designed error messages and logging mechanisms provide valuable information to developers and administrators, enabling them to diagnose and address issues quickly. Monitoring tools that track system performance, resource utilization, and error rates contribute to early detection of anomalies, allowing proactive intervention before failures impact end-users. DevOps practices, emphasizing collaboration between development and operations teams, facilitate a holistic approach to system reliability by integrating development, testing, and deployment processes.

Cybersecurity measures are integral to minimizing system failures, especially in the context of increasing cyber threats. Implementing robust security protocols, including encryption, access controls, and regular security audits, helps protect systems from malicious attacks that could lead to failures. Regularly updating and patching software and systems addresses vulnerabilities, reducing the risk of exploitation. Additionally, educating users about security best practices and implementing multi-factor authentication contribute to a layered defense strategy, enhancing overall system resilience.

In finance, where system failures can have significant economic consequences, implementing disaster recovery and business continuity plans is crucial. These plans outline procedures to ensure the rapid recovery of critical systems in the event of failures or disasters. Regular testing of these plans helps identify potential gaps and ensures that teams can execute recovery processes effectively. Implementing real-time monitoring of financial transactions and market data allows organizations to detect anomalies and potential failures promptly, enabling timely interventions to mitigate risks.

In healthcare, minimizing system failures is paramount to ensuring patient safety and efficient healthcare delivery. Health information systems, including electronic health records (EHRs) and medical devices, must adhere to stringent reliability and safety standards. Regular system audits, compliance checks, and adherence to regulatory frameworks contribute to maintaining the integrity and reliability of healthcare systems. Implementing interoperability standards facilitates seamless information exchange among different healthcare systems, reducing the risk of data discrepancies and improving overall system reliability.

Environmental monitoring systems, particularly in critical sectors such as climate monitoring and natural disaster prediction, employ strategies to minimize failures and ensure the accuracy of data. Deploying redundant sensors and communication channels enhances the reliability of data collection, especially in remote or harsh environments. Implementing machine learning algorithms for anomaly detection in environmental data helps identify abnormal patterns, signaling potential sensor failures or data inaccuracies.

In educational systems, minimizing system failures involves ensuring the reliability of learning management systems (LMS) and digital platforms. Regular system maintenance, updates, and capacity planning contribute to optimal performance and prevent disruptions. Implementing user support mechanisms, including help desks and user guides, enhances user experience and facilitates prompt issue resolution. Furthermore, incorporating user feedback mechanisms allows educational institutions to address issues proactively and make continuous improvements to digital learning systems.

The adoption of artificial intelligence (AI) and machine learning (ML) introduces unique challenges in minimizing system failures. Rigorous testing of AI models, including validation against diverse datasets, helps identify potential biases, inaccuracies, or ethical concerns. Interpretability and explainability measures ensure that AI models can be understood and validated, reducing the risk of unintended consequences. Continuous monitoring of AI systems, including the performance of models in real-world scenarios, contributes to identifying and addressing issues as they arise.

Strategies for minimizing system failures extend to the realm of space exploration and satellite technology. In space missions, redundancy is a fundamental strategy to ensure mission success. Spacecraft often incorporate duplicate systems, such as redundant sensors and communication systems, to mitigate the impact of potential failures in the harsh space environment. Regular communication with and monitoring of satellites allow ground control teams to detect anomalies and initiate corrective actions to prevent mission failures.

In conclusion, minimizing system failures requires a holistic and proactive approach across diverse domains. Strategies encompass rigorous testing in software development, reliability-centered maintenance in engineering, organizational culture in management, redundancy in infrastructure design, error handling in cybersecurity, disaster recovery in finance, compliance in healthcare, environmental monitoring in climate science, user support in education, and interpretability in AI. Embracing a mindset of continuous improvement, investing in robust processes, and fostering interdisciplinary collaboration are fundamental principles in navigating the complexities of modern systems and ensuring their resilience in the face of potential failures.

Redundancy and error recovery mechanisms

Redundancy and error recovery mechanisms are essential strategies employed across various domains to enhance the reliability, resilience, and fault tolerance of complex systems. Redundancy involves the duplication of critical components, functions, or processes within a system to ensure that if one element fails, an alternate can seamlessly take over, preventing disruptions and minimizing the impact on overall system performance. This principle is widely applied in diverse fields, including software development, engineering, infrastructure design, and aerospace.

In the realm of software development, redundancy is a cornerstone of fault-tolerant systems. One common application is the use of redundant servers and load balancing techniques to distribute incoming traffic across multiple servers. In the event of a server failure, the load balancer redirects traffic to healthy servers, ensuring continuous service availability. Redundant storage systems, such as RAID (Redundant Array of Independent Disks), are employed to protect against data loss due to disk failures. Similarly, redundant network paths and communication channels enhance the robustness of distributed systems, ensuring that if one path becomes unavailable, data can still be transmitted through alternative routes.

Engineering systems, particularly those in critical industries such as aerospace and automotive, heavily rely on redundancy to safeguard against component failures. Aircraft, for instance, feature redundant control systems, avionics, and sensors to ensure that critical functions like navigation and communication can persist even in the face of equipment malfunctions. Redundant power systems, such as backup generators or dual power supplies, are integral in engineering design to ensure continuous operation and prevent system failures caused by power outages.

Organizational management also leverages redundancy principles to enhance resilience and mitigate risks. In workforce management, cross-training employees to handle multiple roles introduces redundancy in skills, ensuring that key tasks can still be performed in the absence of specific individuals. Redundant communication channels and contingency plans are vital components of organizational risk management, enabling companies to respond effectively to unexpected events such as natural disasters, cyber-attacks, or disruptions in supply chains.

Infrastructure design, particularly in the context of information technology and data centers, relies on redundancy to prevent service interruptions and data loss. Redundant servers, networking equipment, and power supplies are standard features in data center design. Employing backup systems and failover mechanisms ensures that if one component fails, the redundant systems seamlessly take over, maintaining the continuity of services. Additionally, the use of geographically distributed data centers introduces redundancy at the location level, safeguarding against regional outages or disasters.

Aerospace engineering, where the consequences of system failures can be catastrophic, extensively employs redundancy and error recovery mechanisms. Spacecraft, satellites, and space probes integrate multiple sensors, communication systems, and propulsion units, often in redundant configurations. The redundancy extends to critical subsystems like guidance and navigation, allowing the spacecraft to navigate and make course corrections even if a primary system malfunctions. Error recovery mechanisms involve sophisticated algorithms and protocols that autonomously detect anomalies, isolate faulty components, and trigger corrective actions to restore normal operation.

In the field of cybersecurity, redundancy is a key strategy to enhance the resilience of systems against cyber threats and attacks. Redundant security measures, such as multiple layers of firewalls, intrusion detection systems, and antivirus solutions, create a defense-in-depth approach. This layered security model ensures that even if one security measure fails to detect or prevent an attack, other redundant layers can provide additional protection. Error recovery mechanisms in cybersecurity involve incident response plans, data backup strategies, and rapid detection and mitigation of security incidents to minimize the impact of breaches.

The financial sector employs redundancy and error recovery mechanisms to ensure the continuous availability and security of critical systems. Redundant data centers, backup servers, and failover systems are employed to prevent service disruptions in banking and financial transactions. Error recovery mechanisms involve real-time monitoring of financial transactions, anomaly detection algorithms, and rapid intervention to address potential errors or fraudulent activities. Disaster recovery plans are essential components, detailing procedures for restoring financial systems in the event of unexpected failures or disasters.

Healthcare systems, where patient safety and data integrity are paramount, incorporate redundancy and error recovery mechanisms to ensure continuous operation and prevent critical failures. Electronic health record (EHR) systems employ redundant servers and backup solutions to safeguard patient data. Error recovery mechanisms involve automated alerts for abnormal medical data, enabling healthcare providers to respond promptly to potential errors in diagnostics or patient monitoring. Additionally, redundant medical devices and systems ensure that critical functions, such as life support systems or diagnostic equipment, can continue to operate in the event of component failures.

Environmental monitoring systems, crucial for climate science and disaster prediction, employ redundancy to enhance the reliability of data collection and analysis. Redundant sensors and measurement instruments are deployed to ensure accurate and continuous data acquisition, especially in remote or challenging environments. Error recovery mechanisms involve algorithms for anomaly detection, data validation, and corrective actions to account for potential errors in environmental data. These systems play a critical role in monitoring climate change, natural disasters, and ecological shifts.

In educational systems, redundancy and error recovery mechanisms are essential for ensuring the availability and reliability of digital learning platforms. Redundant servers, load balancing, and failover mechanisms prevent disruptions in online learning environments. Error recovery strategies involve automated backups of educational content, quick identification of potential issues through user feedback, and timely interventions to resolve technical glitches. These mechanisms contribute to a seamless and reliable online learning experience for students and educators.

The adoption of artificial intelligence (AI) and machine learning (ML) introduces specific considerations for redundancy and error recovery. Redundant models and algorithms, often implemented through ensemble methods, enhance the reliability and accuracy of AI systems. Error recovery mechanisms involve continuous monitoring of model performance, algorithmic adjustments, and human intervention in cases where the AI system encounters unforeseen scenarios or makes incorrect predictions. Interpretability and explainability measures further contribute to error recovery by enabling stakeholders to understand and correct AI model behavior.

In conclusion, redundancy and error recovery mechanisms are fundamental strategies employed across diverse domains to enhance the reliability, resilience, and fault tolerance of complex systems. Whether in software development, engineering, organizational management, infrastructure design, aerospace, cybersecurity, finance, healthcare, environmental monitoring, education, or artificial intelligence, these mechanisms play a pivotal role in preventing and mitigating system failures. The integration of redundancy and error recovery principles contributes to the creation of robust and dependable systems capable of withstanding unexpected challenges and ensuring continuous operation in the face of failures.

Examination of well-designed operating systems

An examination of well-designed operating systems reveals a complex interplay of principles, functionalities, and architectural considerations that contribute to their efficiency, reliability, and user satisfaction. At the core of a well-designed operating system is the effective management of hardware resources. This involves intricate mechanisms for task scheduling, memory allocation, and input/output operations to ensure optimal utilization of the underlying hardware components. The orchestration of these functions is a delicate balance, aiming to provide a responsive and seamless computing experience for users.

Well-designed operating systems prioritize user interfaces that are intuitive, efficient, and adaptable. Graphical user interfaces (GUIs) or command-line interfaces (CLIs) are crafted with user experience in mind, enabling users to interact with the system effortlessly. The design often incorporates principles of consistency, simplicity, and responsiveness to create an interface that aligns with user expectations and minimizes the learning curve. Accessibility features further enhance inclusivity, ensuring that users with diverse abilities can navigate and utilize the operating system effectively.

Security is a paramount consideration in the design of operating systems, given the increasing threats in the digital landscape. Well-designed operating systems implement robust security measures, including access controls, encryption, and secure authentication mechanisms. Regular security updates and patches address vulnerabilities, contributing to a proactive defense against potential exploits. Additionally, features such as sandboxing and virtualization create isolated environments, limiting the impact of security breaches and enhancing the overall resilience of the system.

File systems play a crucial role in organizing and managing data within operating systems. A well-designed file system optimizes storage utilization, supports efficient data retrieval, and ensures data integrity. Advanced file systems incorporate features like journaling, snapshots, and versioning, enhancing data protection and recovery capabilities. The seamless integration of file systems with other components of the operating system contributes to a cohesive and reliable storage infrastructure.

Concurrency and multitasking are integral aspects of modern operating systems, allowing users to run multiple applications concurrently. Well-designed operating systems implement efficient process and thread management, enabling parallel execution without compromising system stability. Scheduling algorithms allocate CPU time judiciously, ensuring fair access to resources among running processes. The design also considers mechanisms for inter-process communication and synchronization to facilitate collaboration among concurrently executing tasks.

Memory management is a critical facet of operating system design, influencing system performance and responsiveness. Well-designed operating systems employ strategies such as virtual memory, paging, and caching to optimize memory utilization. Memory protection mechanisms prevent unauthorized access and enhance the overall stability of the system. Efficient memory allocation and deallocation strategies contribute to minimizing memory leaks and optimizing the use of available resources.

Networking capabilities are fundamental in contemporary operating systems, facilitating communication between devices and enabling access to external networks. Well-designed networking components incorporate protocols, drivers, and configurations that ensure seamless connectivity and data exchange. Security measures, including firewalls and encryption, protect networked systems from unauthorized access and data breaches. The integration of networking features with other system components provides users with a comprehensive and interconnected computing environment.

Device drivers and hardware abstraction layers form a crucial bridge between the operating system and underlying hardware components. Well-designed operating systems support a diverse range of hardware configurations through standardized interfaces and well-defined APIs (Application Programming Interfaces). This abstraction layer ensures that applications can interact with hardware components without requiring detailed knowledge of the underlying hardware architecture, enhancing portability and compatibility.

The extensibility of operating systems allows for the integration of third-party applications, drivers, and services. Well-designed operating systems provide developers with well-documented APIs, development frameworks, and software development kits (SDKs) that facilitate the creation of diverse applications. A robust application ecosystem enriches the user experience, offering a variety of tools and functionalities that extend the capabilities of the operating system.

In the context of real-time operating systems (RTOS), which are designed for time-sensitive applications such as embedded systems and control systems, determinism and predictability are paramount.

Well-designed real-time operating systems prioritize tasks with strict timing requirements, ensuring that critical operations are executed within specified time constraints. Scheduling algorithms in RTOS are tailored to meet stringent deadlines, providing a reliable platform for applications where timing accuracy is crucial.

Distributed operating systems extend the traditional operating system model to manage resources and tasks across multiple interconnected machines. Well-designed distributed operating systems implement efficient communication protocols, distributed file systems, and load balancing mechanisms to optimize resource utilization and enhance fault tolerance. Consistency models in distributed systems ensure that data remains coherent across multiple nodes, supporting collaborative and scalable computing environments.

Linux, a well-known example of a well-designed operating system, embodies many of these principles. Its open-source nature fosters collaboration and community-driven development, resulting in a robust, secure, and versatile operating system. Linux's modular architecture, clear separation between the kernel and user-space, and support for a wide range of hardware configurations contribute to its scalability and adaptability. The command-line interface, complemented by various desktop environments, provides users with flexibility and choice in how they interact with the system.

Windows, another prominent operating system, is recognized for its user-friendly graphical interface and extensive compatibility with software applications and hardware devices. The Windows operating system incorporates advanced security features, such as BitLocker encryption and Windows Defender antivirus, to safeguard user data and protect against malware. Windows also supports a rich ecosystem of third-party applications and peripherals, contributing to its widespread adoption in both consumer and enterprise environments.

UNIX, with its roots in the early days of computing, has influenced the design of many operating systems. UNIX-based systems, including variants like FreeBSD and macOS, prioritize stability, security, and a powerful command-line interface. The UNIX philosophy of small, modular tools that do one thing well resonates in these systems, fostering simplicity and composability. macOS, in particular, showcases the integration of UNIX principles with a polished graphical user interface, creating an environment favored by creatives and developers alike.

In conclusion, the examination of well-designed operating systems reveals a synthesis of principles that address diverse aspects of computing. These include resource management, user interface design, security, file systems, concurrency, memory management, networking, hardware abstraction, extensibility, and adaptability to specialized requirements such as real-time and distributed computing. Operating systems like Linux, Windows, and UNIX-based systems exemplify the successful application of these principles, providing users with stable, secure, and versatile computing platforms that form the backbone of modern computing ecosystems. The ongoing evolution of operating systems continues to be shaped by technological advancements, user needs, and the ever-expanding landscape of computing.

Extracting principles from successful implementations

Extracting principles from successful implementations involves a comprehensive examination of diverse domains, from technology to business, education, healthcare, and beyond. One overarching principle is the emphasis on user-centric design. Successful implementations consistently prioritize user experience, ensuring that products or services align with user needs, preferences, and expectations. This principle transcends technological boundaries and resonates in the design of user interfaces, applications, and even organizational processes. A user-centric approach fosters engagement, satisfaction, and loyalty, forming the bedrock of successful implementations across various sectors.

In the realm of technology, a fundamental principle drawn from successful implementations is the pursuit of scalability and adaptability. Systems that can grow seamlessly to accommodate increasing demands while adapting to evolving technological landscapes exhibit a timeless quality. Scalable architectures, modular design, and flexible frameworks underpin the success of platforms like cloud computing services, ensuring they can handle varying workloads, emerging technologies, and changing user requirements. The ability to scale efficiently without compromising performance is a hallmark of successful technological implementations.

Interdisciplinary collaboration emerges as a critical principle from successful implementations, cutting across sectors such as research, business, and innovation. Teams that bring together diverse skill sets, perspectives, and expertise foster creativity, problem-solving, and innovation. Whether in product development, scientific research, or business strategy, the synergy of interdisciplinary collaboration often leads to breakthroughs and holistic solutions. Successful implementations leverage the collective intelligence of multidisciplinary teams to address complex challenges, incorporating perspectives from technology, design, psychology, business, and more.

Agility and adaptability constitute principles derived from successful implementations, particularly in the dynamic landscape of technology and business. Agile methodologies, characterized by iterative development, continuous feedback, and adaptive planning, have become foundational in successful software development and project management. The ability to pivot, respond to changing requirements, and embrace iterative improvement cycles is integral to the success of implementations in rapidly evolving environments. This principle extends beyond software development to organizational structures, where agile frameworks like Scrum and Kanban are applied to enhance adaptability and responsiveness.

The principle of continuous improvement is evident in successful implementations across various domains. Whether through iterative development cycles, feedback loops, or ongoing refinement processes, the commitment to constant enhancement is a common thread. In technology, software updates, patches, and new releases exemplify this principle, delivering improved features, security, and performance. In business, the pursuit of operational excellence involves continuous improvement in processes, products, and services. The ethos of kaizen, emphasizing continuous, incremental improvement, is foundational to the success of implementations in diverse contexts.

In the field of education, successful implementations underscore the principle of personalized and adaptive learning. Tailoring educational experiences to individual student needs, preferences, and learning styles enhances engagement and outcomes. Technology plays a pivotal role in implementing adaptive learning platforms, leveraging data analytics and artificial intelligence to tailor educational content and experiences. The principle of personalization extends beyond formal education to training and professional development, where personalized learning paths contribute to more effective skill acquisition and knowledge retention.

From successful healthcare implementations, the principle of patient-centric care emerges as a guiding ethos. Healthcare systems and technologies that prioritize patient experience, empowerment, and outcomes demonstrate a commitment to holistic well-being. Telemedicine platforms, electronic health records, and patient portals exemplify the integration of technology to enhance patient engagement and access to healthcare services. Patient-centric care extends beyond technology to encompass the human aspects of empathy, communication, and shared decision-making, contributing to successful healthcare implementations.

Environmental sustainability stands out as a principle drawn from successful implementations, reflecting a growing awareness of the need for responsible practices. Whether in technology, manufacturing, urban planning, or business operations, successful implementations increasingly integrate sustainability considerations. Green technologies, energy-efficient practices, and circular economy models are indicative of a commitment to environmental stewardship. Sustainability principles address not only ecological concerns but also social responsibility, ethical sourcing, and the long-term impact of implementations on communities and ecosystems.

In the realm of business, the principle of customer-centricity is a cornerstone of successful implementations. Understanding customer needs, preferences, and behaviors informs product development, marketing strategies, and overall business operations. Customer feedback loops, user testing, and data analytics contribute to the continuous refinement of products and services based on customer insights. The customer-centric principle extends to a focus on building long-term relationships, fostering customer loyalty, and adapting to changing market dynamics through customer-centric business models.

From the successful implementation of artificial intelligence (AI) and machine learning (ML) applications, the principle of ethical and responsible AI emerges as a critical consideration. Recognizing the societal impact of AI, successful implementations prioritize ethical considerations, fairness, transparency, and accountability. Implementing principles like fairness-aware algorithms, ethical AI frameworks, and responsible data practices ensures that AI technologies align with societal values and mitigate potential biases. The ethical and responsible AI principle extends beyond technical considerations to encompass legal, regulatory, and social dimensions.

The principle of inclusivity is evident in successful implementations across various sectors, emphasizing the importance of diversity and accessibility. In technology, inclusive design ensures that products and services cater to a diverse range of users, including those with different abilities and backgrounds. Business strategies that embrace diversity and inclusion foster innovation, creativity, and a positive organizational culture. In education, inclusive practices address diverse learning needs, ensuring that educational resources and environments are accessible to all. The inclusivity principle extends to healthcare, where efforts to reduce health disparities and enhance healthcare access contribute to successful implementations.

Risk management and resilience emerge as principles derived from successful implementations, particularly in the context of technology, business, and critical infrastructure. Successful organizations integrate robust risk management frameworks to identify, assess, and mitigate potential threats. This principle involves proactive measures such as cybersecurity practices, disaster recovery planning, and business continuity strategies. Resilience, the ability to adapt and recover from disruptions, is intrinsic to successful implementations, ensuring that systems can withstand unforeseen challenges and continue to deliver value.

The principle of data privacy and security is paramount in successful implementations, particularly in an era of increasing digitization. Technologies, applications, and business processes that prioritize the protection of user data instill trust and confidence. Implementing strong encryption, secure authentication mechanisms, and compliance with data protection regulations reflects a commitment to safeguarding user privacy. Data privacy and security considerations extend beyond technology to encompass organizational policies, legal compliance, and ethical standards.

Collaborative ecosystems and partnerships constitute a principle drawn from successful implementations, reflecting the recognition that no single entity can address complex challenges in isolation. Collaborative frameworks, alliances, and ecosystems enable organizations to leverage complementary strengths, share resources, and drive innovation. The success of open-source communities, industry consortia, and public-private partnerships underscores the principle of collaborative ecosystems, fostering a collective approach to problem-solving and advancement.

In conclusion, extracting principles from successful implementations reveals a tapestry of guiding ethos that transcend specific domains. User-centric design, scalability and adaptability, interdisciplinary collaboration, agility and adaptability, continuous improvement, personalized and adaptive learning, patient-centric care, environmental sustainability, customer-centricity, ethical and responsible AI, inclusivity, risk management and resilience, data privacy and security, and collaborative ecosystems all contribute to the success of implementations across diverse sectors. These principles serve as guiding lights, shaping the approaches and philosophies that underpin successful endeavors and ensuring that implementations align with societal values, ethical considerations, and the evolving needs of users and stakeholders. As technology continues to advance, and as businesses, education, healthcare, and other sectors evolve, these enduring principles provide a compass for navigating the complexities of successful implementations in an ever-changing landscape.

Chapter 3: Building Blocks: Kernel Architecture and Components

Definition and role in an operating system

An operating system (OS) is a fundamental software component that serves as the intermediary between computer hardware and user applications, providing a cohesive and efficient environment for the execution of tasks. At its core, the operating system manages and controls the underlying hardware resources, such as the central processing unit (CPU), memory, storage devices, input/output (I/O) devices, and network interfaces. It acts as a crucial layer of abstraction, shielding applications from the intricacies of hardware details and offering a standardized interface through which users and software can interact with the computer system.

One of the primary roles of an operating system is to facilitate the execution of user programs and applications. It provides a runtime environment where applications can run, coordinating their access to hardware resources and ensuring that multiple processes can coexist on the same system without interference. The OS accomplishes this through its task scheduling mechanisms, which allocate CPU time to various processes in a manner that optimizes system performance, responsiveness, and fairness.

Memory management is another critical function performed by the operating system. It allocates and deallocates memory space for processes, ensuring that each application has sufficient memory to execute and preventing conflicts between processes that may attempt to access the same memory locations. Through techniques such as virtual memory and paging, the OS enables the illusion of a larger memory space than physically available, enhancing the overall efficiency of memory utilization.

The operating system plays a pivotal role in managing input and output operations, facilitating communication between software applications and external devices such as keyboards, mice, printers, and storage devices. Device drivers, components of the OS, act as intermediaries between the operating system and hardware peripherals, translating high-level commands from software into low-level instructions that the hardware can execute. This abstraction simplifies the development of software applications, as programmers interact with standardized interfaces provided by the OS rather than dealing directly with the intricacies of specific hardware devices.

File system management is integral to the functioning of an operating system, providing a hierarchical structure for organizing and storing data. The file system enables users and applications to create, read, write, and delete files, maintaining a logical organization of data on storage devices. File permissions and security mechanisms implemented by the operating system control access to files, ensuring data integrity and protecting against unauthorized access.

Additionally, the operating system is responsible for handling communication and coordination between different processes running on the system. Inter-process communication (IPC) mechanisms, such as shared memory, message passing, and synchronization tools, allow processes to exchange data, coordinate activities, and achieve mutual exclusion to prevent conflicts. These mechanisms contribute to the creation of robust and collaborative computing environments.

Security is a paramount consideration in operating system design and functionality. The OS implements access control mechanisms, user authentication, and encryption to safeguard the system against unauthorized access, data breaches, and malicious activities. User accounts and permissions ensure that only authorized individuals can perform specific actions or access particular resources, contributing to the overall integrity and confidentiality of the computing environment.

The role of the operating system extends to the management of system resources and their optimization. It oversees the allocation of CPU time, memory, and other resources to various processes, aiming to maximize system throughput and responsiveness. Resource scheduling algorithms, such as round-robin scheduling, priority scheduling, and multi-level queue scheduling, govern the allocation of resources based on predefined criteria. Additionally, the operating system handles system calls, which are requests from user applications for specific services, system information, or resource access, acting as an interface between applications and the kernel.

In the context of networking, the operating system facilitates communication between computers and devices over networks. Network protocols, implemented as part of the operating system's networking stack, govern the transmission and reception of data packets, ensuring reliable and secure communication. The OS manages network interfaces, IP addressing, and routing, enabling applications to leverage network resources seamlessly.

The bootstrapping process, or booting, is a critical phase orchestrated by the operating system when a computer is powered on or restarted. The operating system loader, typically residing in the computer's firmware or on a designated boot device, initiates the loading of the OS kernel into memory. The kernel, the core of the operating system, takes control of the system, initializing hardware components, configuring system settings, and preparing the environment for user interaction.

Beyond these foundational functions, the operating system facilitates the development and execution of software applications through its application programming interfaces (APIs) and libraries.

APIs provide a standardized set of functions and services that applications can leverage without needing to understand the intricacies of the underlying hardware. This abstraction layer simplifies software development, promotes code reusability, and ensures compatibility across different hardware architectures.

The concept of process management is central to the functioning of an operating system. A process, in this context, refers to a program in execution, and the operating system is responsible for creating, scheduling, and terminating processes. Process control blocks (PCBs) maintain information about each process, including its state, program counter, registers, and memory space. Context switching, a fundamental aspect of process management, enables the operating system to switch between different processes, allowing multitasking and concurrent execution.

In the realm of real-time operating systems (RTOS), the operating system is tailored to meet the stringent timing requirements of real-time applications. These applications, found in domains such as aerospace, industrial automation, and medical devices, demand precise and predictable response times. Real-time operating systems prioritize tasks with specific deadlines, implement deterministic scheduling algorithms, and ensure that critical processes receive timely access to system resources.

Distributed operating systems extend the traditional operating system model to manage resources and processes across multiple interconnected machines. Coordination of distributed systems involves mechanisms for communication, synchronization, and data consistency. These systems leverage principles such as fault tolerance, load balancing, and distributed file systems to optimize resource utilization and enhance reliability across a network of interconnected computers.

The role of the operating system also encompasses error handling and recovery mechanisms to ensure system stability and resilience.

When errors occur, the operating system employs various strategies to contain the impact and recover gracefully. Logging, error messages, and system monitoring tools provide diagnostic information to aid in the identification and resolution of issues. Additionally, the operating system may implement mechanisms such as checkpoints and rollback procedures to recover from system failures without compromising data integrity.

Throughout its evolution, the operating system has adapted to the changing landscape of computing, from mainframes and minicomputers to personal computers, servers, mobile devices, and the cloud. The emergence of virtualization technologies has further transformed the role of the operating system, allowing multiple operating system instances to run on a single physical machine. Containerization, exemplified by technologies like Docker, introduces lightweight and portable environments, reshaping the deployment and scalability of applications.

In conclusion, the operating system serves as the linchpin of computing environments, providing essential abstractions, services, and management functions that enable the effective utilization of hardware resources and the execution of diverse software applications. Its role spans a spectrum of responsibilities, from memory and process management to file systems, security, networking, and error recovery. As technology continues to advance, the operating system remains a foundational element, adapting to new paradigms and serving as a bridge between hardware and the evolving needs of users and applications in an ever-changing computing landscape.

Types of kernels (monolithic, microkernel, hybrid)

In the realm of operating systems, the design and structure of the kernel play a pivotal role in shaping the overall functionality, performance, and flexibility of the system. Three main types of kernels have emerged as architectural paradigms: monolithic kernels, microkernels, and hybrid kernels. Each type exhibits distinct characteristics, trade-offs, and applications, influencing the design choices made by operating system developers.

The monolithic kernel represents one of the earliest and simplest kernel architectures. In a monolithic design, the entire operating system, including essential services and device drivers, is implemented as a single, large program running in kernel mode. This unified structure allows for efficient communication and data sharing between different components of the kernel. However, it also presents challenges in terms of complexity and modularity. A change or error in one part of the monolithic kernel can potentially impact the entire system. Despite these challenges, monolithic kernels are known for their performance, as they minimize the overhead associated with inter-module communication. Examples of operating systems employing monolithic kernels include early versions of Unix, Linux, and Windows.

Microkernels represent a departure from the monolithic architecture by adopting a minimalist and modular design philosophy. In a microkernel system, the core functions of the kernel, such as process scheduling, inter-process communication (IPC), and memory management, are implemented as a small and essential nucleus. Other services traditionally included in monolithic kernels, such as file systems, device drivers, and networking protocols, are implemented as separate user-space processes, termed servers. This separation enhances modularity and allows for easier maintenance, debugging, and extensibility. Microkernels aim to provide a reliable and stable foundation, with additional services operating in user space to reduce the impact of errors on the overall system. Notable microkernel-based operating systems include QNX and MINIX.

Hybrid kernels, as the name suggests, blend elements of both monolithic and microkernel architectures. In a hybrid design, a small, essential set of services is implemented in kernel space, similar to a microkernel. However, certain crucial functions, such as device drivers and file systems, may still run in kernel space for improved performance. This hybrid approach seeks to strike a balance between the simplicity and modularity of microkernels and the performance advantages of monolithic kernels. An advantage of hybrid kernels is the ability to achieve a level of performance close to that of monolithic kernels while maintaining the benefits of modularity. Microsoft Windows NT and its successors, including Windows 10, exemplify the hybrid kernel architecture.

The monolithic kernel architecture, with its unified and tightly integrated design, offers advantages in terms of efficiency and performance. Since all components reside in the same address space and can directly communicate, the overhead associated with inter-process communication is minimized. This leads to faster system calls and improved overall throughput. The simplicity of monolithic kernels also facilitates ease of development, as there is less need for complex mechanisms to manage communication between different kernel modules.

However, the monolithic architecture is not without its drawbacks. The tight coupling of components means that a failure or error in one module can potentially affect the entire system. Additionally, updating or modifying one part of the kernel may require recompiling and restarting the entire system, leading to downtime. As the complexity of operating systems and the variety of supported hardware increased, some of these challenges became more pronounced.

Microkernels address some of the limitations of monolithic kernels by promoting a modular and minimalistic design. The core functions essential for managing processes, memory, and communication are kept in a small kernel, while additional services are implemented as separate user-space processes. This separation of concerns enhances the overall modularity of the system, making it easier to understand, maintain, and extend. Microkernels also offer improved fault isolation, as errors in non-essential services do not directly impact the kernel or other critical components. This design promotes system stability and reliability.

Furthermore, microkernels facilitate extensibility by allowing developers to add or replace services without modifying the kernel itself. This modular approach aligns well with the principles of code reuse and separation of concerns. For example, a microkernel-based system can have interchangeable file systems, networking stacks, or device drivers, providing flexibility in tailoring the operating system to different use cases. MINIX, an educational operating system developed by Andrew Tanenbaum, serves as a notable example of a microkernel-based system.

Despite these advantages, microkernels introduce challenges related to performance. Communication between user-space servers and the kernel, which was previously internal to a monolithic kernel, now incurs additional overhead due to inter-process communication. This can lead to slower system calls and reduced overall throughput. While advancements in microkernel research and implementation have mitigated some of these performance issues, they remain a consideration in the evaluation of microkernel-based systems.

Hybrid kernels combine elements of both monolithic and microkernel architectures, aiming to strike a balance between performance and modularity. In a hybrid design, essential services are implemented in kernel space, similar to a microkernel, while certain critical functions, such as device drivers, may still run in kernel space for improved performance. This hybrid approach leverages the benefits of modularity and fault isolation while retaining some of the performance advantages associated with monolithic kernels.

An important advantage of hybrid kernels is the ability to achieve a level of performance that approaches that of monolithic kernels. By retaining critical components in kernel space, hybrid kernels can minimize the performance overhead associated with inter-process communication. This makes them well-suited for applications where performance is a crucial consideration, such as in desktop operating systems like Microsoft Windows NT and its successors.

Hybrid kernels also provide a degree of flexibility in terms of system design. Developers can choose to implement certain components as user-space servers for enhanced modularity or keep them in kernel space for improved performance. This adaptability allows for customization based on specific use cases and requirements. The Windows operating system family, including Windows 10, exemplifies the hybrid kernel architecture employed by Microsoft.

In summary, the choice between monolithic, microkernel, or hybrid kernel architectures involves trade-offs and considerations based on the goals, priorities, and requirements of the operating system. Monolithic kernels prioritize performance and simplicity, while microkernels emphasize modularity, fault isolation, and extensibility. Hybrid kernels seek to combine the strengths of both approaches, offering a balance between performance and modularity. Each architecture has found its niche in different operating systems, contributing to the diversity and adaptability of modern computing environments.

Process management and scheduling

Process management and scheduling are fundamental aspects of operating systems, intricately involved in the orchestration of tasks, efficient resource utilization, and the creation of a responsive computing environment. Process management encompasses a suite of activities related to the lifecycle of processes—programs in execution on a computer system. The operating system, acting as the supervisor, oversees the creation, scheduling, termination, and communication between processes. As processes are the basic units of execution, their effective management is crucial for optimizing system performance and facilitating multitasking.

The process creation phase marks the initiation of a new process within the operating system. This involves allocating the necessary resources, including memory space, for the process to execute. The newly created process inherits attributes from its parent process, such as file descriptors, environment variables, and code segments. Inter-process communication (IPC) mechanisms may be established during creation to facilitate collaboration between processes, allowing them to share data and synchronize their activities.

Once created, processes enter the scheduling phase, a core component of process management. Scheduling refers to the mechanism by which the operating system determines the order in which processes are executed on the CPU. The goal of scheduling is to optimize system throughput, response time, and fairness, ensuring that all processes receive a fair share of CPU time. Various scheduling algorithms, such as round-robin, priority-based, and multi-level queue scheduling, govern the allocation of CPU resources to processes based on predefined criteria.

Round-robin scheduling is a widely used algorithm where each process is assigned a fixed time slice or quantum on the CPU. Processes take turns executing for their allotted time, and the scheduler switches to the next process in the queue when the time slice expires. This ensures fairness and prevents a single process from monopolizing the CPU. Priority-based scheduling assigns priorities to processes, and the scheduler selects the highest-priority process for execution. While effective in ensuring high-priority tasks are addressed promptly, this approach may lead to lower-priority tasks waiting indefinitely.

Multi-level queue scheduling organizes processes into priority queues, each with its own scheduling algorithm. Processes move between queues based on their behavior and resource usage. This approach allows for the efficient handling of diverse workloads, as processes with similar characteristics are grouped together. However, it requires careful tuning of parameters to balance responsiveness and fairness.

The scheduling phase also involves considerations of preemption, which allows the operating system to interrupt the execution of a process to start or resume another. Preemption ensures that high-priority tasks can be addressed promptly and that no process monopolizes the CPU, contributing to a more responsive and equitable system.

Process termination is the final stage in the process lifecycle, where a process concludes its execution. The operating system reclaims resources allocated to the terminated process, freeing up memory and other system assets. Additionally, termination may involve the release of files, network connections, and other resources associated with the process. Proper termination procedures are crucial to prevent resource leaks and ensure the efficient reuse of system resources.

Concurrency and parallelism are inherent aspects of modern computing, and process management plays a central role in facilitating these concepts. Concurrency involves the execution of multiple processes simultaneously, allowing users to run several applications concurrently. Operating systems achieve this by interleaving the execution of processes, giving the illusion of simultaneous execution. Parallelism, on the other hand, involves the simultaneous execution of tasks on multiple processors or cores, providing true concurrency and enhancing system performance. Process management in a parallel environment requires coordination and synchronization mechanisms to avoid conflicts and ensure the correct execution of parallel tasks.

Thread management is an extension of process management that introduces the concept of threads—lightweight, independent units of execution within a process. Threads share the same address space and resources, allowing for efficient communication and data sharing. Thread creation, scheduling, and termination are managed by the operating system, providing a flexible and responsive platform for concurrent execution. Multi-threaded applications leverage threads to perform multiple tasks concurrently, enhancing performance and responsiveness.

Synchronization and communication mechanisms become crucial in a multi-threaded environment to prevent race conditions and ensure data consistency. Techniques such as locks, semaphores, and condition variables are employed to coordinate the execution of threads and avoid conflicts. Synchronization is essential to maintain the integrity of shared data structures and prevent issues such as data corruption or unpredictable behavior.

In addition to process and thread management, the operating system handles inter-process communication (IPC) to facilitate collaboration and data exchange between processes. IPC mechanisms include shared memory, message passing, pipes, and sockets. Shared memory allows processes to share a common region of memory for communication, while message passing involves the exchange of data through explicit messages. Pipes and sockets enable communication between processes running on different machines or across a network. IPC mechanisms contribute to the creation of cohesive and collaborative computing environments, allowing processes to work together to achieve complex tasks.

Real-time operating systems (RTOS) introduce a specialized dimension to process management, focusing on tasks with stringent timing requirements. Real-time tasks must complete within specified deadlines to ensure the correct functioning of systems such as embedded devices, industrial automation, and control systems. RTOS employ deterministic scheduling algorithms and priority-based schemes to guarantee timely execution of real-time tasks. Ensuring predictable response times and minimizing latency is critical in scenarios where timing accuracy is paramount.

The concept of multi-core and multi-processor systems further complicates process management, introducing the need for efficient load balancing and resource allocation. Operating systems must adapt to the distributed nature of resources and ensure that processes are allocated to cores or processors in a manner that maximizes system throughput. Load balancing algorithms distribute tasks evenly across available processors, preventing situations where some processors are idle while others are overloaded.

In distributed systems, where processes span multiple machines, distributed process management becomes essential. Coordination, communication, and synchronization across networked nodes are critical for achieving consistency and reliability. Distributed systems employ protocols, algorithms, and distributed databases to ensure that processes running on different machines can collaborate seamlessly and share data in a coordinated manner.

Fault tolerance is a crucial consideration in process management, especially in mission-critical systems where system failures can have severe consequences. Operating systems implement mechanisms such as checkpointing, redundancy, and error recovery to enhance the resilience of processes. Checkpointing involves saving the state of a process at specific intervals, allowing for recovery in case of a failure. Redundancy involves duplicating critical components or processes to ensure continued operation even if one instance fails. Error recovery mechanisms detect and correct errors to prevent cascading failures and maintain system stability.

In conclusion, process management and scheduling are integral components of operating systems, playing a foundational role in the execution, coordination, and efficient utilization of resources. The lifecycle of processes—from creation and scheduling to termination—involves intricate mechanisms and algorithms that balance the goals of responsiveness, fairness, and resource efficiency. As computing environments evolve with the advent of multi-core processors, distributed systems, and real-time requirements, the principles of process management continue to adapt to meet the demands of diverse applications and ensure the smooth functioning of modern operating systems.

Memory management and virtual memory

Memory management is a critical function of operating systems, responsible for the efficient allocation, utilization, and protection of a computer's memory resources. It encompasses a range of activities, including managing the physical and virtual memory spaces, ensuring processes have access to the required memory, and preventing conflicts between different processes. In the context of modern operating systems, memory management plays a pivotal role in providing a cohesive and responsive environment for applications while abstracting the complexities of underlying hardware.

At the core of memory management is the concept of physical memory, referring to the actual RAM (Random Access Memory) installed in a computer. Physical memory is finite, and the operating system must judiciously allocate it to various processes running concurrently. During the execution of a program, the operating system assigns portions of physical memory to store the program's code, data, and stack. This allocation is dynamic, with memory being allocated and deallocated as processes start, run, and terminate.

One key aspect of memory management is addressing, a mechanism that enables the operating system to uniquely identify each byte in memory. In systems with a 32-bit address space, each memory address corresponds to a 32-bit binary number, allowing for the addressing of 2^{32} (approximately 4 billion) distinct memory locations. More recently, 64-bit systems have become prevalent, providing an even larger address space and accommodating the increasing demands of modern applications.

Virtual memory, an extension of physical memory, plays a crucial role in overcoming the limitations of finite RAM. Virtual memory allows the operating system to create an illusion of a larger memory space than is physically available by leveraging a combination of RAM and secondary storage, such as hard drives or SSDs. This abstraction enables the execution of larger programs and facilitates efficient multitasking, as the operating system can temporarily store portions of less frequently used programs or data in secondary storage, freeing up RAM for more immediate needs.

The operating system achieves virtual memory through a technique known as paging. In a paged memory system, physical memory is divided into fixed-size blocks called pages, and the secondary storage is divided into corresponding blocks called page frames. When a program is loaded into memory, its address space is divided into pages, and the operating system maintains a page table to track the mapping between virtual pages and physical page frames. When a program accesses a portion of its virtual memory that is not currently in RAM, a page fault occurs, prompting the operating system to retrieve the required page from secondary storage and load it into an available page frame.

Another approach to virtual memory management is segmentation, which divides a program's address space into segments, each serving a specific purpose such as code, data, or stack. Each segment is independently managed, allowing for flexibility in memory allocation. Segmentation, however, can lead to fragmentation, where memory is divided into small, non-contiguous blocks, potentially impacting system performance.

The demand paging strategy enhances the efficiency of virtual memory systems by bringing in pages only when they are required, rather than loading the entire program into memory at the start. This approach minimizes the initial loading time and conserves memory resources. However, it introduces the possibility of page faults, which occur when a program accesses a page that is not currently in RAM. The operating system must then handle the page fault by bringing the required page into memory, which may involve swapping out a less frequently used page to secondary storage.

Page replacement algorithms are employed to determine which page to evict when a page fault occurs and a free page frame is needed. Common page replacement algorithms include the Least Recently Used (LRU), First-In-First-Out (FIFO), and Optimal algorithms. LRU replaces the page that has not been used for the longest time, while FIFO replaces the oldest page. The Optimal algorithm, although impractical to implement in real-time, serves as a benchmark by selecting the page that will not be used for the longest time in the future.

Memory protection is an integral aspect of memory management, ensuring that processes do not interfere with each other's memory space. Each process is assigned its own address space, isolated from other processes. The operating system enforces protection mechanisms, preventing processes from accessing unauthorized memory regions and ensuring the integrity and security of the system. Unauthorized access attempts result in memory protection violations and may lead to termination of the offending process.

In addition to memory protection, the operating system employs memory isolation to shield processes from one another. Each process perceives its address space as if it were the only program running on the system. This isolation prevents unintended interactions between processes, enhancing system stability and security.

Memory management extends beyond the allocation and deallocation of memory to include mechanisms for optimizing memory usage. One such mechanism is memory caching, where frequently accessed data is stored in a small, high-speed memory known as a cache. Caching exploits the principle of temporal and spatial locality, anticipating that recently accessed data is likely to be accessed again in the near future. By maintaining a cache of frequently used data, the operating system enhances overall system performance and reduces the latency associated with fetching data from slower storage devices.

Shared memory is another memory management technique that facilitates communication and collaboration between processes. In a shared memory system, multiple processes can access a common region of memory, enabling them to exchange data efficiently. Shared memory is particularly useful in scenarios where processes need to communicate or synchronize their activities, as it provides a fast and direct means of inter-process communication.

In distributed systems, where processes span multiple machines, distributed memory management becomes essential. Coordination, communication, and synchronization across networked nodes are critical for achieving consistency and reliability. Distributed systems employ protocols, algorithms, and distributed databases to ensure that processes running on different machines can collaborate seamlessly and share data in a coordinated manner.

Memory fragmentation, a common challenge in memory management, can occur in two forms: external fragmentation and internal fragmentation. External fragmentation arises when free memory blocks are scattered throughout the address space, making it challenging to allocate contiguous blocks of memory to processes. Internal fragmentation occurs when allocated memory blocks are larger than necessary, resulting in wasted memory. Techniques such as compaction, which involves relocating processes to consolidate free memory, and dynamic memory allocation algorithms aim to mitigate the effects of fragmentation.

Dynamic memory allocation allows processes to request and release memory dynamically during runtime. The operating system provides memory allocation functions, such as malloc() and free() in C, to facilitate dynamic memory management. Heap memory, where dynamically allocated memory resides, is managed by the operating system to ensure efficient utilization and prevent memory leaks, where allocated memory is not properly released.

In conclusion, memory management is a multifaceted aspect of operating systems, encompassing the allocation, utilization, and protection of physical and virtual memory. The evolution of memory management techniques, from simple physical memory allocation to sophisticated virtual memory systems, reflects the ongoing effort to address the challenges posed by finite memory resources. Memory protection, isolation, and optimization mechanisms contribute to the creation of robust and responsive computing environments, while dynamic memory allocation and distributed memory management cater to the diverse needs of modern applications and distributed systems.

Interaction between the kernel and hardware

The interaction between the kernel and hardware forms a fundamental bridge in the architecture of operating systems, facilitating the seamless communication and coordination necessary for the effective utilization of a computer's resources. At the heart of this interaction lies the kernel, the core component of an operating system responsible for managing hardware resources and providing a uniform interface for user applications. The kernel operates in privileged mode, often referred to as kernel mode or supervisor mode, enabling it to execute privileged instructions and directly access hardware components.

The kernel interacts with hardware through a set of routines known as device drivers. Device drivers serve as intermediaries between the kernel and specific hardware devices, translating high-level commands issued by the operating system into low-level instructions understandable by the hardware. These drivers encapsulate the intricacies of hardware communication, allowing the kernel to communicate with diverse devices such as storage controllers, network interfaces, graphics cards, and input/output peripherals.

Central to the interaction between the kernel and hardware is the concept of system calls. System calls provide a controlled entry point for user applications to request services from the kernel. When a user program requires access to hardware resources or privileged operations, it issues system calls to the kernel. These system calls act as a boundary between user space, where applications run, and kernel space, where the operating system and device drivers reside.

The kernel orchestrates the allocation and management of hardware resources, ensuring fair and secure access for multiple applications. For instance, the kernel regulates access to the central processing unit (CPU) through scheduling algorithms, determining which processes are granted CPU time and in what order. This scheduling is crucial for achieving system responsiveness, efficiency, and fairness in the execution of diverse applications.

Memory management is another critical aspect of the kernel's interaction with hardware. The kernel is responsible for overseeing the allocation and deallocation of memory space for processes, ensuring that each application has access to the required memory while preventing conflicts between processes. The kernel manages both physical and virtual memory, utilizing techniques such as paging and segmentation to optimize memory usage and provide an abstraction layer for user applications.

The interaction between the kernel and storage devices is vital for data persistence and retrieval. File systems, managed by the kernel, organize and store data on storage devices such as hard drives and solid-state drives. The kernel communicates with storage controllers through device drivers to read and write data, maintaining file structures, and ensuring data integrity. Storage management involves handling file permissions, managing file hierarchies, and executing file operations requested by user applications.

Network communication represents another realm of interaction between the kernel and hardware. The kernel manages network interfaces through network device drivers, enabling communication over local area networks (LANs) or wide area networks (WANs). Network protocols, implemented in the kernel, govern the transmission and reception of data packets, ensuring reliable and secure communication between devices. The kernel handles tasks such as IP address assignment, routing, and packet filtering to facilitate seamless network connectivity.

The bootstrapping process, or booting, marks a crucial phase in the interaction between the kernel and hardware. When a computer is powered on or restarted, the initial control is passed to a special program known as the bootloader. The bootloader, residing in the computer's firmware or on a designated boot device, loads the kernel into memory and transfers control to the kernel. During this process, the kernel initializes hardware components, configures system settings, and prepares the environment for the execution of user applications.

The kernel's interaction with hardware extends to interrupt handling, a mechanism that enables hardware devices to signal the CPU about specific events or conditions that require attention. Interrupts serve as a means for hardware devices to communicate with the kernel asynchronously. When an interrupt occurs, the CPU interrupts its current execution and transfers control to the appropriate interrupt handler in the kernel. This handler addresses the event signaled by the interrupt, such as input from a keyboard, data arrival on a network interface, or completion of a storage operation.

Security is a paramount consideration in the interaction between the kernel and hardware. The kernel enforces access control mechanisms, ensuring that only authorized processes and users can perform privileged operations or access specific hardware resources. User authentication, implemented by the kernel, validates the identity of users and applications, preventing unauthorized access to sensitive system components.

In modern computing environments, virtualization technologies have introduced new dimensions to the interaction between the kernel and hardware. Hypervisors, operating at a layer above the kernel, enable the simultaneous execution of multiple virtual machines on a single physical machine. The kernel of each virtual machine interacts with a virtualized set of hardware resources provided by the hypervisor. This abstraction allows for resource isolation, enhanced scalability, and efficient resource utilization in virtualized environments.

The development of graphics processing units (GPUs) has introduced complexities in the interaction between the kernel and hardware. GPUs, originally designed for rendering graphics, are now utilized for parallel processing tasks such as scientific simulations, machine learning, and general-purpose computing. The kernel interacts with GPUs through specialized drivers, offloading parallelizable tasks to the GPU for accelerated computation. This interaction requires coordination between the CPU and GPU to ensure data synchronization and efficient task execution.

Embedded systems represent another domain where the interaction between the kernel and hardware is crucial. In embedded environments, operating systems tailored for specific hardware configurations manage devices with resource constraints. The kernel in embedded systems oversees real-time requirements, power management, and efficient utilization of limited resources to ensure optimal performance in devices ranging from IoT devices to embedded controllers in automotive systems.

The interaction between the kernel and hardware is not static but evolves with advancements in hardware technology and the changing landscape of computing. The kernel serves as a mediator, providing a standardized interface for applications while efficiently managing and abstracting the complexities of diverse hardware components. As computing architectures continue to evolve, from traditional desktops and servers to mobile devices, edge computing, and the cloud, the kernel's role in facilitating seamless interaction with an increasingly diverse array of hardware remains pivotal in shaping the efficiency, security, and responsiveness of modern computing environments.

Strategies for efficient input/output operations

Efficient input/output (I/O) operations are crucial for the overall performance and responsiveness of computer systems. I/O operations involve the transfer of data between a computer and external devices, such as storage devices, network interfaces, and user input devices. Strategies for optimizing I/O operations encompass a range of techniques, from hardware-level optimizations to software-driven approaches, all aimed at minimizing latency, maximizing throughput, and ensuring smooth interaction between the computer and its peripherals.

At the hardware level, optimizing I/O performance often involves advancements in storage and communication technologies. For storage devices, the transition from traditional hard disk drives (HDDs) to solid-state drives (SSDs) has been a transformative development. SSDs, with no moving parts and faster access times, significantly reduce latency in reading and writing data. Additionally, technologies like Non-Volatile Memory Express (NVMe) further enhance SSD performance by providing a more efficient communication interface between the storage device and the system.

Caching mechanisms play a pivotal role in I/O optimization, both at the hardware and software levels. Caching involves storing frequently accessed data in a high-speed memory, such as RAM or dedicated cache memory. This helps reduce the need for repeated access to slower storage devices. In hardware, disk controllers often incorporate caching strategies to prefetch data and optimize the order of read and write operations. At the software level, operating systems employ file system caches to store frequently accessed data in system memory, reducing the time required to retrieve information from secondary storage.

Parallelism is a key strategy for improving I/O efficiency, leveraging multiple processing units or cores to perform I/O operations concurrently. Parallel I/O is particularly beneficial in scenarios involving large datasets, as it allows multiple read or write operations to occur simultaneously. Modern operating systems and file systems support parallel I/O through techniques like asynchronous I/O operations and parallel file systems. Asynchronous I/O enables programs to initiate I/O operations and continue processing other tasks while waiting for the completion of the I/O requests, reducing idle time and improving overall system efficiency.

Buffering is a fundamental technique employed to enhance I/O performance by minimizing the number of direct interactions with external devices. Buffering involves temporarily storing data in a buffer or cache before it is read or written to a storage device. This allows the system to perform more efficient block transfers, reducing the overhead associated with individual data transfers. Buffers can be implemented at various levels, including application-level buffering within programs, kernel-level buffering within the operating system, and hardware-level buffering within storage controllers.

I/O scheduling algorithms are integral to optimizing the order in which I/O requests are serviced, particularly in scenarios with multiple competing requests. These algorithms determine the sequence in which pending I/O operations are executed, aiming to minimize seek times and maximize throughput. Common I/O scheduling algorithms include First-Come-First-Serve (FCFS), Shortest Seek Time First (SSTF), and Elevator (SCAN or C-SCAN). SSTF, for instance, prioritizes servicing the I/O request with the shortest seek time, reducing the physical movement of disk heads and improving overall I/O efficiency.

Caching can also be implemented at the application level through the use of in-memory data structures. For example, databases often employ caching mechanisms to store frequently accessed data in memory, reducing the need to repeatedly fetch information from persistent storage. This in-memory caching strategy enhances data retrieval speed and responsiveness, particularly for read-heavy workloads.

Optimizing network I/O involves strategies for efficient communication between systems over networks. Techniques such as pipelining and batch processing help streamline the transfer of data, reducing the overhead associated with individual network transactions. Pipelining allows multiple network requests to be initiated before receiving the responses, enabling continuous data flow and minimizing idle time. Batch processing involves bundling multiple data transfers into a single larger transaction, reducing the per-operation overhead and improving network efficiency.

Compression and decompression algorithms play a role in I/O optimization, particularly when dealing with large datasets. Compressing data before writing it to storage or transmitting it over a network reduces the amount of data that needs to be transferred, saving both time and bandwidth. However, it's essential to strike a balance between the computational cost of compression and the benefits gained in terms of reduced I/O times and network utilization.

Efficient error handling is a critical aspect of I/O optimization, ensuring that the system can gracefully recover from I/O errors without causing disruptions. Error recovery mechanisms, such as error-correcting codes (ECC) in memory and error detection and correction in storage systems, help maintain data integrity. Additionally, retry mechanisms and graceful degradation strategies enable the system to continue functioning even in the presence of transient I/O errors, minimizing the impact on overall system reliability.

File system optimizations contribute significantly to I/O efficiency, focusing on the organization and management of data on storage devices. Techniques like defragmentation, which reorganizes fragmented files on a storage medium, reduce seek times and improve sequential read and write performance. File system journaling, a method for recording changes to file systems, enhances recovery after unexpected system failures, ensuring the consistency of stored data.

I/O prioritization allows the system to assign different priorities to various I/O operations based on their importance or urgency. This ensures that critical tasks, such as real-time processing or user interactions, receive preferential treatment in terms of I/O access. Prioritization mechanisms are particularly relevant in multitasking environments, where numerous applications may compete for I/O resources.

Optimizing I/O performance in virtualized environments involves strategies that account for the shared nature of hardware resources among multiple virtual machines. Techniques such as I/O virtualization, where a hypervisor mediates access to I/O devices for virtual machines, help prevent contention and ensure fair allocation of I/O resources. Additionally, technologies like paravirtualization, which involves collaboration between guest operating systems and the hypervisor for efficient I/O handling, contribute to improved performance in virtualized environments.

In conclusion, strategies for efficient input/output operations span a spectrum of hardware and software techniques, each contributing to the overall responsiveness and performance of computer systems. These strategies encompass advancements in storage and communication technologies, parallelism, caching, buffering, scheduling algorithms, network optimizations, compression, error handling, file system optimizations, I/O prioritization, and considerations for virtualized environments. The holistic approach to I/O optimization involves a careful balance between these techniques, considering the specific requirements and characteristics of the computing environment to achieve optimal efficiency in data transfer and communication with external devices.

Design principles and file organization

Design principles and file organization are fundamental aspects of constructing efficient and accessible storage systems, playing a crucial role in managing and retrieving data in a structured manner. These principles guide the architecture of file systems, defining how information is stored, accessed, and organized on storage devices. The design of file systems revolves around optimizing performance, reliability, and scalability while adhering to principles that ensure data integrity and ease of use.

One of the fundamental design principles in file organization is hierarchical structuring, where files are organized in a tree-like hierarchy of directories or folders. This hierarchical arrangement provides a logical and intuitive organization of data, allowing users to navigate through levels of directories to locate specific files. The root directory serves as the top-level container, branching into subdirectories that can further branch into additional levels. This hierarchical structure enhances the ease of file management and helps users create a meaningful organization for their data.

Another key design principle is the abstraction of physical storage details from users through logical addressing. The file system presents a logical view of data to users, abstracting away the physical details of storage devices. Files are identified by logical addresses, such as filenames or paths, rather than physical addresses on storage media. This abstraction simplifies file access and management, allowing users to interact with data in a more intuitive manner without needing to concern themselves with the intricacies of storage hardware.

File naming conventions are essential for effective file organization and retrieval. Meaningful and descriptive filenames contribute to the overall usability of a file system. Naming conventions often include alphanumeric characters, allowing for flexibility and readability. Some file systems also support the use of extensions to denote file types, aiding users in identifying the nature of a file. Well-designed naming conventions contribute to a user-friendly experience and facilitate efficient data management.

File attributes, such as permissions, timestamps, and ownership information, are critical components of file organization and access control. Permissions determine who can read, write, or execute a file, ensuring data security and privacy. Timestamps record information about the creation, modification, and access times of files, aiding in version control and auditing. Ownership information associates files with specific users or groups, facilitating accountability and access management. These attributes collectively contribute to a robust system for organizing and securing data.

The concept of directories or folders extends beyond mere organization; it also supports logical partitioning and access control. Directories enable users to group related files together, providing a structured means of organization. Additionally, directories contribute to access control by allowing administrators to set permissions at different directory levels, restricting or granting access to specific users or groups. This hierarchical access control model enhances security and ensures that users can only interact with files for which they have the appropriate permissions.

File systems employ data structures such as file allocation tables (FAT), indexed allocation, and extent-based allocation to manage the physical allocation of data on storage devices. The choice of allocation method influences factors like storage efficiency, access speed, and fragmentation. FAT systems maintain a table that maps logical clusters to physical addresses, providing a straightforward but potentially less efficient approach. Indexed allocation uses an index structure to store pointers to data blocks, offering faster access times but introducing overhead. Extent-based allocation assigns continuous blocks of storage to files, minimizing fragmentation but potentially leading to inefficient use of space.

Efficient file organization necessitates strategies for managing free space and handling file growth. File systems implement techniques like free space bitmaps and linked lists to track available storage space. Free space bitmaps maintain a bitmap indicating the occupied and vacant blocks, enabling quick identification of free space. Linked lists utilize pointers to connect free blocks, simplifying space management but potentially introducing fragmentation. Dynamic file growth mechanisms, such as extending file allocation or utilizing techniques like preallocation, allow file systems to adapt to changing storage needs without unnecessary overhead.

Journaling is a design principle employed to enhance the reliability and recoverability of file systems. Journaling involves maintaining a log, or journal, of changes made to the file system. In the event of a system crash or unexpected shutdown, the file system can use the journal to recover and restore the system to a consistent state. This ensures data integrity and reduces the risk of file system corruption. Journaling is particularly crucial for file systems that prioritize reliability, such as those used in critical server environments.

Security considerations are integral to file organization, with access control mechanisms and encryption playing pivotal roles. Access control lists (ACLs) and permissions regulate user and group access to files and directories. Encryption safeguards data by encoding it in a manner that only authorized users can decipher. File systems may implement encryption at various levels, including file-level encryption, directory-level encryption, or full-disk encryption. These security measures are crucial for protecting sensitive data and maintaining the confidentiality and integrity of information stored in the file system.

Fault tolerance and redundancy are essential design principles in file organization to mitigate the impact of hardware failures. Redundant array of independent disks (RAID) configurations provide fault tolerance by distributing data across multiple disks, enabling continued operation even if one disk fails. RAID levels, such as RAID 1 (mirroring) and RAID 5 (striping with parity), offer varying degrees of redundancy and performance. These configurations enhance data availability and reliability, crucial considerations in systems where uninterrupted access to data is paramount.

File compression is a strategy employed to optimize storage space and enhance data transfer efficiency. Compressed files occupy less space on storage media, reducing storage costs and accelerating data transmission over networks. Compression algorithms, such as ZIP or GZIP, are utilized to compress and decompress files. However, it's essential to strike a balance between compression ratios and computational overhead, as excessive compression may result in increased processing time.

File system journaling is a design principle employed to enhance the reliability and recoverability of file systems. Journaling involves maintaining a log, or journal, of changes made to the file system. In the event of a system crash or unexpected shutdown, the file system can use the journal to recover and restore the system to a consistent state. This ensures data integrity and reduces the risk of file system corruption. Journaling is particularly crucial for file systems that prioritize reliability, such as those used in critical server environments.

Security considerations are integral to file organization, with access control mechanisms and encryption playing pivotal roles. Access control lists (ACLs) and permissions regulate user and group access to files and directories. Encryption safeguards data by encoding it in a manner that only authorized users can decipher. File systems may implement encryption at various levels, including file-level encryption, directory-level encryption, or full-disk encryption. These security measures are crucial for protecting sensitive data and maintaining the confidentiality and integrity of information stored in the file system.

Fault tolerance and redundancy are essential design principles in file organization to mitigate the impact of hardware failures. Redundant array of independent disks (RAID) configurations provide fault tolerance by distributing data across multiple disks, enabling continued operation even if one disk fails. RAID levels, such as RAID 1 (mirroring) and RAID 5 (striping with parity), offer varying degrees of redundancy and performance. These configurations enhance data availability and reliability, crucial considerations in systems where uninterrupted access to data is paramount.

File compression is a strategy employed to optimize storage space and enhance data transfer efficiency. Compressed files occupy less space on storage media, reducing storage costs and accelerating data transmission over networks. Compression algorithms, such as ZIP or GZIP, are utilized to compress and decompress files. However, it's essential to strike a balance between compression ratios and computational overhead, as excessive compression may result in increased processing time.

In conclusion, the design principles and file organization strategies implemented in file systems are integral to creating structured, efficient, and reliable storage solutions. These principles address hierarchical structuring, logical addressing, naming conventions, file attributes, directory organization, data structure choices, free space management, journaling, security, fault tolerance, and compression. By adhering to these principles, file systems provide a foundation for effective data management, storage optimization, and reliable access to information, supporting diverse computing environments ranging from personal devices to enterprise-scale storage systems.

Security considerations in file management

Security considerations in file management are paramount in ensuring the confidentiality, integrity, and availability of data stored within a computing system. The management of files encompasses various aspects, ranging from access control and encryption to auditing and protection against malicious activities. One of the foundational elements of file security is access control, which involves regulating user and system permissions to determine who can read, write, or execute files. Access control mechanisms, implemented through permission settings and access control lists (ACLs), play a crucial role in preventing unauthorized access and ensuring that only authorized users can interact with specific files or directories.

Encryption is a fundamental security measure employed in file management to safeguard data from unauthorized access during storage or transmission. File-level encryption involves encoding the contents of individual files, rendering them unreadable without the appropriate decryption key. This encryption ensures that even if unauthorized users gain access to the storage medium, the encrypted files remain secure. Full-disk encryption extends this protection to the entire storage device, adding an additional layer of security against physical theft or unauthorized access.

File auditing mechanisms contribute to security by providing a record of file access and modifications. Auditing allows administrators to track user activities, detect suspicious behavior, and investigate security incidents. File system audit logs capture information such as who accessed a file, when the access occurred, and the type of action performed. These logs aid in compliance with security policies, facilitate forensic analysis, and contribute to the overall security posture of the system.

Secure deletion or data shredding is a security consideration that ensures the permanent removal of sensitive data from storage media. Simply deleting a file does not guarantee its complete elimination, as remnants may still exist on the storage device. Secure deletion methods, such as overwriting data multiple times or employing cryptographic techniques, ensure that deleted files cannot be easily recovered. This practice is especially crucial when dealing with classified or sensitive information to prevent unauthorized retrieval.

File integrity verification is essential for detecting and mitigating data tampering or corruption. Hash functions generate unique cryptographic checksums, or hash values, for files based on their content. Periodically verifying the integrity of files by comparing their current hash values with previously generated values allows administrators to identify unauthorized modifications. File integrity monitoring tools automate this process, providing real-time alerts when discrepancies are detected, enabling prompt responses to potential security incidents.

In the context of collaborative environments, version control systems contribute to file security by maintaining a history of file changes and facilitating the identification of authorized modifications. Versioning allows users to roll back to previous states of files, aiding in the recovery from unintentional changes or malicious activities. Version control is particularly crucial in scenarios where multiple users collaborate on shared documents, ensuring data consistency and accountability.

Security considerations extend to the physical protection of storage media to prevent unauthorized access or tampering. Physical security measures, such as access controls, surveillance, and secure storage environments, help safeguard storage devices from theft, vandalism, or tampering. Encrypting data on portable storage devices, such as USB drives, adds an extra layer of protection in case of loss or theft. Combining physical and logical security measures strengthens overall file management security.

Secure file transfer mechanisms are critical for protecting data during transmission over networks. Protocols like Secure File Transfer Protocol (SFTP) or protocols layered with Secure Sockets Layer (SSL) or Transport Layer Security (TLS) encryption ensure that files are transmitted securely, preventing eavesdropping and man-in-the-middle attacks. Secure file transfer mechanisms are especially vital when exchanging sensitive information over public networks, offering end-to-end encryption to safeguard data in transit.

Security patches and updates play a crucial role in maintaining file management security by addressing vulnerabilities in file system software. Regularly updating the operating system, file system, and associated security software ensures that known vulnerabilities are patched, reducing the risk of exploitation by malicious actors. Timely patching is a proactive measure to address emerging security threats and maintain the resilience of file management systems.

File system journaling contributes to security by enhancing the recoverability and consistency of the file system in the event of system crashes or unexpected shutdowns. The journal maintains a log of changes made to the file system, allowing for the restoration of the system to a consistent state. This not only improves data integrity but also helps prevent file system corruption that could be exploited by attackers to compromise the security of stored data.

Security awareness and training for users and administrators are integral components of file management security. Educating users about best practices, password hygiene, and the risks associated with sharing sensitive files helps create a security-conscious culture. Administrators need to stay informed about emerging threats, implement security policies, and conduct regular security audits to identify and address potential vulnerabilities in the file management infrastructure.

File management security is closely tied to the broader realm of cybersecurity. Antivirus software, intrusion detection systems, and firewalls contribute to overall system security by detecting and preventing malicious activities that may impact file integrity or compromise sensitive data. Implementing a defense-in-depth strategy, which combines multiple layers of security controls, helps create a robust security posture that extends beyond file management to safeguard the entire computing environment.

In conclusion, security considerations in file management are multifaceted and essential for ensuring the confidentiality, integrity, and availability of stored data. Access control, encryption, auditing, secure deletion, integrity verification, physical security, secure file transfer, patch management, journaling, and user awareness collectively contribute to a comprehensive security framework. By adopting these measures, organizations can mitigate the risk of unauthorized access, data breaches, and other security incidents, fostering a secure and resilient file management environment in the face of evolving cybersecurity challenges.

Common issues and solutions in kernel development

Kernel development, the process of designing and implementing the core component of an operating system responsible for managing system resources, poses various challenges that developers must navigate. Common issues in kernel development span a range of areas, including device drivers, memory management, process scheduling, and security. One frequent challenge is the development of stable and efficient device drivers. Device drivers act as intermediaries between the kernel and hardware, translating high-level commands into instructions understood by specific devices. Ensuring compatibility with diverse hardware configurations, handling interrupts, and managing power states are intricate tasks that demand meticulous attention to detail.

Memory management presents another common challenge in kernel development. Efficiently allocating and deallocating memory, preventing memory leaks, and handling virtual memory require robust solutions. Developers often grapple with the intricacies of page tables, addressing modes, and ensuring that the kernel's memory footprint is optimized. The balance between performance and reliability in memory management is crucial, as errors in this domain can lead to system instability, crashes, or security vulnerabilities.

Process scheduling is a critical aspect of kernel development that demands careful design to achieve fairness, responsiveness, and optimal system resource utilization. Designing scheduling algorithms that cater to both interactive and computational workloads, managing process priorities, and handling real-time constraints are complex tasks. Developers must address issues related to preemption, context switching overhead, and the efficient allocation of CPU time to ensure a responsive and efficient operating system.

Security considerations in kernel development are paramount, as the kernel is the heart of the operating system, governing access to system resources. Vulnerabilities in the kernel can lead to severe security breaches, and developers face the challenge of implementing robust access control mechanisms, protecting against privilege escalation, and mitigating the impact of potential exploits. Regular security audits, code reviews, and adherence to best practices are crucial to maintaining a secure kernel environment.

Maintaining compatibility and interoperability across different hardware architectures is a persistent challenge in kernel development. Achieving portability requires careful consideration of architecture-specific details, such as instruction set architectures, memory layouts, and hardware-specific optimizations. Developers often need to write architecture-specific code or use abstraction layers to ensure that the kernel can run seamlessly on a diverse range of hardware platforms.

Concurrency and synchronization issues present significant challenges in kernel development, given that the kernel must handle multiple tasks concurrently. Developers must contend with race conditions, deadlocks, and ensuring proper synchronization mechanisms to avoid data corruption or system instability. Locking strategies, such as mutexes and semaphores, need to be implemented judiciously to strike a balance between performance and correctness.

Real-time constraints and predictability are crucial in certain applications, such as embedded systems or critical infrastructure. Kernel developers face challenges in meeting stringent timing requirements, minimizing interrupt latencies, and providing deterministic behavior. Real-time scheduling policies and mechanisms for prioritizing time-sensitive tasks require careful design and implementation to ensure reliable and predictable system behavior.

Debugging and profiling kernel code pose unique challenges compared to user-space applications. Traditional debugging tools may not be as readily available, and developers often rely on specialized kernel debugging tools, kernel probes, and tracepoints. The lack of a traditional user interface in the kernel necessitates creative approaches for debugging, such as printk statements, kernel logs, and remote debugging setups.

Maintaining backward compatibility while introducing new features or making changes to the kernel is an ongoing concern. Kernel developers need to consider the impact of modifications on existing user-space applications, libraries, and device drivers. API and ABI stability are crucial for ensuring that updates to the kernel do not break existing software, and developers must carefully manage the deprecation and removal of older interfaces.

Documentation is a perennial challenge in kernel development. The complex nature of kernel internals requires comprehensive and accurate documentation to aid developers in understanding the intricacies of the codebase. Clear and up-to-date documentation facilitates collaboration among developers, contributes to the learning curve for newcomers, and enables the development of robust kernel modules and extensions.

Solutions to these challenges often involve a combination of meticulous design, thorough testing, collaboration within the open-source community, and adherence to established best practices. Continuous integration systems, automated testing frameworks, and code review processes are integral to identifying and addressing issues early in the development cycle. Engaging with the community through mailing lists, forums, and collaborative development platforms fosters knowledge exchange and collective problem-solving.

In addressing device driver challenges, developers employ strategies such as using hardware abstraction layers (HALs) to isolate hardware-specific details, adopting well-defined APIs for driver development, and leveraging frameworks like the Linux kernel's Device Model. Memory management challenges are tackled through careful algorithm design, the use of advanced data structures, and the implementation of memory protection mechanisms to prevent unauthorized access.

In the realm of process scheduling, developers explore scheduling policies tailored to specific use cases, optimizing context switch overhead, and incorporating real-time scheduling mechanisms. Security challenges are mitigated through rigorous code audits, the application of security principles like the principle of least privilege, and the integration of security-enhancing features such as Control Flow Integrity (CFI) and Address Space Layout Randomization (ASLR).

To address hardware compatibility challenges, kernel developers embrace modular design principles, ensuring that drivers can be loaded and unloaded dynamically. The Linux kernel, for instance, employs a modular architecture, enabling the addition or removal of kernel modules at runtime, promoting flexibility and ease of adaptation to different hardware configurations.

Concurrency and synchronization issues are tackled through the use of appropriate synchronization primitives, such as spinlocks, mutexes, and read-write locks. Developers employ careful design patterns, such as lock-free data structures, to minimize contention and enhance parallelism. Real-time constraints are met through the implementation of real-time scheduling policies, kernel preemption, and the reduction of interrupt latencies through techniques like interrupt coalescing.

Debugging challenges are addressed through the use of specialized tools, such as kprobes, ftrace, and dynamic kernel instrumentation frameworks. Profiling tools, like perf and SystemTap, aid in understanding the performance characteristics of the kernel. Backward compatibility concerns are managed through versioning, deprecation warnings, and communication with user-space developers to facilitate a smooth transition to new interfaces.

Documentation efforts involve maintaining accurate and comprehensive documentation within the kernel source code, as well as external documentation sources. Projects like kernel documentation in the Linux kernel source tree aim to provide in-depth information on various aspects of kernel development. Emphasizing the importance of detailed commit messages, inline code comments, and external documentation resources contributes to the overall understanding of the kernel codebase.

In conclusion, kernel development presents a myriad of challenges spanning device drivers, memory management, process scheduling, security, hardware compatibility, concurrency, real-time constraints, debugging, backward compatibility, and documentation. Developers employ a combination of best practices, collaborative approaches, rigorous testing, and specialized tools to address these challenges and ensure the creation of robust, efficient, and secure kernel systems. The evolution of open-source development models and community engagement further enhances the collective effort to overcome these challenges and advance the field of kernel development.

Balancing performance and stability

Balancing performance and stability is a perpetual challenge in the realm of software development, demanding careful consideration and strategic decision-making to optimize both aspects without compromising one for the other. This delicate equilibrium is particularly crucial in the development of operating systems, applications, and software systems where users expect a seamless experience marked by responsiveness, efficiency, and reliability.

The pursuit of performance often involves optimizing code, enhancing algorithmic efficiency, and leveraging hardware capabilities to deliver swift and resource-efficient execution. Developers strive to minimize execution times, reduce latency, and optimize memory usage to provide users with a responsive and fluid experience. Techniques such as code profiling, compiler optimizations, and parallelization play a pivotal role in achieving performance gains. However, the quest for enhanced performance introduces complexities and trade-offs that can potentially impact system stability.

One of the primary trade-offs in the performance-stability equation lies in the realm of software complexity. Introducing intricate optimizations or utilizing cutting-edge techniques may boost performance but can also introduce a higher likelihood of bugs, vulnerabilities, and unintended consequences. Balancing the desire for performance gains with the need for robustness requires a nuanced approach, with developers carefully weighing the benefits of optimizations against the potential risks of introducing complexity.

Concurrency and parallelism, while instrumental in improving performance by leveraging multi-core architectures, pose challenges in terms of stability. Managing shared resources, avoiding race conditions, and ensuring consistent behavior in a multi-threaded environment demand meticulous synchronization and error-handling mechanisms. The pursuit of parallelism to enhance performance must be tempered with comprehensive testing, debugging, and validation to mitigate the risks of concurrency-related issues that can compromise system stability.

In the context of operating systems, kernel development, and system-level software, optimizing I/O operations is a critical aspect of performance enhancement. Efficiently managing input and output, minimizing disk latency, and optimizing file systems contribute to a responsive system. However, aggressive I/O optimizations can introduce challenges related to data consistency, reliability, and potential data corruption. Striking a balance involves implementing caching mechanisms, asynchronous I/O, and error recovery strategies to enhance performance without compromising data integrity.

The deployment of aggressive compiler optimizations is another facet of the performance-stability trade-off. Compiler flags and optimizations can significantly improve execution speed by leveraging advanced code generation techniques. However, certain optimizations may lead to unexpected behaviors, especially when interacting with specific hardware or relying on assumptions about the underlying system. Developers must carefully evaluate the impact of compiler optimizations on both performance and stability, considering factors such as platform variability and compatibility.

In the pursuit of performance gains, the choice of data structures and algorithms becomes pivotal. Opting for highly optimized algorithms or data structures tailored to specific use cases can yield impressive speed improvements. However, the selection of complex or specialized structures may introduce a higher risk of implementation errors, memory leaks, or unexpected edge cases that could compromise stability. Achieving the right balance involves a nuanced evaluation of the trade-offs between algorithmic efficiency and code simplicity.

Memory management is a critical arena where the trade-off between performance and stability becomes evident. Efficient memory allocation and deallocation contribute to improved performance by reducing overhead and minimizing memory footprint. However, aggressive memory optimizations can lead to issues such as memory leaks, fragmentation, or undefined behavior. Striking a balance involves implementing robust memory management strategies, utilizing garbage collection mechanisms, and conducting thorough testing to identify and rectify potential memory-related issues.

In the domain of application development, graphical user interfaces (GUIs) provide a tangible interface for users to interact with software. The design and implementation of visually appealing and responsive GUIs are crucial for user satisfaction and perceived performance. However, introducing sophisticated graphical elements, animations, or dynamic content can strain system resources and impact stability. Developers must carefully optimize rendering processes, consider resource constraints, and implement graceful degradation mechanisms to ensure that the user experience remains stable even under varying conditions.

Maintaining a balance between performance and stability is particularly challenging in the context of real-time systems, where stringent timing constraints coexist with the demand for high performance. Real-time systems, prevalent in applications such as embedded systems, industrial control, and telecommunications, require predictable and deterministic behavior. Achieving optimal performance without violating real-time requirements necessitates specialized scheduling algorithms, prioritization mechanisms, and careful consideration of system resource utilization.

Security considerations add an additional layer of complexity to the performance-stability trade-off. Aggressive security measures, such as extensive encryption, access controls, and intrusion detection mechanisms, can introduce computational overhead and potentially impact performance. Striking the right balance involves implementing security measures without unduly compromising performance, adopting efficient encryption algorithms, and conducting regular security audits to identify and address vulnerabilities.

Continuous integration and continuous deployment (CI/CD) practices play a crucial role in managing the performance-stability trade-off in a dynamic development environment. Automated testing, code analysis, and deployment pipelines enable developers to catch performance bottlenecks, stability issues, and regressions early in the development cycle. CI/CD practices facilitate rapid iteration, allowing developers to implement optimizations and stability enhancements iteratively while minimizing the risk of introducing major issues.

User expectations and the specific use case of a software system also influence the optimal balance between performance and stability. In certain scenarios, such as scientific computing or high-performance computing, users may prioritize raw computational speed over other considerations. In contrast, applications focused on critical infrastructure, financial transactions, or healthcare may place a higher emphasis on stability and reliability. Understanding user requirements and tailoring the performance-stability trade-off to align with these expectations is essential for delivering a software solution that meets user needs.

In conclusion, balancing performance and stability in software development is a nuanced and ongoing process that demands careful consideration of trade-offs, thoughtful decision-making, and a commitment to iterative refinement. Developers must navigate the complexities of optimizing code for speed while ensuring that system behavior remains predictable, reliable, and secure. Strategies such as thorough testing, code profiling, continuous integration, and a user-centric approach contribute to achieving an optimal equilibrium between performance and stability, fostering the creation of robust and high-performing software systems.

Chapter 4: In the Code's Realm: Programming Paradigms for OS Development

Imperative vs. declarative programming

Imperative and declarative programming represent contrasting paradigms that shape the way developers express and structure their code. These programming styles dictate how instructions are written and executed, influencing the overall design, readability, and maintainability of software systems. Imperative programming, rooted in specifying explicit steps for achieving a desired outcome, emphasizes the detailed control flow and the sequence of actions to be performed by the computer. In this paradigm, developers articulate how to achieve a particular result, often relying on statements and loops that modify the program's state incrementally. The imperative style closely mirrors the machine's execution model, making it well-suited for tasks that require fine-grained control over computation.

In contrast, declarative programming abstracts away the control flow and emphasizes describing the desired outcome without specifying the step-by-step procedure for achieving it. Instead of instructing the computer on how to perform a task, developers using declarative languages focus on describing what they want to achieve, leaving the implementation details to the underlying system. This paradigm encourages a more concise and expressive code, as developers can articulate the intent of their programs without delving into the minutiae of execution. Declarative programming aligns with higher-level abstractions and allows for more natural expression of complex logic, making it well-suited for tasks involving data manipulation, transformations, and queries.

Imperative programming often involves mutable state, where variables can be modified during the program's execution. This mutable state, while providing fine-grained control, introduces challenges related to side effects, concurrency, and debugging. Managing state changes becomes crucial, and unexpected modifications can lead to bugs that are difficult to trace. In imperative languages, such as C, Java, or Python, developers are responsible for explicitly updating variables and managing memory, which can make code more error-prone and complex, especially in large codebases.

Declarative programming, on the other hand, tends to favor immutability and avoids explicit state modifications. In languages like SQL for databases or functional programming languages like Haskell or Lisp, once a value is assigned, it typically remains unchanged. This immutability simplifies reasoning about the behavior of programs, making it easier to understand, test, and maintain. Declarative languages often promote a more functional style, where functions are treated as first-class citizens, enabling higher-order functions, pure functions, and composition of functions to create more modular and reusable code.

The paradigm shift from imperative to declarative programming is evident in various domains. In web development, the shift towards declarative frameworks, such as React in JavaScript, has gained popularity. React allows developers to describe the user interface in terms of components and their states, letting the framework handle the underlying rendering and updates. This declarative approach simplifies the development of complex user interfaces, encourages code reuse, and enhances the maintainability of large codebases.

In database management, SQL exemplifies declarative programming by allowing users to express queries for data retrieval, modification, or deletion without specifying how the database engine should execute them. This separation of concerns between the what and the how abstracts away the complexity of database operations, enabling efficient query optimization and providing a high level of expressiveness for working with structured data.

The advent of declarative configuration languages, such as YAML or JSON, in system configuration and infrastructure as code further exemplifies the shift towards expressing the desired state rather than imperatively defining the steps to reach that state. Tools like Ansible or Terraform leverage this approach to define infrastructure setups and configurations in a concise and readable manner, promoting automation, consistency, and scalability.

Despite the advantages of declarative programming, there are scenarios where imperative paradigms are more suitable. Performance-critical applications or systems that require low-level control over hardware often benefit from the explicit nature of imperative languages. In scenarios like embedded systems or systems programming, languages like C or assembly provide the precise control needed for efficient resource management and execution.

Imperative programming's emphasis on control flow is also advantageous in scenarios where step-by-step execution is essential. For example, algorithms that involve intricate state transitions, procedural generation of content, or low-level optimizations may be more naturally expressed in an imperative style. In these contexts, the clarity of step-by-step instructions can facilitate understanding and debugging.

It's important to note that programming languages and paradigms exist on a spectrum, and many languages allow a mix of both imperative and declarative elements. For instance, Python, which is often considered imperative, incorporates declarative features, especially in libraries like NumPy for numerical computing or Pandas for data manipulation. Similarly, functional programming languages, while predominantly declarative, may have imperative constructs for certain operations.

In conclusion, imperative and declarative programming represent two fundamental approaches to expressing the logic of a program. Imperative programming emphasizes explicit control flow, mutable state, and step-by-step instructions, providing fine-grained control but often leading to more complex and error-prone code. Declarative programming, on the other hand, focuses on describing the desired outcome without specifying the detailed execution steps, promoting immutability and abstraction. Each paradigm has its strengths and weaknesses, and the choice between them depends on factors such as the nature of the problem, readability, maintainability, and the specific requirements of the application or system being developed. The evolving landscape of programming languages continues to incorporate elements from both paradigms, offering developers a spectrum of tools to express their ideas and build software systems that balance performance and maintainability.

Low-level vs. high-level programming languages

The distinction between low-level and high-level programming languages encapsulates a fundamental dichotomy in the way developers interact with computers, influencing the efficiency, abstraction, and expressiveness of the software development process. Low-level programming languages, such as assembly languages and machine code, operate in close proximity to the hardware, providing a one-to-one correspondence with the architecture's instruction set. Programmers working in low-level languages have granular control over the hardware resources, including memory addresses, registers, and processor instructions. This proximity allows for precise optimization and fine-tuning of code to exploit hardware capabilities fully. However, low-level languages demand a deep understanding of the hardware architecture, leading to code that is often intricate, error-prone, and less portable across different platforms.

Contrastingly, high-level programming languages, such as Python, Java, or C++, abstract away hardware details and provide a more human-readable and expressive syntax. These languages operate at a higher level of abstraction, offering built-in constructs and functionalities that simplify complex operations. Programmers in high-level languages focus on problem-solving and algorithmic design without delving into the intricacies of memory management or processor instructions. This abstraction fosters code readability, reusability, and portability, making high-level languages more accessible for a broader range of developers. However, the convenience of abstraction comes with a trade-off in terms of performance, as high-level languages may introduce overhead due to additional layers of interpretation or compilation.

Low-level programming languages are well-suited for tasks that demand maximum control over system resources, such as embedded systems, device drivers, or operating system kernels. In these contexts, the ability to manipulate hardware directly and optimize for specific architectures is crucial for achieving optimal performance. Assembly languages, for example, provide a symbolic representation of machine code, allowing programmers to write instructions that directly correspond to the processor's native commands. While this level of control is powerful, it requires meticulous attention to detail, and the resulting code is often less portable and harder to maintain than higher-level alternatives.

In contrast, high-level programming languages prioritize developer productivity and code maintainability. The abstraction provided by these languages enables rapid application development and simplifies the implementation of complex algorithms. High-level languages often feature automatic memory management, alleviating developers from manual memory allocation and deallocation, a common source of errors in low-level programming. This abstraction layer also enhances code portability, as high-level programs are typically written independently of the underlying hardware architecture, allowing for easier migration across platforms.

The advent of high-level languages has democratized software development, enabling a broader range of individuals to engage in programming without the need for an in-depth understanding of hardware intricacies. Python, for instance, has gained widespread popularity due to its readability and versatility, making it accessible for beginners while remaining powerful enough for diverse applications, from web development to scientific computing. Java, with its "write once, run anywhere" philosophy, exemplifies portability, as Java programs can run on any device with a Java Virtual Machine (JVM), abstracting away hardware-specific details.

Low-level languages, however, retain their relevance in specific domains where performance is paramount. Game development, for instance, often relies on low-level languages like C++ to achieve the computational efficiency required for real-time graphics rendering and physics simulations. Similarly, firmware development for embedded systems demands low-level programming to interact directly with hardware components, such as sensors or microcontrollers, where every clock cycle matters.

The choice between low-level and high-level languages depends on the nature of the project, the desired trade-offs between control and productivity, and the specific requirements of the application. Some programming languages, like C, offer a middle ground, providing a balance of low-level features, such as manual memory management, with high-level abstractions for structured programming. C has been widely used in systems programming, where direct control over hardware resources is necessary, while still maintaining a level of abstraction that makes it more readable than pure assembly language.

Low-level languages shine in scenarios where deterministic performance, minimal resource overhead, and intimate control over hardware are paramount. Real-time systems, operating systems, and certain embedded applications demand the precision that low-level programming provides. Kernel development, for example, often involves writing low-level code to interact with hardware devices and manage system resources efficiently. However, the complexity and potential for errors in low-level code necessitate a high level of expertise and careful consideration of security implications.

High-level languages, on the other hand, have become the cornerstone of modern software development due to their ease of use and versatility. Web development, data science, artificial intelligence, and a myriad of other domains benefit from the abstraction and productivity gains offered by high-level programming languages. Frameworks and libraries built on top of these languages further accelerate development by providing pre-built solutions for common tasks, allowing developers to focus on application-specific logic.

The evolution of programming languages reflects ongoing efforts to bridge the gap between low-level and high-level paradigms. Just-in-time (JIT) compilers, for instance, attempt to combine the efficiency of low-level languages with the abstraction of high-level languages by translating high-level code into machine code at runtime. This approach aims to deliver performance comparable to low-level languages while retaining the convenience of high-level abstractions.

In conclusion, the choice between low-level and high-level programming languages is a nuanced decision shaped by project requirements, development goals, and the level of control needed over hardware resources. Low-level languages excel in scenarios where precise control, performance optimization, and hardware interaction are critical. High-level languages prioritize developer productivity, code readability, and portability, making them well-suited for a wide range of applications. As technology evolves, the programming landscape continues to adapt, offering a spectrum of languages and tools that cater to diverse development needs and strike a balance between abstraction and control.

Understanding the role of assembly in OS development

The role of assembly language in operating system (OS) development is foundational, serving as a bridge between the hardware architecture and higher-level programming languages. Assembly language is a low-level programming language that is specific to a particular computer architecture, providing a symbolic representation of machine code instructions that directly correspond to the processor's native commands. In OS development, assembly language plays a crucial role in several key aspects, encompassing bootstrapping, hardware interaction, kernel initialization, and system-level control.

One of the primary functions of assembly language in OS development is in the bootstrapping process. The bootstrapping sequence is the set of operations that occur when a computer is powered on or restarted. During this phase, the system firmware, such as the BIOS (Basic Input/Output System) or UEFI (Unified Extensible Firmware Interface), loads a small piece of code known as the bootloader into memory. This bootloader, often written in assembly language, is responsible for initiating the OS loading process. The bootloader's role is to set up the initial environment, load the OS kernel into memory, and transfer control to the kernel, marking the transition from firmware execution to OS execution.

Once the OS kernel gains control, assembly language continues to play a pivotal role in interacting with and managing hardware resources. The kernel, being the core component of an OS, requires direct access to hardware to perform essential functions such as managing memory, handling interrupts, and communicating with peripheral devices. Assembly language is instrumental in crafting the low-level routines that facilitate these interactions. Instructions written in assembly allow the OS to manipulate registers, control hardware interrupts, and configure device controllers to establish a foundational layer of communication with the underlying hardware.

Memory management, a critical aspect of OS functionality, relies heavily on assembly language. The OS kernel must be adept at allocating and deallocating memory, setting up page tables, and managing memory protection mechanisms. Assembly instructions enable the OS to work with physical and virtual memory addresses, control memory access permissions, and implement efficient algorithms for memory allocation. The intricate dance between the kernel and memory, orchestrated through assembly code, ensures that the OS can utilize available memory resources effectively and provide a stable and secure environment for executing processes.

Interrupt handling is another vital role of assembly language in OS development. Interrupts are signals generated by hardware or software events that require the CPU's immediate attention. Examples include a keypress on the keyboard, a mouse movement, or a request from a peripheral device. Assembly language is employed to write the interrupt service routines (ISRs) that respond to these interrupts. ISRs manage the context switch from normal execution to handling the interrupt, process the interrupt, and restore the system's state once the interrupt is serviced. The ability to precisely control the sequence of operations during interrupt handling is critical for the OS to maintain stability and responsiveness.

The development of system calls, which are interfaces through which user-level processes can request services from the kernel, is another domain where assembly language proves indispensable. Assembly is used to define the calling conventions for system calls, specifying how arguments are passed to the kernel, how the kernel returns values, and how control is transferred between user-level code and the kernel. The precision and control provided by assembly language are crucial for ensuring the compatibility and interoperability of system calls across different programming languages and user-space applications.

Security considerations in OS development also benefit from the use of assembly language. Techniques such as implementing secure boot processes, enforcing access control mechanisms, and isolating user processes rely on low-level operations that are expressed most effectively in assembly. Assembly language allows developers to implement features like address space layout randomization (ASLR) and control flow integrity (CFI), enhancing the OS's resistance to various forms of attacks, including buffer overflows and code injection vulnerabilities.

Furthermore, performance optimization is a key consideration in OS development, and assembly language provides a level of control over the hardware that is essential for achieving optimal performance. Kernel developers can use assembly instructions to fine-tune critical sections of code, utilize processor-specific features, and exploit hardware-level parallelism. This level of control is particularly important in scenarios where every CPU cycle matters, such as in real-time systems, embedded systems, or high-performance computing environments.

The role of assembly language in OS development extends beyond the kernel itself. Device drivers, which are specialized pieces of software that enable the OS to communicate with hardware devices, often involve assembly code. Writing device drivers in assembly allows developers to harness the full capabilities of hardware and optimize performance for specific devices. Assembly language provides the necessary flexibility to configure and control the behavior of device controllers, ensuring seamless integration with the OS.

Despite its power and versatility, the use of assembly language in OS development comes with challenges. Writing and maintaining assembly code require a deep understanding of the underlying hardware architecture, making it less portable across different platforms.

Additionally, debugging and testing assembly code can be more challenging compared to higher-level languages, as tools for these tasks are often less sophisticated in the low-level programming domain.

In conclusion, assembly language is a linchpin in the development of operating systems, providing the necessary tools for interfacing with hardware, managing system resources, and implementing critical functionalities. From the early stages of bootstrapping through kernel initialization, interrupt handling, memory management, system calls, security enforcement, and device driver development, assembly language is woven into the fabric of OS development. While higher-level languages offer abstraction and ease of development, the precision and control afforded by assembly are indispensable for crafting the intricate dance between software and hardware that defines the core of an operating system. As technology evolves, the role of assembly language continues to adapt, ensuring that OS developers can strike a delicate balance between efficiency, control, and abstraction in the ever-changing landscape of computing.

Writing basic assembly code

Writing basic assembly code involves crafting instructions at the lowest level of abstraction that a computer's central processing unit (CPU) can understand. Assembly language serves as a human-readable representation of machine code, allowing programmers to interact directly with the underlying hardware architecture. In the context of writing basic assembly code, understanding the fundamentals of the assembly language syntax, registers, memory access, and basic instructions is essential. The process typically begins with selecting an assembly language that corresponds to the target CPU architecture, as different processors have distinct instruction sets. As an illustrative example, let's consider the x86 architecture, which is widely used in personal computers.

The assembly language syntax for x86 architecture is mnemonic-based, with each mnemonic representing a specific machine code instruction. An assembly program consists of a series of instructions, often written in a human-readable format with mnemonics, operands, and comments. The assembler, a tool in the software development toolkit, translates this assembly code into machine code that the CPU can execute directly.

A fundamental concept in assembly language is registers. Registers are small, fast storage locations within the CPU that hold data temporarily during program execution. x86 architecture, for instance, includes general-purpose registers like EAX, EBX, ECX, and EDX, each capable of holding 32 bits of data. These registers play a central role in basic assembly code as they are used for arithmetic operations, data manipulation, and storing intermediate values.

Memory access is another critical aspect of assembly programming. In x86 assembly, memory is typically addressed using a combination of segment registers and offsets. Instructions such as MOV (move) allow data to be transferred between registers and memory. For example, to load a value from memory into the EAX register, one might use the instruction `MOV EAX, [MemoryAddress]`. Conversely, storing a value from a register into memory would involve `MOV [MemoryAddress], EAX`. Understanding memory addressing modes, which specify how operands are calculated, is crucial for effective use of memory in assembly code.

Basic arithmetic and logic operations are the building blocks of assembly code. Instructions like ADD (addition), SUB (subtraction), MUL (multiplication), and DIV (division) enable manipulation of numerical values in registers. Logical operations such as AND, OR, and XOR facilitate bitwise manipulations. These operations, often accompanied by conditional jumps (JE, JNE, etc.), allow the implementation of control flow structures like loops and conditional statements.

Branching and control flow are integral to any programming language, and assembly is no exception. Jumps and conditional jumps are used to alter the flow of execution based on specific conditions. For instance, the JMP (jump) instruction unconditionally transfers control to a specified address, while JE (jump if equal) and JNE (jump if not equal) allow conditional branching based on the results of a preceding comparison.

To illustrate these concepts, let's consider a simple assembly program that calculates the sum of two numbers. The x86 assembly code might look like this:

```
section .data
num1 dd 10 ; Define the first number as a doubleword (32 bits)
num2 dd 20 ; Define the second number as a doubleword
section .text
global _start ; Entry point for the program
_start:
; Load num1 into EAX register
mov eax, [num1]
; Add num2 to EAX register
add eax, [num2]
; Exit the program with the result in EAX
mov ebx, eax ; Move the result to EBX register (return value)
mov eax, 1 ; System call number for exit
int 0x80 ; Invoke the kernel to exit the program
```

In this example, the program starts by defining two doubleword variables in the `.data` section. The `.text` section contains the actual code. It uses the `MOV` and `ADD` instructions to load the values from memory into the `EAX` register, perform the addition, and store the result. The program then exits, returning the result in the `EBX` register.

Understanding the underlying hardware architecture is crucial when writing basic assembly code. It requires careful consideration of register usage, memory addressing, and the sequence of instructions to achieve the desired computation. Assembly programming demands precision and attention to detail, as developers are essentially providing instructions directly to the CPU. While higher-level languages offer abstraction and ease of development, delving into assembly language provides a profound insight into the inner workings of a computer's central processing unit and the low-level operations that drive program execution.

Importance of C in OS development

The importance of the C programming language in the development of operating systems (OS) is deeply ingrained in the history and evolution of system-level software. C's significance lies in its combination of efficiency, portability, and low-level capabilities, making it a versatile tool for building the intricate layers of an operating system that directly interact with hardware and manage system resources.

At the core of C's importance in OS development is its ability to provide a level of abstraction that strikes a delicate balance between hardware specificity and programmer productivity. Operating systems serve as an intermediary between application software and the underlying hardware, translating high-level commands into instructions the hardware can execute. C, with its low-level features and ability to interact with memory and hardware directly, empowers OS developers to express the intricacies of these translations effectively.

Efficiency is paramount in the realm of operating systems, where every instruction cycle matters. C's syntax and features are crafted to map closely to the machine instructions, allowing developers to write code that is both concise and efficient. Direct manipulation of memory addresses and pointers in C facilitates precise control over system resources, a crucial aspect of OS development where efficient memory management and hardware interaction are fundamental.

C's portability across different architectures is another key factor in its importance. Operating systems often need to run on diverse hardware platforms with varying architectures, and C's design emphasizes portability without sacrificing low-level control. The abstraction provided by C shields developers from the intricacies of individual hardware architectures while still allowing them to write code that interacts closely with the hardware when necessary.

The kernel, the core component of an operating system, is where C truly shines in OS development. The kernel manages essential tasks such as process scheduling, memory management, file systems, and device drivers. C's ability to work at a low level, coupled with its features for structured programming, enables the implementation of these complex functionalities. C's syntax is well-suited for expressing algorithms, data structures, and system-level logic, making it an ideal language for the development of robust and efficient kernels.

Memory management is a critical aspect of OS development, and C provides the necessary tools to control and manipulate memory effectively. Pointers and manual memory allocation allow developers to implement sophisticated memory management systems tailored to the specific needs of the operating system. C's flexibility in managing memory is crucial for creating stable and efficient systems, preventing issues like memory leaks and fragmentation.

C's support for system programming constructs, such as structures and unions, enhances the organization and representation of data within an operating system. These features contribute to the creation of efficient data structures that facilitate tasks like file system management and process control. The ability to define custom data types and structures in C allows OS developers to model and manipulate the complex relationships and hierarchies inherent in system-level functionalities.

Device drivers, essential for enabling the OS to communicate with hardware components, are often written in C. C's direct access to memory and hardware registers, along with its ability to interface with assembly language, makes it well-suited for writing efficient and hardware-specific code. Device drivers play a crucial role in facilitating communication between the OS and peripherals such as storage devices, network interfaces, and graphics cards. C's capabilities allow developers to implement drivers that optimize performance and ensure seamless integration with the OS.

The development of Unix, one of the pioneering operating systems, played a pivotal role in establishing C as the language of choice for OS development. Unix, created at Bell Labs in the early 1970s by Ken Thompson, Dennis Ritchie, and others, was initially implemented in assembly language. However, recognizing the need for a more portable and maintainable solution, Thompson and Ritchie developed C, eventually rewriting Unix in their newly created language. This decision had a profound impact on the field, solidifying C's reputation as a language suitable for systems programming and OS development.

The influence of Unix and C extends beyond its historical roots. Many modern operating systems, including Linux and its variants, BSD Unix, and even components of Windows, are written in C. The POSIX standard, which defines a set of APIs for compatibility between Unix-like operating systems, further underscores the enduring importance of C in OS development. The widespread adoption of Unix and its derivatives has cemented C as a lingua franca for system-level programming, creating a rich ecosystem of tools, libraries, and best practices that continue to shape OS development.

The open-source nature of many operating systems has contributed to the prominence of C in OS development. The transparency and collaborative nature of open-source projects facilitate peer review, knowledge sharing, and continuous improvement. C's readability and expressiveness enable developers to contribute effectively to large and complex codebases, fostering a community-driven approach to OS development.

Security considerations are paramount in operating system development, and C provides the tools necessary for implementing secure and robust systems. While C does not prevent all types of programming errors, its low-level features allow developers to implement security measures, such as stack canaries, memory protection, and input validation, directly within the code. Additionally, the fine-grained control offered by C is crucial for addressing security vulnerabilities and conducting thorough code audits.

The influence of C in OS development extends to the application programming interfaces (APIs) exposed to application developers. Many OS APIs are designed with compatibility in mind, allowing programs written in C to seamlessly interact with the underlying system. The standard C library (libc) provides a set of functions that abstract away many OS-specific details, enabling application developers to write code that is portable across different operating systems.

Despite its enduring significance, C is not without its challenges in the context of OS development. Memory-related errors, such as buffer overflows and pointer arithmetic mistakes, pose potential security risks and require careful handling. Modern programming languages with memory safety features, such as Rust, aim to address these challenges while retaining low-level control, sparking discussions about their potential role in OS development.

In conclusion, the importance of C in operating system development stems from its unique combination of efficiency, portability, and low-level capabilities. C's ability to provide a balance between abstraction and hardware control makes it an ideal language for crafting the intricate layers of an operating system. From kernel development and memory management to device drivers and security considerations, C has proven its resilience and adaptability over decades. The historical roots of C in the development of Unix, coupled with its widespread use in modern operating systems, solidify its role as a foundational language in the landscape of system-level programming. As the field evolves, C continues to be a linchpin for those who navigate the complexities of operating system development, ensuring that systems remain efficient, reliable, and capable of interfacing seamlessly with diverse hardware architectures.

System-level programming techniques

System-level programming techniques encompass a set of principles and practices that enable developers to create software that interacts closely with the underlying hardware and manages system resources efficiently. This level of programming delves into the intricacies of operating systems, device drivers, and other software components that form the foundation of computing systems. System-level programming is characterized by a focus on low-level details, memory management, hardware interaction, and optimization for performance. Understanding and employing these techniques are crucial for crafting robust, efficient, and reliable software at the heart of modern computing systems.

One fundamental aspect of system-level programming is memory management. Efficiently managing memory is essential for system stability and performance. Techniques such as manual memory allocation and deallocation, using pointers, and implementing custom memory management algorithms are common in system-level programming. Developers must be mindful of memory leaks, where allocated memory is not properly deallocated, and issues such as buffer overflows, which can compromise system security. Employing these memory management techniques allows system-level programmers to finely control how memory is allocated, used, and released, ensuring optimal performance and minimizing the risk of memory-related errors.

Another critical technique in system-level programming is the handling of interrupts. Interrupts are signals generated by hardware or software events that require immediate attention from the CPU. System-level programmers must develop Interrupt Service Routines (ISRs) to manage these interrupts. ISRs handle events such as keyboard input, mouse movements, or disk I/O, ensuring that the system responds promptly. Effective interrupt handling is vital for real-time systems and contributes to the overall responsiveness and reliability of the operating system.

Concurrency and synchronization techniques are essential in system-level programming to manage multiple tasks or processes running concurrently. Operating systems often deal with parallel execution, where several processes or threads execute simultaneously. System-level programmers employ synchronization mechanisms, such as locks, semaphores, and mutexes, to coordinate access to shared resources and prevent race conditions. Understanding these concurrency techniques is crucial for preventing data corruption and ensuring the correct execution of system-level code in a multi-tasking environment.

Device drivers, key components of system-level software, require specialized programming techniques. Device drivers facilitate communication between the operating system and hardware devices, such as graphics cards, network interfaces, or storage devices. System-level programmers must write efficient and robust device drivers that interact directly with hardware registers and manage device-specific functionalities. Employing techniques like memory-mapped I/O and direct hardware access allows device drivers to optimize performance and ensure seamless integration with the operating system.

Optimizing code for performance is a constant consideration in system-level programming. Low-level languages like C and assembly language are often employed to write critical sections of code that require maximum efficiency. Profiling tools and performance analysis techniques help identify bottlenecks and areas for optimization. Techniques such as loop unrolling, instruction pipelining, and cache optimization contribute to squeezing out the maximum computational power from the underlying hardware. System-level programmers must balance the trade-off between performance and readability, choosing optimizations judiciously based on the specific requirements of the system.

File system management is another domain that demands specialized techniques in system-level programming. Developing file systems involves designing data structures, implementing file access protocols, and ensuring data integrity. Techniques for handling file I/O efficiently, managing directories, and implementing file permissions are crucial for creating reliable and performant file systems. Understanding the intricacies of file system structures, such as inodes and directory entries, allows system-level programmers to implement features like file versioning, access control, and efficient storage allocation.

Security considerations are paramount in system-level programming. Techniques for secure coding, input validation, and implementing robust authentication and authorization mechanisms are critical in preventing security vulnerabilities. Buffer overflows, injection attacks, and privilege escalation are common security threats that system-level programmers must guard against. Employing encryption algorithms, secure communication protocols, and regular security audits are essential techniques to ensure the integrity and confidentiality of system-level code.

In addition to traditional system-level programming, the emergence of virtualization and containerization technologies has introduced new techniques. Virtualization allows multiple operating systems to run on a single physical machine, and techniques such as hypervisors and virtual machines are employed to manage these virtualized environments. Containerization, exemplified by technologies like Docker, relies on techniques such as namespace isolation and cgroup control to provide lightweight, portable, and isolated environments for applications. System-level programmers working with virtualization and containers must understand these techniques to create efficient and secure virtualized environments.

Networking is a critical aspect of modern system-level programming, especially in the context of distributed systems and cloud computing. Techniques for implementing network protocols, socket programming, and ensuring reliable communication are essential skills for system-level programmers. Understanding the intricacies of networking protocols, such as TCP/IP, and employing techniques like load balancing, fault tolerance, and distributed data storage contribute to the development of robust and scalable distributed systems.

Error handling and recovery techniques play a crucial role in system-level programming to ensure the robustness of software in the face of unexpected situations. System-level programmers must implement strategies for graceful error recovery, logging, and diagnostics to facilitate debugging and troubleshooting. Techniques such as checksums, error-correcting codes, and transactional processing contribute to the reliability of system-level code, especially in scenarios where data consistency is paramount.

Collaboration and version control techniques are vital for managing complex system-level projects involving multiple developers. Version control systems, such as Git, facilitate collaborative development by allowing programmers to track changes, merge code contributions, and roll back to previous versions. Techniques like modularization, code documentation, and coding standards enhance the maintainability and readability of system-level codebases, fostering collaboration and easing the integration of contributions from different developers.

The evolution of system-level programming continues to be shaped by advancements in hardware architectures, emerging technologies, and the increasing complexity of computing systems. System-level programmers must adapt to new challenges and employ evolving techniques to address the demands of contemporary computing environments. The principles of efficiency, reliability, security, and collaboration remain at the forefront of system-level programming, guiding developers as they navigate the intricate landscape of operating systems, device drivers, and system-level software. Through a combination of foundational knowledge, experience, and an ongoing commitment to learning, system-level programmers contribute to the development of the robust and sophisticated software infrastructure that underpins the digital world.

Applying OOP principles to kernel and system design

Applying Object-Oriented Programming (OOP) principles to kernel and system design represents a paradigm shift in the traditional approach to operating system development. OOP, with its emphasis on encapsulation, inheritance, and polymorphism, introduces a more modular and extensible framework for building complex systems. In the realm of kernel and system design, where efficiency, performance, and robustness are paramount, leveraging OOP principles introduces a set of challenges and opportunities that reshape the landscape of system-level software.

Encapsulation, a key OOP principle, involves bundling data and the methods that operate on that data into a single unit known as a class. In the context of kernel design, encapsulation allows developers to create well-defined and self-contained abstractions for representing system components. For instance, device drivers, crucial elements in system-level programming, can be encapsulated within classes that hide the intricacies of hardware interaction. Encapsulation enhances modularity and maintainability, isolating the implementation details of individual components and allowing for easier modifications or replacements without affecting the entire system.

Inheritance, another fundamental OOP concept, facilitates the creation of hierarchical relationships between classes, enabling the reuse of code and promoting a structured design. In kernel and system design, inheritance can be applied to create a hierarchy of abstractions that mirrors the hierarchical structure of hardware and software components. For example, a generic file system class could serve as a base class, with specific file systems inheriting and extending its functionality. Inheritance fosters code reuse, reducing redundancy and promoting a more organized and scalable architecture.

Polymorphism, the ability of objects to take multiple forms, further enhances the adaptability and extensibility of kernel and system design. Polymorphism allows developers to write code that can work with objects of various types, providing a level of flexibility crucial in the dynamic and evolving landscape of system-level programming. For instance, polymorphic interfaces can be employed to interact with different types of devices through a unified interface, enabling the system to seamlessly accommodate new hardware without extensive modifications.

The application of OOP principles to kernel and system design is exemplified in the development of microkernels. Microkernels, a modular approach to kernel design, embody the OOP principles of encapsulation and abstraction. In a microkernel architecture, the core functionality of the kernel is minimized, and essential services are implemented as separate, interchangeable modules. Each module encapsulates a specific set of functionalities, such as process management, file systems, or device drivers, within well-defined interfaces. This modular and encapsulated structure enhances maintainability and allows for the dynamic loading and unloading of components, facilitating system updates and customization without requiring a full system reboot.

In the realm of device drivers, OOP principles can be applied to create a unified and extensible framework. Using encapsulation, each device driver can be encapsulated within a class, hiding the low-level details of hardware interaction. Inheritance allows for the creation of a hierarchy of device driver classes, where common functionalities are inherited from a base class, and specific functionalities are implemented in derived classes. Polymorphism enables the development of a generic interface that can interact with different types of devices through a unified set of methods, providing a consistent and extensible framework for handling diverse hardware components.

File systems, crucial components in operating systems, can benefit from OOP principles to enhance their design and extensibility. Each file system type can be encapsulated within a class, with common functionalities defined in a base class and specific features implemented in derived classes. Inheritance allows for the creation of a hierarchy of file system classes, enabling code reuse and providing a modular structure that accommodates the diverse requirements of different file system types. Polymorphism enables a generic file system interface to interact with various file system implementations, allowing the operating system to support multiple file system types seamlessly.

The implementation of networking protocols is another area where OOP principles can be applied to enhance system design. Encapsulation allows for the creation of classes representing different network protocols, such as TCP/IP or UDP, each encapsulating its specific functionalities. Inheritance facilitates the creation of a hierarchy of protocol classes, promoting code reuse and extensibility. Polymorphism enables the development of a unified networking interface that can interact with different protocols, allowing the system to support a variety of networking technologies without compromising the coherence of the overall design.

Concurrency and synchronization mechanisms, critical aspects of kernel and system design, can also benefit from OOP principles. Encapsulation allows for the creation of classes representing synchronization primitives, such as locks or semaphores, each encapsulating its specific implementation details. Inheritance enables the development of a hierarchy of synchronization classes, with common functionalities defined in a base class and specific features implemented in derived classes. Polymorphism facilitates the creation of a generic interface for synchronization, allowing the system to employ different synchronization mechanisms based on specific requirements.

The application of OOP principles to kernel and system design, however, introduces challenges that need careful consideration. The potential overhead introduced by OOP features such as dynamic dispatch and object-oriented abstractions must be weighed against the performance requirements of system-level software. Kernel code often operates in a resource-constrained environment, and excessive abstraction or indirection may impact the efficiency and responsiveness of the system. Balancing the benefits of OOP principles with the need for minimal overhead is a nuanced task that requires a deep understanding of the specific requirements and constraints of the target system.

Furthermore, the adoption of OOP principles in kernel and system design requires a paradigm shift in the mindset of system-level programmers. Traditional approaches to operating system development often rely on procedural languages and imperative programming styles. Transitioning to OOP necessitates a shift towards a more object-centric and design-oriented methodology, which may pose challenges in terms of training, legacy code compatibility, and established development practices.

In conclusion, the application of Object-Oriented Programming principles to kernel and system design introduces a paradigm shift that redefines the way system-level software is conceptualized and developed. Encapsulation, inheritance, and polymorphism provide a modular, extensible, and maintainable framework for building complex operating systems. Microkernels exemplify the successful application of OOP principles in kernel design, promoting modularity and flexibility. Device drivers, file systems, networking protocols, and synchronization mechanisms can all benefit from the structured and hierarchical approach enabled by OOP. However, the potential trade-offs in terms of performance overhead and the need for a shift in programming paradigms highlight the nuanced nature of incorporating OOP principles into the traditionally low-level domain of kernel and system design. As the landscape of computing evolves, the thoughtful application of OOP principles can contribute to the development of more robust, modular, and adaptable system-level software architectures.

Benefits and challenges of OOP in OS development

Object-Oriented Programming (OOP) brings both benefits and challenges to the realm of Operating System (OS) development, introducing a paradigm shift in how system-level software is conceptualized and designed. The adoption of OOP principles, such as encapsulation, inheritance, and polymorphism, offers several advantages that can enhance the development, maintenance, and extensibility of operating systems. However, these benefits come with their own set of challenges, ranging from potential performance overhead to the need for a fundamental shift in the mindset of system-level programmers.

One of the primary benefits of OOP in OS development is the concept of encapsulation. Encapsulation allows developers to bundle data and the methods that operate on that data into a single unit known as a class. This results in well-defined and self-contained abstractions, providing a modular and organized structure for representing various components of the operating system. In the context of device drivers, for example, encapsulation enables the isolation of hardware interaction details within a driver class, making it easier to understand, maintain, and replace specific components without affecting the entire system. This modular approach enhances code readability and maintainability, crucial aspects in the complex and evolving landscape of operating systems.

Inheritance, another fundamental OOP concept, facilitates the creation of hierarchical relationships between classes, enabling the reuse of code and promoting a structured design. In the context of

OS development, inheritance can lead to a more organized and scalable architecture. For instance, a base class representing a generic file system can be extended by specific file system classes that inherit common functionalities. This hierarchy allows for code reuse, reducing redundancy, and providing a flexible framework for accommodating different file system types. Inheritance, therefore, contributes to the development of a coherent and extensible structure, fostering modularity and ease of maintenance in the complex environment of operating systems.

Polymorphism, the ability of objects to take multiple forms, introduces flexibility and adaptability into OS development. Polymorphism allows developers to write code that can work with objects of various types through a unified interface. In the context of networking protocols, for example, polymorphism enables the creation of a generic networking interface that can interact with different protocols seamlessly. This adaptability is crucial in the dynamic landscape of operating systems, where new technologies and protocols may be introduced over time. Polymorphism allows for a unified and extensible design that accommodates diverse requirements without sacrificing the coherence of the overall system.

The application of OOP principles is exemplified in the development of microkernels. Microkernels, which embody the OOP principles of encapsulation and abstraction, provide a modular approach to kernel design. The core functionality of the kernel is minimized, and essential services are implemented as separate, interchangeable modules. Each module encapsulates a specific set of functionalities within well-defined interfaces. This modular and encapsulated structure enhances maintainability and allows for the dynamic loading and unloading of components, facilitating system updates and customization without requiring a full system reboot. Microkernels, therefore, demonstrate how OOP principles can be leveraged to create a flexible and extensible foundation for operating systems.

However, the adoption of OOP in OS development comes with its set of challenges. One significant concern is the potential performance overhead introduced by OOP features, such as dynamic dispatch and object-oriented abstractions. Operating systems often operate in resource-constrained environments where every computational cycle counts. The additional layers of abstraction introduced by OOP may result in increased memory usage and slower execution times. Balancing the benefits of OOP, such as modularity and maintainability, with the need for minimal overhead becomes a critical consideration, especially in performance-critical components of the operating system, such as the kernel.

Another challenge lies in the need for a fundamental shift in the mindset of system-level programmers. Traditional approaches to operating system development often rely on procedural languages and imperative programming styles. Transitioning to OOP necessitates a shift towards a more object-centric and design-oriented methodology. This shift may pose challenges in terms of training existing developers, compatibility with legacy code, and the need to establish new development practices. Adapting to OOP requires a reevaluation of established conventions and a commitment to embracing a more structured and modular approach to system-level software.

Additionally, the complexity introduced by OOP can lead to potential challenges in debugging and understanding the flow of execution. In deeply embedded and resource-constrained environments, debugging tools may be limited, making it challenging to trace the interactions between objects and diagnose issues efficiently. The intricate relationships between classes and their interactions may require specialized tools and techniques to ensure the robustness and reliability of the operating system.

Security considerations also come into play when applying OOP principles in OS development. The encapsulation of data and methods within classes can enhance security by restricting access to sensitive information. However, the potential for vulnerabilities, such as privilege escalation through inheritance hierarchies or polymorphic interfaces, must be carefully considered. Ensuring secure coding practices and conducting thorough security audits become imperative when implementing OOP in operating systems where robustness and integrity are paramount.

Despite these challenges, the benefits of OOP in OS development are significant. The modular, extensible, and maintainable nature of OOP design aligns well with the evolving requirements of modern operating systems. The encapsulation of functionalities within classes allows for a more intuitive and organized representation of system components. Inheritance promotes code reuse and hierarchy, fostering a structured and scalable design. Polymorphism enables adaptability to changing requirements and technologies. Microkernels exemplify how OOP principles can be leveraged to create flexible and dynamic foundations for operating systems. While overcoming the challenges requires careful consideration and adaptation, the potential benefits make OOP an enticing paradigm for shaping the future of system-level software. As the field of operating system development continues to evolve, the judicious application of OOP principles holds the promise of creating more resilient, modular, and adaptable operating systems that meet the demands of contemporary computing environments.

Handling multiple processes and threads

Handling multiple processes and threads is a fundamental aspect of modern operating systems, and it involves intricate design considerations to ensure efficient utilization of resources, responsiveness, and system stability. A process is an independent instance of a running program, while threads represent individual units of execution within a process. The coordination and management of multiple processes and threads are critical in achieving multitasking, parallelism, and responsiveness, which are essential for meeting the demands of contemporary computing environments.

In the context of processes, an operating system employs a variety of mechanisms to create, manage, and terminate these independent units of execution. Process creation involves allocating resources such as memory, file descriptors, and a process control block (PCB) to store information about the process. Context switching is a crucial operation that allows the operating system to switch between different processes, preserving their states and ensuring a seamless transition. Scheduling algorithms, such as round-robin or priority-based scheduling, dictate the order in which processes are granted access to the CPU, optimizing for factors like fairness, throughput, or response time.

Inter-process communication (IPC) mechanisms play a pivotal role in facilitating communication and coordination between different processes. Techniques like shared memory, message passing, and semaphores enable processes to exchange data and synchronize their activities. These mechanisms are vital for collaborative tasks and coordination between independent processes, fostering a modular and distributed approach to system-level programming.

Threads, on the other hand, provide a lighter-weight alternative to processes and share the same address space. Threads within a process can execute concurrently, allowing for parallelism and improved performance. Thread creation, synchronization, and communication are critical aspects of managing multithreaded applications. Thread creation involves allocating a separate stack for each thread and managing their execution contexts. Synchronization mechanisms, such as locks, semaphores, and condition variables, prevent race conditions and ensure orderly access to shared resources. Thread communication is facilitated by techniques like thread-safe data structures and inter-thread signaling, enabling collaboration and data sharing among threads within a process.

The distinction between processes and threads introduces a trade-off between isolation and resource efficiency. Processes provide a higher level of isolation, as each has its own memory space and resources, reducing the risk of one process affecting the stability of others. However, this isolation comes with a higher overhead in terms of resource consumption. Threads, sharing the same address space, offer more efficient communication and resource utilization but increase the complexity of synchronization and introduce the potential for data conflicts.

In the development of parallel and concurrent systems, the application of threads becomes crucial. Multi-core processors and parallel computing architectures leverage threads to exploit parallelism, enhancing overall system performance. Thread pools, where a group of threads is pre-allocated and managed, streamline the creation and destruction of threads, mitigating the overhead associated with dynamic thread creation. Parallel algorithms, designed to execute tasks concurrently, benefit from thread-based parallelism, enabling efficient utilization of available processing resources.

However, managing threads introduces challenges related to synchronization and coordination. Race conditions, where multiple threads access shared data concurrently, may lead to unpredictable behavior and data corruption. Deadlocks, situations where threads are unable to proceed due to circular dependencies on resources, pose a threat to system stability. Careful design and the use of synchronization primitives are essential to mitigate these challenges and ensure the reliable execution of multithreaded applications.

The concept of thread safety becomes paramount when multiple threads access shared data or resources concurrently. Thread-safe data structures, atomic operations, and the use of locks or other synchronization mechanisms prevent data corruption and ensure the consistency of shared information. However, the indiscriminate use of locks can lead to performance bottlenecks and contention for resources, necessitating a balance between synchronization and parallelism.

In modern operating systems, thread-level parallelism is complemented by higher-level abstractions such as parallel programming frameworks and libraries. Technologies like OpenMP and Intel Threading Building Blocks (TBB) provide high-level constructs for expressing parallelism, allowing developers to focus on algorithmic design while the underlying framework manages the intricacies of thread creation, synchronization, and load balancing. These abstractions simplify the development of parallel applications, making it more accessible to a broader range of programmers.

Real-time operating systems (RTOS) introduce additional considerations for handling processes and threads, particularly in environments where strict timing constraints must be met. RTOS employs priority-based scheduling algorithms to ensure timely execution of time-critical tasks. The deterministic behavior of threads in an RTOS is essential for applications such as robotics, aerospace, and industrial control systems, where precise timing and responsiveness are critical for system functionality and safety.

Asynchronous programming models, such as event-driven and callback-based approaches, offer an alternative to traditional multithreading for handling concurrency. These models leverage asynchronous I/O operations and event loops to manage concurrent tasks without the need for explicit multithreading. Asynchronous programming is prevalent in scenarios where responsiveness and scalability are essential, such as web servers handling numerous concurrent connections.

In conclusion, the effective handling of multiple processes and threads is a cornerstone of modern operating system design. Operating systems must balance the need for resource isolation, efficient utilization, and responsiveness to cater to diverse application requirements. The careful design of process and thread management mechanisms, along with robust synchronization and communication techniques, is essential for creating stable, efficient, and scalable systems. The evolution of computing architectures, from single-core to multi-core and parallel systems, emphasizes the importance of threads in achieving optimal performance. However, challenges related to synchronization, race conditions, and deadlock prevention require continuous innovation and refinement in system-level programming. As the computing landscape continues to evolve, the effective management of processes and threads remains a dynamic area of research and development, shaping the foundations of modern operating systems.

Strategies for efficient parallel programming in operating systems

Efficient parallel programming in operating systems is a multi-faceted challenge that involves employing a range of strategies to harness the full potential of modern multicore and parallel computing architectures. These strategies aim to optimize performance, ensure scalability, and minimize synchronization overhead, all while maintaining the stability and responsiveness of the system. One key approach is the careful design of parallel algorithms and data structures that can exploit parallelism without introducing bottlenecks or contention. Developers often leverage task parallelism, dividing a large computation into smaller tasks that can be executed concurrently. This strategy, exemplified by techniques such as parallel loops and parallel recursive algorithms, ensures a balanced distribution of workloads across available cores.

Another crucial strategy for efficient parallel programming is the use of synchronization mechanisms to manage access to shared resources and prevent data corruption. Locks, semaphores, and atomic operations play a pivotal role in coordinating the execution of parallel threads or processes. However, the judicious use of synchronization is essential to avoid bottlenecks and contention. Fine-grained locking, where locks are applied to specific portions of shared data, can reduce contention but requires careful design to avoid deadlock and ensure correctness. Additionally, lock-free and wait-free algorithms, which minimize the reliance on locks, offer alternatives for achieving efficient parallelism by reducing contention and enhancing scalability.

Parallel programming frameworks and libraries provide a higher-level abstraction, enabling developers to express parallelism without delving into low-level details. Technologies like OpenMP, Intel Threading Building Blocks (TBB), and CUDA for GPU programming offer constructs for parallelizing computations, managing threads, and exploiting hardware accelerators. These frameworks automate many aspects of parallel programming, simplifying the development process and making it more accessible to a broader range of programmers. The use of parallel libraries encourages code reusability and facilitates the creation of scalable applications without the need for intricate manual parallelization.

Task scheduling is a critical aspect of efficient parallel programming, ensuring that available resources are utilized optimally. Dynamic load balancing, where tasks are dynamically distributed among available threads based on their computational load, helps prevent underutilization of cores and maximizes overall throughput. Techniques such as work-stealing, commonly employed in parallel runtime systems, dynamically assign tasks to idle threads, minimizing contention and ensuring a balanced distribution of workloads. The careful design and implementation of a scheduler are paramount for achieving efficient parallelism across diverse applications and workloads.

Data parallelism, a strategy where the same operation is performed on multiple data elements concurrently, is a cornerstone of efficient parallel programming. Vectorization and parallelization of loops, for instance, enable operations on arrays or vectors to be parallelized, exploiting the SIMD (Single Instruction, Multiple Data) capabilities of modern processors. This strategy enhances throughput and computational efficiency, particularly in numerical and scientific computing applications. GPU programming, exemplified by frameworks like CUDA and OpenCL, extends data parallelism to accelerate computations by leveraging the massive parallelism inherent in graphics processing units.

Asynchronous programming models offer an alternative paradigm for efficient parallelism by focusing on non-blocking operations and event-driven architectures. In such models, tasks are initiated asynchronously, and the system continues processing other tasks while waiting for results. Event-driven frameworks, including Node.js for server-side JavaScript and asyncio in Python, exemplify this approach, providing a scalable and responsive way to handle numerous concurrent operations without the need for explicit multithreading. Asynchronous programming is well-suited for applications with high I/O or event-driven workloads, where responsiveness and scalability are crucial.

The development of parallel debugging and profiling tools is instrumental in identifying bottlenecks, analyzing performance, and ensuring the correctness of parallel programs. Profilers designed for parallel environments can highlight areas of contention, guide optimization efforts, and provide insights into the efficiency of parallel algorithms. Debugging tools for parallel programming must address challenges unique to concurrency, such as race conditions and deadlocks. Advanced debugging techniques, including thread-specific breakpoints and visualization tools, aid developers in understanding the intricate interactions between parallel threads and diagnosing issues in complex parallel applications.

The concept of speculative parallelization introduces a strategy where the system attempts to parallelize certain tasks speculatively, anticipating that they can be executed concurrently without dependencies. Speculative parallelization mechanisms, including compiler-based approaches and runtime optimizations, aim to identify and exploit parallelism dynamically. However, speculative parallelization introduces challenges related to correctness, as the system must account for potential dependencies and rollback mechanisms in case of mis-speculation. This strategy is particularly relevant in scenarios where the static analysis of dependencies is challenging, and runtime decisions can lead to more effective parallelization.

In the context of operating systems, efficient parallel programming extends beyond application-level parallelism to the design of the operating system kernel itself. Multicore-aware kernel schedulers, lock-free data structures, and parallel file systems are examples of strategies employed to harness the power of parallel architectures. Kernel-level parallelism introduces challenges related to synchronization, real-time constraints, and ensuring the responsiveness of critical system services. Techniques such as parallel I/O and asynchronous system calls contribute to the overall efficiency of the operating system, particularly in scenarios where high-throughput and low-latency operations are essential.

In conclusion, efficient parallel programming in operating systems involves a multifaceted approach that spans algorithm design, synchronization mechanisms, parallel programming frameworks, and runtime optimizations. Developers must strike a balance between exploiting parallelism for improved performance and mitigating the challenges associated with contention, synchronization, and correctness. As the landscape of parallel computing continues to evolve with emerging architectures and technologies, the application of efficient parallel programming strategies remains a dynamic and vital area of research and development. The judicious use of parallelism in operating systems is crucial for meeting the ever-increasing demands of computational workloads, enhancing overall system performance, and ensuring a responsive and scalable computing environment.

Chapter 5: The Dance of Devices: Drivers and Hardware Interaction

Definition and purpose in operating systems

An operating system (OS) serves as the fundamental software layer that facilitates communication and coordination between hardware components and application software within a computing device. It acts as a mediator, providing a set of essential services and functionalities that enable users to interact with the computer system seamlessly. The primary purpose of an operating system is to manage the underlying hardware resources efficiently, ensuring optimal utilization and smooth operation of various software applications.

At its core, an operating system serves as an abstraction layer, shielding users and application programs from the intricacies of hardware intricacies. It achieves this by providing a consistent and standardized interface, commonly known as the user interface, through which users can interact with the system. This interface could take the form of a command-line interface (CLI) or a graphical user interface (GUI), offering users a familiar environment to execute commands, launch applications, and manage files.

Resource management is a central function of operating systems, encompassing the allocation and deallocation of system resources such as CPU time, memory, and input/output (I/O) devices. The OS employs various scheduling algorithms to ensure fair and efficient utilization of the CPU, preventing any one program from monopolizing system resources. Memory management involves allocating and deallocating memory space for processes, swapping data between RAM and secondary storage, and handling virtual memory to extend the apparent size of the available RAM.

File systems, another critical component of operating systems, facilitate the organization, storage, and retrieval of data on storage devices. Operating systems implement file systems to manage files and directories, providing a hierarchical structure for organizing data. This abstraction simplifies the interaction between users and storage devices, allowing for easy navigation and manipulation of files.

In addition to resource management and file systems, operating systems play a crucial role in ensuring the security and integrity of a computing environment. They implement user authentication mechanisms, access control policies, and encryption techniques to safeguard sensitive data and prevent unauthorized access. Operating systems also incorporate error-handling mechanisms to detect and recover from system failures, contributing to the overall reliability of the computing system.

Communication between hardware devices and software applications is facilitated by device drivers, which are specialized programs that act as intermediaries between the operating system and hardware components. The OS abstracts the underlying hardware details, allowing application software to interact with devices through standardized interfaces. This abstraction layer promotes compatibility, enabling applications to run on a variety of hardware configurations without requiring modification.

Furthermore, the concept of multitasking is integral to modern operating systems, allowing multiple processes to run concurrently. The OS employs scheduling algorithms to switch between tasks rapidly, giving users the illusion of simultaneous execution. Multitasking enhances system efficiency by maximizing CPU utilization and responsiveness.

Network support is another essential aspect of operating systems, enabling communication between devices over local and wide-area networks. Operating systems incorporate network protocols and services, facilitating tasks such as data transfer, remote access, and network configuration. This connectivity is vital in today's interconnected world, supporting collaboration and resource sharing across different computing devices.

The evolution of operating systems has seen the emergence of different types, each tailored to specific computing environments. Real-time operating systems (RTOS) prioritize timely and deterministic execution of tasks, making them suitable for applications like embedded systems and control systems. Mobile operating systems, designed for smartphones and tablets, focus on power efficiency, user interface responsiveness, and app management. Server operating systems optimize resource utilization for hosting and managing network services, ensuring high availability and reliability.

In conclusion, operating systems serve as the backbone of modern computing, providing a crucial layer of abstraction and coordination between hardware components and software applications. Their multifaceted role encompasses resource management, file systems, security, communication, and support for various computing environments. Operating systems play an indispensable role in shaping the user experience, ensuring the efficient utilization of hardware resources, and fostering a stable and secure computing environment.

Types of device drivers and their roles

Device drivers are integral components of operating systems that facilitate communication between the operating system and hardware devices. They serve as intermediary software layers, translating high-level commands from the operating system into low-level instructions that the hardware can understand. The diverse types of device drivers play distinct roles in managing specific classes of hardware, ensuring seamless integration and optimal functionality within a computing environment.

One prominent category of device drivers is the display driver, responsible for enabling communication between the operating system and graphics hardware. Display drivers are crucial for rendering graphical elements on computer screens, supporting various resolutions, color depths, and refresh rates. They translate graphical commands from the operating system into signals that the graphics card can interpret, ensuring the accurate display of images and user interfaces. Display drivers also play a role in graphics acceleration, enhancing the performance of graphics-intensive applications by offloading certain processing tasks to the graphics hardware.

Another essential type of device driver is the printer driver, designed to facilitate the interaction between the operating system and printers. Printers vary widely in terms of models, capabilities, and connectivity options. Printer drivers act as translators, converting print job data generated by applications into a format that the specific printer can understand. They handle tasks such as formatting, spooling, and managing print queues. Printer drivers enable users to print documents with diverse layouts, fonts, and graphics, ensuring compatibility between applications and a wide range of printer models.

Storage device drivers are instrumental in managing the communication between the operating system and storage devices, such as hard disk drives (HDDs), solid-state drives (SSDs), and optical drives. These drivers facilitate tasks such as reading and writing data, managing file systems, and ensuring data integrity. Storage device drivers implement protocols like SATA, SCSI, or NVMe, allowing the operating system to interact with storage devices at the hardware level. They play a crucial role in supporting features like disk caching, error correction, and wear leveling in the context of SSDs.

Network interface card (NIC) drivers are essential for enabling communication between the operating system and network hardware. NIC drivers implement networking protocols and manage the flow of data between the computer and the network. They handle tasks such as packet encapsulation and decapsulation, error detection and correction, and network address translation. NIC drivers play a crucial role in supporting various networking technologies, including Ethernet, Wi-Fi, and Bluetooth, ensuring seamless connectivity and data exchange between devices in local and wide-area networks.

Audio drivers are responsible for managing the interaction between the operating system and audio hardware components, such as sound cards and integrated audio controllers. Audio drivers interpret high-level audio commands from the operating system, converting them into signals that the audio hardware can process. They support tasks such as audio playback, recording, and signal processing. Audio drivers also play a role in implementing features like surround sound, equalization, and audio effects, contributing to the overall audio experience of a computing system.

Input device drivers are designed to handle the communication between the operating system and input devices like keyboards, mice, and touchpads. These drivers interpret user input signals and translate them into commands that the operating system and applications can understand. Input device drivers support functionalities such as key mapping, gesture recognition, and cursor control. They enable users to interact with the computer system through various input methods, contributing to the versatility and user-friendliness of computing devices.

USB drivers play a crucial role in managing the communication between the operating system and USB (Universal Serial Bus) devices. USB is a widely used interface for connecting peripherals such as external drives, printers, cameras, and input devices. USB drivers handle tasks like device recognition, configuration, and data transfer.

They ensure the seamless integration of USB devices with the operating system, supporting features like plug-and-play and hot-swapping. USB drivers also play a role in managing power delivery to USB devices and enforcing standards for compatibility.

Peripheral component interconnect (PCI) drivers are essential for handling communication between the operating system and PCI-based hardware components, including expansion cards and integrated peripherals. PCI is a standard interface used for connecting internal hardware components within a computer. PCI drivers facilitate the enumeration and configuration of PCI devices, enabling the operating system to recognize and utilize these components. They ensure that the operating system can interact with PCI devices efficiently and take advantage of their specific functionalities.

Bluetooth drivers are specific to devices equipped with Bluetooth technology, such as wireless keyboards, mice, headphones, and mobile devices. Bluetooth drivers enable the operating system to communicate with Bluetooth-enabled devices, supporting tasks like device pairing, data transfer, and wireless connectivity. These drivers implement Bluetooth protocols and manage the establishment of connections between devices, ensuring a seamless and secure wireless communication experience.

Camera drivers are designed to facilitate communication between the operating system and imaging devices, including built-in webcams and external cameras. Camera drivers interpret commands related to image capture, video recording, and camera settings. They play a crucial role in supporting video conferencing, online streaming, and other applications that utilize camera input. Camera drivers also handle tasks such as image processing, resolution adjustment, and color balance to deliver a satisfactory visual experience.

In conclusion, the myriad types of device drivers fulfill specialized roles in managing the communication between the operating system and various hardware components. Display drivers contribute to the rendering of graphics on screens, printer drivers enable compatibility with a wide range of printers, storage device drivers manage data storage and retrieval, NIC drivers facilitate network connectivity, audio drivers enhance the audio experience, input device drivers interpret user input, USB drivers handle communication with USB devices, PCI drivers manage internal hardware components, Bluetooth drivers support wireless communication, and camera drivers enable the use of imaging devices. Together, these drivers form a critical layer that ensures the seamless integration and optimal performance of diverse hardware components within a computing environment.

Abstraction techniques for diverse hardware

Abstraction techniques for diverse hardware play a crucial role in the development and functionality of modern computing systems, allowing software to interact with hardware in a standardized and simplified manner. One prominent abstraction technique is the use of high-level programming languages, which enable developers to write code without having to be concerned about the intricate details of specific hardware architectures. By providing a set of common commands and syntax, these languages allow programmers to express complex algorithms and functionalities in a way that is independent of the underlying hardware, fostering portability and ease of development across a wide range of computing devices.

Another key abstraction technique is the implementation of Application Programming Interfaces (APIs) and libraries. APIs define a set of functions and protocols that serve as an interface between software applications and hardware components. By utilizing APIs, developers can access specific hardware functionalities without needing to understand the intricate details of the hardware itself. This abstraction layer simplifies the development process, as programmers can focus on the broader aspects of their applications while relying on standardized APIs to interact with diverse hardware components.

Operating systems play a central role in hardware abstraction by providing a unified and standardized interface for applications. The operating system abstracts hardware details, such as memory management, process scheduling, and file systems, presenting a consistent environment to applications regardless of the underlying hardware architecture. This abstraction allows software to run seamlessly on different platforms, promoting interoperability and facilitating the development of software that can be deployed on a variety of hardware configurations.

Virtualization is a powerful abstraction technique that enables the creation of virtual instances of hardware resources. Virtual machines (VMs) and containers abstract the underlying physical hardware, allowing multiple operating systems and applications to run concurrently on the same physical machine. This abstraction enhances resource utilization, flexibility, and scalability, as developers can create and deploy applications without being constrained by the specific hardware characteristics of the hosting environment.

In the realm of graphics and multimedia, Graphics Processing Unit (GPU) abstraction is crucial for efficient and scalable rendering. APIs like OpenGL and DirectX provide a high-level interface for developers to interact with GPUs, allowing them to offload complex graphics tasks without delving into the intricate details of GPU architectures. This abstraction facilitates the development of graphics-intensive applications such as video games, simulations, and multimedia editing software.

Network abstraction is fundamental for communication between devices over diverse network architectures. Protocols such as Transmission Control Protocol (TCP) and Internet Protocol (IP) provide a standardized way for devices to communicate over networks, abstracting the underlying complexities of data transmission and routing. This abstraction allows developers to create networked applications without the need to understand the intricacies of the various networking technologies.

Device drivers represent a specific form of hardware abstraction, translating high-level commands from the operating system into low-level instructions that hardware components can understand. By providing a standardized interface, device drivers enable seamless interaction between the operating system and peripherals, such as printers, storage devices, and input devices. This abstraction ensures that applications can utilize diverse hardware components without being tightly coupled to their specific implementations.

Middleware, a layer of software that resides between the operating system and application software, serves as an abstraction framework for distributed systems. Middleware abstracts the complexities of communication, data synchronization, and resource management in distributed environments. This abstraction allows developers to build distributed applications without directly dealing with the intricacies of network protocols, enabling the creation of scalable and interoperable systems.

In the context of storage, File System abstraction is essential for organizing and accessing data on diverse storage devices. File systems provide a standardized way to store and retrieve data, abstracting the specifics of underlying storage technologies. This abstraction allows applications to interact with data in a uniform manner, regardless of whether it is stored on a traditional hard disk drive, solid-state drive, or network-attached storage.

In the realm of embedded systems, abstraction techniques are employed to simplify the development of firmware and software for devices with limited resources. Hardware Abstraction Layers (HALs) provide a level of abstraction that shields developers from the intricacies of the underlying hardware, enabling them to focus on writing code that interacts with sensors, actuators, and other embedded components. This abstraction is particularly valuable in the Internet of Things (IoT) era, where a diverse array of connected devices requires efficient and scalable software development.

In conclusion, abstraction techniques for diverse hardware are essential for simplifying the development process, promoting portability, and enhancing the scalability of software across a wide range of computing environments. High-level programming languages, APIs, operating systems, virtualization, graphics APIs, network protocols, device drivers, middleware, file systems, and embedded systems abstraction layers collectively form a comprehensive framework that allows developers to create software without being burdened by the intricacies of the underlying hardware. These abstraction techniques are foundational to the versatility, interoperability, and efficiency of modern computing systems.

Ensuring compatibility and portability

Ensuring compatibility and portability are critical objectives in the design and development of software systems, aiming to maximize the reach and usability of applications across diverse computing environments. Compatibility refers to the ability of a software application to function correctly and seamlessly on different hardware configurations, operating systems, and software dependencies. Achieving compatibility involves creating software that can adapt to varying specifications, ensuring that it operates as intended regardless of the specific environment in which it is deployed. Portability, on the other hand, encompasses the ease with which software can be transferred or adapted to different platforms, enabling it to run efficiently and consistently across a range of devices and systems.

One fundamental approach to ensuring compatibility is through adherence to industry standards. Standards define common specifications and protocols that facilitate interoperability between different components of a computing system. By designing software in accordance with established standards, developers ensure that their applications can communicate with hardware devices, operating systems, and other software components using universally accepted protocols. For example, adherence to networking standards allows applications to communicate seamlessly across diverse network architectures, fostering compatibility between different devices and systems.

In the realm of operating systems, achieving compatibility involves designing software that can operate seamlessly across various platforms. This often requires careful consideration of system calls, file system structures, and other OS-specific functionalities. Abstraction layers, such as those provided by high-level programming languages and middleware, play a crucial role in shielding applications from the intricacies of different operating systems, promoting compatibility by providing a consistent interface regardless of the underlying platform.

Cross-platform development is a key strategy for ensuring both compatibility and portability. This approach involves creating software that can run on multiple operating systems without requiring significant modifications. Technologies such as Java, which leverages the Java Virtual Machine (JVM), enable developers to write code once and run it on different platforms. Similarly, frameworks like Xamarin and Electron facilitate the creation of cross-platform applications that can be deployed on diverse devices, including desktops, mobile devices, and the web. Cross-platform development streamlines the software deployment process, reducing the need for platform-specific code modifications and testing.

Virtualization is another powerful technique for achieving compatibility and portability. Virtual machines (VMs) and containers allow software to run in isolated environments, abstracting away the underlying hardware and operating system. This abstraction ensures that applications can be easily moved between different environments without being affected by variations in the hosting infrastructure. Cloud computing platforms leverage virtualization extensively, enabling the deployment of software across a variety of virtualized environments with minimal adjustments.

Compatibility testing is a crucial aspect of software development, involving the systematic evaluation of an application's performance across different configurations and environments. This testing process aims to identify and address potential issues related to hardware variations, operating system differences, and software dependencies. Automated testing tools and frameworks help streamline the compatibility testing process, allowing developers to assess their applications across a broad spectrum of scenarios efficiently.

Ensuring compatibility with diverse hardware configurations is paramount for reaching a broad user base. Hardware abstraction layers, such as device drivers, provide a standardized interface for software to interact with hardware components. By developing software that relies on these abstraction layers, developers can ensure compatibility with a wide range of devices, from printers and graphics cards to network adapters and storage devices. Compatibility with various input devices, such as keyboards, mice, and touchscreens, is also essential, and ensuring support for industry-standard input protocols enhances user experience across different hardware setups.

In the context of web development, achieving compatibility across different browsers is a significant challenge. Web standards, such as those established by the World Wide Web Consortium (W3C), provide guidelines for creating web pages that can be rendered consistently across various browsers. Web developers employ techniques like responsive design and feature detection to ensure that websites and web applications adapt to different screen sizes and capabilities, offering a seamless experience to users regardless of the browser or device they are using.

Open standards and open-source software contribute significantly to compatibility and portability. Open standards ensure that specifications are publicly available, allowing developers to implement them without restrictions. Open-source software, with its transparent and collaborative development model, often prioritizes compatibility across diverse systems. Projects like the Linux operating system and the Apache web server exemplify the success of open-source initiatives in achieving broad compatibility and portability.

The use of containerization technologies, such as Docker, has become increasingly popular for achieving portability. Containers encapsulate an application and its dependencies, ensuring that it can run consistently across different environments. This approach simplifies the deployment process, as containers provide a self-contained and isolated runtime environment for applications. Container orchestration platforms, like Kubernetes, further enhance portability by automating the deployment, scaling, and management of containerized applications across diverse computing environments.

Ensuring compatibility and portability is particularly crucial in the context of mobile app development. The fragmentation of the mobile ecosystem, with various devices running different operating systems and versions, poses challenges for developers seeking to reach a broad user base. Cross-platform frameworks, such as React Native and Flutter, allow developers to create mobile applications that can run on both iOS and Android devices, minimizing the effort required for platform-specific development. Additionally, responsive design practices and adaptive layouts ensure that mobile apps provide a consistent user experience across various screen sizes and resolutions.

In conclusion, ensuring compatibility and portability is a multifaceted challenge that spans hardware configurations, operating systems, browsers, and diverse computing environments. Adherence to industry standards, cross-platform development, virtualization, compatibility testing, hardware abstraction layers, open standards, open-source software, containerization, and mobile app development practices are essential strategies for achieving these objectives.

As technology continues to evolve, the pursuit of compatibility and portability remains a foundational principle in the creation of robust and versatile software systems that can thrive in the ever-changing landscape of computing.

Protocols for communication

Protocols for communication constitute the fundamental frameworks that govern the exchange of data and information between different entities within a networked environment. These protocols establish the rules and conventions that enable seamless and standardized communication, ensuring that devices and systems can interact effectively. At various layers of the OSI (Open Systems Interconnection) model, a conceptual framework used to understand network interactions, specific communication protocols dictate how data is encapsulated, transmitted, and received.

Starting at the lowest layer, the physical layer protocols govern the transmission of raw binary data over physical media such as cables and wireless channels. Protocols like Ethernet and Wi-Fi define the electrical and mechanical characteristics of the hardware connections, specifying how bits are encoded, transmitted, and received. Ethernet, for example, employs protocols like TCP/IP for higher-layer communication.

Moving up the OSI model, the data link layer protocols handle the reliable transmission of data frames between directly connected nodes in a network. Protocols such as Point-to-Point Protocol (PPP) and High-Level Data Link Control (HDLC) govern this layer, managing the framing, addressing, and error detection of data packets. PPP is commonly used in establishing direct connections, while HDLC is employed in synchronous communication links.

The network layer protocols, such as Internet Protocol (IP), play a crucial role in routing data across interconnected networks. IP provides logical addressing and routing functionality, enabling the transmission of data packets between devices on different networks. The version 4 of Internet Protocol (IPv4) and the newer IPv6 are widely used in the addressing and routing of data packets over the Internet and other networks.

Transport layer protocols focus on end-to-end communication between devices, ensuring reliable and error-checked delivery of data. Transmission Control Protocol (TCP) is a connection-oriented protocol that guarantees the delivery of data in the correct order and handles retransmission of lost or corrupted packets. User Datagram Protocol (UDP), on the other hand, is connectionless and is often used in scenarios where low overhead and faster transmission are prioritized, such as real-time applications.

At the higher layers of the OSI model, various application layer protocols facilitate communication between software applications. The Hypertext Transfer Protocol (HTTP) governs the exchange of hypertext documents on the World Wide Web, providing the foundation for web communication. HTTPS, a secure variant of HTTP, adds a layer of encryption using protocols like Transport Layer Security (TLS) or its predecessor, Secure Sockets Layer (SSL), ensuring the confidentiality and integrity of data exchanged between web browsers and servers.

Simple Mail Transfer Protocol (SMTP) is a widely used protocol for sending email messages, while Post Office Protocol version 3 (POP3) and Internet Message Access Protocol (IMAP) are protocols used by email clients to retrieve messages from mail servers. These application layer protocols enable the seamless exchange of electronic mail across the Internet.

File Transfer Protocol (FTP) is a protocol that governs the transfer of files between computers on a network. It provides a standard set of commands for uploading, downloading, and managing files on remote servers. Secure File Transfer Protocol (SFTP) and FTP Secure (FTPS) are secure variants of FTP that use encryption to protect data during transmission.

In the realm of voice and video communication, Real-time Transport Protocol (RTP) is a key protocol that facilitates the real-time transmission of audio and video over IP networks. RTP works in conjunction with Real-time Transport Control Protocol (RTCP), which provides feedback on the quality of the transmission and helps manage network resources.

Beyond these widely recognized communication protocols, the Internet is reliant on the Domain Name System (DNS) for translating human-readable domain names into IP addresses, facilitating the routing of data to the intended destination. DNS operates as a distributed hierarchical system, ensuring efficient and reliable resolution of domain names to IP addresses.

Emerging technologies such as the Internet of Things (IoT) introduce communication protocols designed to cater to the unique requirements of interconnected devices. The Message Queuing Telemetry Transport (MQTT) protocol, for instance, is lightweight and well-suited for scenarios where low bandwidth and minimal power consumption are crucial, making it a popular choice for IoT applications.

In industrial settings, the Modbus protocol is widely used for communication between industrial control systems and devices. Modbus facilitates the exchange of data between devices over serial communication, contributing to the interoperability of diverse industrial automation equipment.

Security protocols, such as the aforementioned TLS and SSL, are crucial for protecting data during transmission. These protocols use cryptographic techniques to encrypt data, preventing unauthorized access and ensuring the confidentiality and integrity of sensitive information.

While these protocols provide a framework for communication within a networked environment, the Internet Protocol suite, commonly known as TCP/IP, serves as the cornerstone of modern networking. TCP/IP encompasses a comprehensive suite of protocols, including IP, TCP, UDP, and others, that collectively enable the seamless communication of data across the global network that is the Internet.

In conclusion, communication protocols form the backbone of modern networking, facilitating the exchange of data between devices, systems, and applications. From the physical layer protocols that govern raw data transmission to the application layer protocols that enable the exchange of web pages, emails, and multimedia content, these protocols collectively ensure the interoperability, reliability, and security of communication in diverse computing environments. As technology continues to evolve, new protocols will likely emerge to address the specific requirements of emerging applications and communication scenarios, further shaping the landscape of networked communication.

Interrupts and their role in device interaction

Interrupts play a pivotal role in the intricate dance of communication and coordination between a computer's central processing unit (CPU) and peripheral devices, ensuring efficient and responsive interaction within a computing system. At their core, interrupts are signals generated by external devices or internal events that divert the CPU's attention from its current task to handle a specific event or request. This mechanism allows devices to gain the CPU's focus precisely when needed, avoiding the inefficiency of constant polling and allowing the CPU to dedicate its processing power to other tasks when no immediate attention is required.

The interaction between interrupts and devices is deeply rooted in the concept of asynchronous events. Peripheral devices, ranging from keyboards and mice to storage devices and network interfaces, operate independently of the CPU's clock and initiate interactions with the system as needed. For example, when a user presses a key on the keyboard, an interrupt signal is generated to notify the CPU that input is awaiting processing. This asynchronous nature ensures that the CPU is not bogged down by continuous monitoring of devices and can focus on executing instructions efficiently.

Interrupts are classified into various types, each serving a specific purpose in facilitating device interaction. Hardware interrupts, triggered by external devices, are a common type. For instance, a network interface may generate a hardware interrupt to inform the CPU that a data packet has been received. Another type is software interrupts, which are initiated by specific instructions in a program. These instructions act as signals to the CPU to switch to a specific routine or handle a specific task. Software interrupts are commonly used for system calls, allowing applications to request services from the operating system.

One of the key roles of interrupts in device interaction is to ensure timely and precise response to external events. Take, for example, the case of real-time systems where immediate response is critical. Interrupts enable devices to interrupt the CPU's ongoing tasks, allowing time-sensitive events, such as sensor readings or control signals in industrial automation, to be processed promptly. This capability is crucial in applications where a delayed response could lead to system failures or compromised performance.

Interrupt service routines (ISRs) are the heart of interrupt-driven device interaction. When an interrupt is triggered, the CPU suspends its current task, saves its state, and transfers control to the ISR associated with the interrupting event. The ISR executes the necessary operations to handle the event, such as reading data from a device, updating system variables, or initiating a response. Once the ISR completes its task, the CPU restores its previous state and resumes the interrupted task. The ISR's efficiency is paramount, as it determines how quickly the system can respond to interrupts and interact with devices.

Device drivers, specialized software components, play a crucial role in the interaction between interrupts and devices. These drivers act as intermediaries, translating the generic interrupt signals into device-specific actions. For instance, a printer driver interprets an interrupt from the printing hardware, manages the data transfer, and ensures that the printed output aligns with the user's request. Device drivers encapsulate the intricacies of device communication, allowing applications to interact with devices through a standardized interface while abstracting the low-level details handled by interrupts.

The interrupt request (IRQ) system is a mechanism used to prioritize and manage interrupt signals from multiple devices. Each device is assigned a specific IRQ line, and the CPU responds to interrupts based on their priority levels. This system ensures that critical interrupts, such as those from a system clock or a high-priority device, are serviced promptly. The IRQ system thus contributes to the efficient handling of simultaneous or overlapping interrupt requests from various devices within the system.

Interrupts also play a crucial role in managing system resources and ensuring fair access among competing devices. Priority levels assigned to interrupts help the CPU allocate processing time appropriately. For example, in a multitasking environment, where multiple applications are running concurrently, interrupts enable the CPU to allocate time slices to different tasks based on priority. This ensures that critical tasks, such as real-time processes or user input handling, receive timely attention without compromising the overall system performance.

Beyond their role in handling device-related events, interrupts contribute significantly to power management in modern computing systems. Devices can utilize low-power states when not actively processing data, and interrupts serve as a mechanism to wake them up when needed. This approach enhances energy efficiency, particularly in mobile devices where conserving battery power is crucial.

Interrupts thus enable a balance between responsiveness and power conservation, ensuring that devices are active only when required.

Interrupts are also instrumental in error handling and recovery. When a device encounters an error condition, it can generate an interrupt to alert the CPU. The CPU can then execute error-handling routines, log the issue, and potentially initiate recovery procedures. This capability enhances the robustness and reliability of computing systems, allowing them to respond to faults, malfunctions, or unexpected events in a controlled manner.

The relationship between interrupts and devices extends to input/output (I/O) operations, where devices communicate with the CPU to send or receive data. Devices, such as hard drives or network interfaces, use interrupts to signal the completion of data transfers or to request attention when a specific I/O operation is ready to proceed. This asynchronous I/O model, facilitated by interrupts, ensures that the CPU is not idle while waiting for I/O operations to complete, enhancing overall system efficiency.

In the context of inter-device communication, interrupts enable devices to signal each other or coordinate their actions. For instance, in a networked environment, devices may use interrupts to notify each other of specific events, synchronize data transfer, or manage shared resources. This capability is foundational in building complex systems where devices need to collaborate and exchange information to achieve collective goals.

Interrupts also contribute to the security of computing systems. Security features, such as access control mechanisms and encryption, can be initiated through interrupts. For example, a security module may generate an interrupt to request user authentication when accessing sensitive data. Interrupt-driven security measures enhance the protection of critical information and resources within a computing environment.

In conclusion, interrupts serve as the dynamic conduits through which devices communicate with the CPU in a computing system. Their role is multifaceted, encompassing responsiveness to external events, precise handling of time-sensitive tasks, resource management, power conservation, error handling, and facilitating inter-device communication. The interaction between interrupts and devices, orchestrated by interrupt service routines and device drivers, underpins the efficiency, reliability, and versatility of modern computing systems. As technology advances and computing architectures evolve, the role of interrupts remains integral in shaping the dynamic and responsive nature of device interaction within the broader context of computing ecosystems.

Design considerations for plug-and-play support

Designing systems with plug-and-play support is a complex endeavor that involves addressing a myriad of considerations to ensure seamless integration and usability for users interacting with various hardware components. Plug-and-play, often abbreviated as PnP, refers to the ability of a system to automatically detect and configure hardware devices without requiring manual intervention from users or system administrators. The successful implementation of plug-and-play functionality enhances user experience, reduces the technical barriers associated with hardware installation, and allows for the dynamic connection of devices. Several design considerations are crucial to achieving effective plug-and-play support.

At the forefront of plug-and-play design is the need for standardized hardware interfaces and communication protocols. Establishing and adhering to industry-accepted standards ensure that devices can communicate effectively with the system, regardless of their specific manufacturers. Protocols such as USB (Universal Serial Bus), Thunderbolt, and Bluetooth exemplify standardized interfaces that enable plug-and-play capabilities across a diverse range of devices, including peripherals, storage, and audiovisual equipment. Standardization fosters interoperability, allowing users to connect devices seamlessly without worrying about compatibility issues.

The development of consistent and well-documented device drivers is another critical consideration for plug-and-play support. Device drivers act as intermediary software between the operating system and hardware devices, translating high-level commands from the system into instructions that the hardware can understand. Designing robust and universally compatible device drivers is essential for ensuring that the system can recognize and configure newly connected devices automatically. Additionally, the availability of driver updates and a centralized repository for drivers contribute to the long-term compatibility and stability of plug-and-play functionality.

A comprehensive approach to device enumeration and identification is vital for effective plug-and-play support. When a new device is connected, the system must be able to identify the type, model, and capabilities of the device accurately. Mechanisms like Plug and Play BIOS (PnP BIOS) and Universal Plug and Play (UPnP) protocols assist in the automatic detection and configuration of devices by providing standardized methods for querying device information. This information is crucial for the system to load the appropriate device drivers, allocate resources, and ensure seamless integration of the new hardware.

Power management considerations play a significant role in plug-and-play design, especially in mobile and energy-efficient computing environments. Devices often have varying power requirements, and the system needs to manage power distribution dynamically based on the connected devices. The Advanced Configuration and Power Interface (ACPI) standard is instrumental in facilitating power management for plug-and-play systems. ACPI enables the operating system to control the power state of individual devices, allowing for efficient power usage and extending battery life in portable devices.

Dynamic resource allocation is a key consideration to prevent conflicts and ensure optimal performance in plug-and-play systems. Devices may share common system resources, such as interrupt request lines (IRQs), memory addresses, and I/O ports. The system must have mechanisms in place to allocate these resources dynamically, avoiding conflicts when multiple devices are connected simultaneously. Resource Allocation Protocols and Plug and Play Operating System (PnP OS) settings contribute to effective resource management, ensuring that connected devices receive the necessary resources without compromising system stability.

User interface design is integral to the plug-and-play experience, focusing on providing users with clear and intuitive methods for interacting with connected devices. User-friendly interfaces should convey information about connected devices, such as their status, capabilities, and any required actions. Device icons, notifications, and wizards can guide users through the process of connecting and configuring new hardware components, minimizing the need for technical expertise. A well-designed user interface enhances the accessibility and adoption of plug-and-play functionality, catering to both novice and experienced users.

Error handling and feedback mechanisms are essential to address situations where plug-and-play encounters issues, such as incompatible devices or driver conflicts. The system should be equipped to provide informative error messages, guiding users on how to resolve problems or seek additional support. Diagnostic tools, event logs, and error reporting mechanisms contribute to troubleshooting and resolving issues related to plug-and-play functionality. Effective error handling ensures that users can identify and rectify problems swiftly, minimizing disruptions to their computing experience.

Security considerations are paramount in plug-and-play design to mitigate potential risks associated with connecting external devices to the system. Devices can introduce security vulnerabilities, and the system must implement robust security measures to protect against malware, unauthorized access, or data breaches. Secure device authentication, encryption protocols, and adherence to security standards contribute to a secure plug-and-play environment. Additionally, the system should regularly update device drivers and firmware to address security vulnerabilities and ensure a resilient security posture.

Scalability is a fundamental design consideration, especially in environments where a diverse range of devices may be connected to the system. Plug-and-play support should scale seamlessly as the number and complexity of connected devices increase. The system's architecture should accommodate a growing ecosystem of devices without sacrificing performance or stability. Scalability considerations extend to both hardware and software components, ensuring that the plug-and-play infrastructure remains responsive and adaptable to the evolving landscape of connected devices.

Integration with system management tools and frameworks is crucial for effective plug-and-play functionality, particularly in enterprise environments where centralized management is essential. System administrators should have the ability to monitor and control plug-and-play activities across multiple devices within a network. Integration with tools like Microsoft System Center Configuration Manager (SCCM) or third-party device management solutions facilitates centralized device configuration, monitoring, and updates. A well-integrated management framework streamlines the administration of plug-and-play functionality, enhancing efficiency in large-scale deployments.

In conclusion, designing for plug-and-play support requires a holistic approach that addresses standardized hardware interfaces, robust device drivers, effective device enumeration, power management, resource allocation, user interface design, error handling, security measures, scalability, and integration with system management tools. By carefully considering these factors, developers can create systems that deliver a seamless and user-friendly experience, allowing users to connect and use devices effortlessly while ensuring the compatibility, reliability, and security of the plug-and-play infrastructure. As technology continues to evolve, the design considerations for plug-and-play support will play a crucial role in shaping the user experience and fostering innovation in the realm of connected devices and computing ecosystems.

Dynamic device recognition and configuration

Dynamic device recognition and configuration constitute a pivotal aspect of modern computing systems, enabling seamless integration and utilization of diverse hardware components without requiring manual intervention. The term "dynamic" implies an adaptive and automatic process wherein the system identifies connected devices in real-time, configures them appropriately, and ensures their optimal functionality. This dynamic capability significantly enhances user experience, as it eliminates the need for users to navigate through intricate configuration settings or install drivers manually. The overarching goal is to create a plug-and-play environment where devices are recognized on-the-fly, configured according to their specifications, and made ready for immediate use, contributing to the versatility and accessibility of computing ecosystems.

At the core of dynamic device recognition is the utilization of standardized communication protocols and interfaces. By adhering to established industry standards, such as USB (Universal Serial Bus), Thunderbolt, or Bluetooth, devices ensure a common language for interacting with the system. These protocols define the rules and conventions for data exchange between the device and the operating system, allowing for a consistent method of communication that transcends device manufacturers and models. Standardization is foundational for dynamic recognition, as it provides a universal framework that facilitates the automatic detection and configuration of devices by the system.

The process of dynamic device recognition begins with the physical connection of a device to the system. In scenarios where a user plugs in a USB flash drive or connects a peripheral device, the system's hardware layer plays a crucial role. Physical layer protocols, such as those governing USB or Thunderbolt, facilitate the transmission of signals and electrical interactions between the device and the system. The physical layer serves as the gateway for the dynamic recognition process, allowing the system to detect the presence of a new device and initiate the subsequent configuration steps.

A key component in dynamic device recognition is the presence of Plug and Play (PnP) functionality within the operating system. PnP is a set of technologies and standards that enable the automatic configuration of hardware devices without user intervention. When a device is connected, the operating system utilizes PnP mechanisms to identify the device and initiate the necessary steps for configuring it. These mechanisms include querying the device for identification information, checking against a database of known devices, and determining the appropriate device drivers to load. PnP transforms the connection of a new device into a seamless and automated process, aligning with the principles of dynamic device recognition.

The role of device drivers in dynamic recognition is paramount. Device drivers serve as the bridge between the operating system and the specific hardware characteristics of a device. In a dynamic recognition scenario, the operating system, through its PnP mechanisms, queries the device for identification information, such as Vendor IDs (VIDs) and Product IDs (PIDs). Using this information, the system can identify the device model and version. Once identified, the system searches its database or external repositories for the corresponding device driver. If the driver is available, it is loaded into the system, enabling the device to function seamlessly. This dynamic loading of drivers ensures that the system remains adaptable to a wide array of devices, even those not present during the initial installation of the operating system.

To facilitate dynamic device recognition, the system relies on standardized methods for device enumeration. Enumeration is the process of systematically identifying and assigning unique identifiers to connected devices. Protocols like Universal Plug and Play (UPnP) play a significant role in enumeration by providing a standardized framework for devices to announce their presence on the network and communicate essential information. UPnP enables dynamic device discovery and configuration in networked environments, allowing devices to seamlessly integrate into the ecosystem without requiring manual intervention.

Power management considerations are integral to dynamic device recognition, particularly in scenarios where devices may have varying power requirements. The system needs to manage power distribution dynamically based on the connected devices to optimize energy usage and extend battery life in mobile devices. The Advanced Configuration and Power Interface (ACPI) standard plays a crucial role in power management for plug-and-play systems. ACPI enables the operating system to control the power state of individual devices, allowing for efficient power usage and ensuring that devices are active only when needed.

Dynamic resource allocation is another critical aspect of the recognition process. As devices are connected and identified, the system must allocate resources such as interrupt request lines (IRQs), memory addresses, and I/O ports dynamically to prevent conflicts and ensure optimal performance. Resource Allocation Protocols and Plug and Play Operating System (PnP OS) settings contribute to effective resource management. These mechanisms enable the system to allocate resources intelligently, avoiding clashes when multiple devices are connected simultaneously. Dynamic resource allocation is crucial for accommodating the diverse range of devices that users may connect to the system.

User interfaces are essential components in the dynamic device recognition process, providing users with feedback and control over the connected devices. User-friendly interfaces convey information about the status and configuration of connected devices, offering transparency and facilitating user understanding. Device icons, notifications, and wizards guide users through the process of connecting and configuring new hardware components, minimizing the need for technical expertise. A well-designed user interface enhances the accessibility and adoption of plug-and-play functionality, catering to both novice and experienced users.

Error handling and feedback mechanisms are critical considerations in dynamic device recognition to address situations where issues may arise, such as incompatible devices or driver conflicts. The system should be equipped to provide informative error messages, guiding users on how to resolve problems or seek additional support. Diagnostic tools, event logs, and error reporting mechanisms contribute to troubleshooting and resolving issues related to dynamic device recognition. Effective error handling ensures that users can identify and rectify problems swiftly, minimizing disruptions to their computing experience.

Security considerations are paramount in the dynamic device recognition process to mitigate potential risks associated with connecting external devices to the system. Devices can introduce security vulnerabilities, and the system must implement robust security measures to protect against malware, unauthorized access, or data breaches. Secure device authentication, encryption protocols, and adherence to security standards contribute to a secure dynamic device recognition environment. Additionally, the system should regularly update device drivers and firmware to address security vulnerabilities and ensure a resilient security posture.

Scalability is a fundamental consideration for dynamic device recognition, especially in environments where a diverse range of devices may be connected to the system. The design should accommodate a growing ecosystem of devices without sacrificing performance or stability. The system's architecture should scale seamlessly as the number and complexity of connected devices increase. Scalability considerations extend to both hardware and software components, ensuring that the dynamic recognition infrastructure remains responsive and adaptable to the evolving landscape of connected devices.

Integration with system management tools and frameworks is crucial for effective dynamic device recognition, particularly in enterprise environments where centralized management is essential. System administrators should have the ability to monitor and control dynamic recognition activities across multiple devices within a network. Integration with tools like Microsoft System Center Configuration Manager (SCCM) or third-party device management solutions facilitates centralized device configuration, monitoring, and updates. A well-integrated management framework streamlines the administration of dynamic device recognition, enhancing efficiency in large-scale deployments.

In conclusion, dynamic device recognition and configuration represent a cornerstone in the evolution of computing systems towards seamless integration and user-friendly experiences. The dynamic nature of this process, driven by standardized protocols, intelligent resource allocation, user interfaces, error handling mechanisms, and security considerations, ensures that users can effortlessly connect and use a diverse array of devices without the complexities of manual configuration. As technology continues to advance, the design considerations for dynamic device recognition will remain instrumental in shaping the future of computing ecosystems, enabling enhanced interoperability and adaptability in the face of an ever-expanding landscape of connected devices.

Strategies for improving device efficiency

Improving device efficiency is a multifaceted challenge that involves optimizing various aspects of hardware, software, and system architecture to enhance performance, reduce energy consumption, and streamline overall functionality. These strategies encompass a range of approaches, from hardware innovations and intelligent power management to software optimization and streamlined communication protocols. By adopting a holistic perspective, developers and engineers can design devices that not only meet user expectations for speed and responsiveness but also contribute to sustainability and resource efficiency.

At the hardware level, one fundamental strategy for improving device efficiency is to leverage advancements in semiconductor technology. Shrinking transistor sizes, transitioning to more efficient materials, and adopting innovative chip architectures contribute to enhanced processing capabilities while minimizing energy consumption. The development of System-on-Chip (SoC) designs, which integrate multiple functions onto a single chip, allows for improved efficiency by reducing the need for inter-chip communication and optimizing the use of resources.

Power-efficient components and subsystems play a crucial role in overall device efficiency. Manufacturers can focus on selecting energy-efficient processors, memory modules, and other essential components. Additionally, advancements in display technologies, such as organic light-emitting diode (OLED) and low-power LCDs, contribute to improved energy efficiency in devices with visual interfaces. Power-efficient components not only enhance the device's performance but also extend battery life in portable devices, addressing a critical consideration in modern computing.

Effective power management strategies are integral to optimizing device efficiency, particularly in battery-powered devices. Dynamic Voltage and Frequency Scaling (DVFS) techniques enable devices to adjust their voltage and clock frequency dynamically based on the workload, reducing power consumption during periods of low activity and ramping up performance when needed. Advanced Power Management (APM) and Advanced Configuration and Power Interface (ACPI) standards provide frameworks for controlling power states, allowing devices to transition between active and low-power states intelligently.

In the realm of software, optimization plays a pivotal role in improving device efficiency. Efficient algorithms, well-structured code, and optimized data storage and retrieval mechanisms contribute to faster and more resource-efficient computation. Compilation techniques, such as Just-In-Time (JIT) compilation and code optimization, enhance the execution speed of software, ensuring that the device's resources are utilized efficiently. Additionally, adopting lightweight and modular software architectures reduces the overall system footprint and enhances responsiveness.

Parallel computing is a powerful strategy for improving device efficiency, especially in the context of multi-core processors. By designing software to take advantage of parallelism, developers can distribute computational tasks across multiple cores, enabling faster execution and improved overall performance. Parallel processing is particularly relevant in applications that involve complex calculations, simulations, or data processing, where breaking down tasks into parallel threads can lead to significant efficiency gains.

Efficient memory management is crucial for optimizing device performance. Utilizing advanced memory technologies, such as high-speed and low-latency RAM (Random Access Memory), contributes to faster data access and retrieval. Caching mechanisms, both at the hardware and software levels, reduce the need to fetch data from slower storage, improving response times. Additionally, memory compression techniques and algorithms help minimize the amount of data transferred between storage and memory, further enhancing efficiency.

Streamlining communication protocols and data transfer mechanisms is essential for improving device efficiency, especially in networked and interconnected environments. Efficient networking protocols, such as Transmission Control Protocol (TCP) variants optimized for high-latency or low-bandwidth scenarios, contribute to faster and more reliable data transmission. The adoption of lightweight communication protocols, as seen in IoT (Internet of Things) devices, ensures efficient exchange of information without unnecessary overhead.

The integration of Artificial Intelligence (AI) and machine learning algorithms presents opportunities for improving device efficiency through predictive and adaptive capabilities. AI algorithms can analyze usage patterns, predict user behavior, and adapt device settings dynamically to optimize performance and energy consumption. Machine learning models can be employed for predictive maintenance, identifying potential hardware issues before they escalate, contributing to increased device reliability and efficiency.

Energy harvesting technologies offer a sustainable approach to improving device efficiency, especially in scenarios where battery replacement or recharging is impractical. Devices can harness ambient energy sources, such as solar, kinetic, or thermal energy, to supplement or replace traditional power sources. Energy harvesting technologies contribute to prolonged device lifetimes, reduce environmental impact, and enhance the overall efficiency of devices in remote or resource-constrained settings.

Adopting a modular design philosophy allows for the creation of customizable and upgradeable devices, enabling users to replace or upgrade specific components without discarding the entire device.

This strategy enhances resource efficiency by extending the lifecycle of devices and reducing electronic waste. Modular designs also facilitate easier repairs, contributing to a more sustainable and environmentally conscious approach to device manufacturing.

In the context of networked devices, edge computing is emerging as a strategy to improve efficiency by processing data closer to the source, reducing the need for extensive data transmission to centralized servers. Edge computing architectures enable real-time data processing, lower latency, and reduced bandwidth usage, enhancing overall system efficiency. This approach is particularly relevant in applications where rapid decision-making is critical, such as IoT deployments and autonomous systems.

Cross-platform development frameworks offer an efficient strategy for building applications that can run on multiple operating systems and devices with minimal modifications. Technologies like Xamarin, Flutter, and React Native allow developers to write code once and deploy it across various platforms, reducing development time and effort. Cross-platform development enhances resource efficiency by streamlining the software development process and ensuring a consistent user experience across different devices and operating systems.

Security measures are integral to improving device efficiency by safeguarding against potential threats and ensuring the reliability of device operations. Implementing robust security protocols, encryption algorithms, and secure boot mechanisms protects devices from unauthorized access, data breaches, and malicious attacks. Security measures contribute to the overall efficiency of devices by preserving the integrity of software, protecting user data, and maintaining the reliability of critical functions.

Lifecycle management practices, including regular software updates and firmware upgrades, contribute to the long-term efficiency of devices. Manufacturers and developers can address performance issues, introduce optimizations, and enhance security by providing timely updates to the device's software and firmware. Additionally, end-of-life considerations, including responsible recycling and disposal practices, contribute to the overall sustainability and efficiency of the device lifecycle.

In conclusion, strategies for improving device efficiency span a wide spectrum of hardware and software considerations, encompassing advancements in semiconductor technology, power management, software optimization, parallel computing, memory management, communication protocols, AI integration, energy harvesting, modular design, edge computing, cross-platform development, security measures, and lifecycle management practices. The holistic integration of these strategies enables the creation of devices that not only deliver superior performance but also prioritize energy efficiency, sustainability, and user experience. As technology continues to evolve, the pursuit of efficient device design remains a dynamic and multifaceted endeavor, driving innovation and shaping the landscape of computing ecosystems.

Balancing device interaction with overall system performance

Balancing device interaction with overall system performance is a nuanced challenge that lies at the heart of designing efficient and user-friendly computing ecosystems. In the dynamic landscape of modern devices, ranging from smartphones and laptops to IoT (Internet of Things) devices and industrial systems, the seamless integration of diverse hardware components while maintaining optimal system performance is a delicate equilibrium. This equilibrium is crucial to ensure that users can interact with connected devices effectively without compromising the overall efficiency and responsiveness of the entire system. Achieving this delicate balance involves addressing multiple facets, including hardware capabilities, software optimization, resource allocation, and user interface design.

One of the fundamental considerations in balancing device interaction with system performance is the hardware's processing power and capabilities. The central processing unit (CPU), graphics processing unit (GPU), and other specialized hardware components collectively determine the system's computational prowess. To accommodate diverse devices seamlessly, the system must possess sufficient processing power to handle concurrent interactions and complex tasks. Multi-core processors and parallel processing architectures play a crucial role in distributing computational loads efficiently, enabling devices to interact with the system without causing undue strain on overall performance.

Memory management is a pivotal aspect of the delicate balance between device interaction and system performance. Efficient utilization of Random Access Memory (RAM) ensures that the system can handle concurrent tasks and maintain responsiveness during device interactions. Effective caching mechanisms and optimized memory allocation contribute to minimizing latency in data retrieval and storage. Balancing the needs of connected devices for rapid data access with the overall system's requirement for smooth operation involves intelligent memory management strategies that prioritize critical tasks and allocate resources dynamically based on usage patterns.

Resource allocation is a critical consideration in optimizing overall system performance while facilitating device interactions. Devices often share common resources, such as CPU cycles, memory bandwidth, and I/O (Input/Output) throughput. The system must intelligently allocate these resources to ensure that device interactions do not lead to bottlenecks or performance degradation. Advanced scheduling algorithms, such as those used in modern operating systems, prioritize tasks based on their importance and urgency, contributing to a balanced allocation of resources that caters to both system-wide and device-specific requirements.

Power management strategies play a significant role in maintaining the delicate balance between device interaction and overall system performance, especially in battery-powered devices. Dynamic Voltage and Frequency Scaling (DVFS) techniques allow the system to adjust the voltage and clock frequency dynamically based on workload, conserving power during periods of low activity and ramping up performance when required. Power-efficient hardware components, coupled with intelligent power management policies, contribute to extended battery life and sustained overall system performance during device interactions.

The design of communication protocols and data transfer mechanisms is instrumental in harmonizing device interaction with overall system performance. Efficient networking protocols, such as Transmission Control Protocol (TCP) variants optimized for high-latency or low-bandwidth scenarios, contribute to faster and more reliable data transmission between devices and the system. As devices communicate with the system, streamlined protocols reduce the impact on overall performance, ensuring that the system's resources are utilized judiciously and do not become a bottleneck during data exchange.

Parallel computing emerges as a strategic approach to strike a balance between device interaction and system performance, particularly in the era of multi-core processors. By designing software to leverage parallelism, tasks can be distributed across multiple cores, allowing for faster execution and improved overall system performance. Parallel processing architectures are particularly advantageous in applications that involve complex calculations, simulations, or data processing, where breaking down tasks into parallel threads can lead to significant efficiency gains without compromising device responsiveness.

Effective user interface design is a crucial aspect of balancing device interaction with overall system performance. The user interface serves as the primary point of interaction between users and devices, influencing the user experience and shaping expectations. Well-designed interfaces provide intuitive controls, real-time feedback, and responsive interactions, ensuring that users can engage with devices seamlessly. User interfaces should be optimized to minimize latency, prioritize critical interactions, and maintain a consistent experience across different devices, contributing to a harmonious balance between device-specific interactions and system-wide performance.

Error handling and feedback mechanisms play a critical role in maintaining the delicate equilibrium between device interaction and overall system performance. As devices interact with the system, the occurrence of errors or unexpected events is inevitable. Effective error handling mechanisms provide users with informative feedback, guiding them on how to resolve issues or seek additional support. By swiftly addressing errors and minimizing disruptions, these mechanisms contribute to a smoother user experience without compromising the stability of the overall system.

Security considerations are integral to the delicate balance between device interaction and overall system performance. Devices interacting with the system may introduce potential security vulnerabilities. Robust security measures, including secure communication protocols, encryption algorithms, and secure boot mechanisms, are essential to safeguard against unauthorized access, data breaches, and malicious attacks. Balancing security requirements with the need for seamless device interactions ensures that the system remains resilient and reliable without compromising user safety or data integrity.

Scalability is a key consideration in maintaining a balanced relationship between device interaction and overall system performance. As the number and complexity of connected devices increase, the system's architecture should scale seamlessly to accommodate growing demands. Scalability considerations extend to both hardware and software components, ensuring that the system can handle diverse devices and interactions without sacrificing performance or responsiveness. A scalable architecture contributes to the long-term sustainability of the system in dynamic and evolving computing environments.

In the context of networked devices, edge computing emerges as a strategic approach to optimize overall system performance while facilitating device interactions. Edge computing architectures process data closer to the source, reducing the need for extensive data transmission to centralized servers. This approach leads to lower latency, reduced bandwidth usage, and real-time data processing, enhancing the overall efficiency of the system. Balancing the processing capabilities between edge devices and centralized systems ensures that device interactions are seamless, responsive, and well-integrated into the broader computing ecosystem.

Lifecycle management practices, including regular software updates and firmware upgrades, contribute to the sustained balance between device interaction and overall system performance. Timely updates address performance issues, introduce optimizations, and enhance security, ensuring that the system remains efficient and reliable throughout its lifecycle. End-of-life considerations, including responsible recycling and disposal practices, contribute to a sustainable and environmentally conscious approach, reinforcing the delicate balance between device-specific interactions and the broader system's efficiency.

In conclusion, balancing device interaction with overall system performance is a multifaceted challenge that requires a holistic and integrated approach. Considerations span hardware capabilities, software optimization, resource allocation, power management, communication protocols, parallel computing, user interface design, error handling, security measures, scalability, edge computing, and lifecycle management. The delicate equilibrium between seamless device interactions and sustained system performance is crucial for delivering an optimal user experience while ensuring the overall efficiency and reliability of computing ecosystems. As technology continues to advance, the pursuit of this delicate balance remains a dynamic and evolving endeavor, shaping the landscape of connected devices and computing systems.

Chapter 6: Securing the Citadel: Operating System Security Measures

The critical role of security in operating systems

The critical role of security in operating systems is a cornerstone of modern computing, safeguarding sensitive data, preserving user privacy, and ensuring the integrity and reliability of digital environments. Operating systems serve as the foundational layer that manages hardware resources, facilitates communication between software applications and hardware components, and provides a platform for users to interact with their devices. In this pivotal role, security considerations are paramount to protect against a myriad of threats, ranging from malicious software and cyber-attacks to unauthorized access and data breaches.

Security in operating systems begins with robust access control mechanisms that govern user privileges and permissions. User authentication and authorization protocols ensure that only authorized individuals or entities can access specific resources and perform designated actions. The principle of least privilege guides the allocation of permissions, limiting users and applications to the minimum level of access required for their intended tasks. Effective access control mitigates the risk of unauthorized access, minimizing the potential for malicious activities or inadvertent system compromises.

Authentication mechanisms play a pivotal role in verifying the identity of users and entities interacting with the operating system. Password-based authentication, biometric methods, and multi-factor authentication enhance the reliability of user identity verification. Strong authentication mechanisms are crucial to prevent unauthorized access and protect against password-related vulnerabilities, such as brute force attacks. Multi-factor authentication, combining multiple forms of identification, adds an additional layer of security, further reducing the risk of unauthorized access.

Encryption is a fundamental component of operating system security, serving to protect data in transit and at rest. Secure communication protocols, such as Transport Layer Security (TLS) and Secure Sockets Layer (SSL), encrypt data during transmission, preventing eavesdropping and man-in-the-middle attacks. Disk encryption technologies, such as BitLocker and FileVault, secure data stored on devices, ensuring that even if physical access is gained, the data remains unintelligible without proper decryption credentials. Encryption safeguards sensitive information and reinforces the confidentiality and privacy of user data.

Vulnerability management and patching are critical aspects of operating system security, addressing known vulnerabilities and weaknesses that could be exploited by malicious actors. Operating system vendors regularly release security patches and updates to address identified vulnerabilities and improve system resilience. Timely application of these patches is essential to close potential security loopholes, minimizing the risk of exploitation. Automated update mechanisms and centralized patch management tools streamline the process of keeping operating systems secure and up-to-date.

Malware protection is a central focus of operating system security, as malicious software poses a constant threat to the integrity and functionality of digital systems. Antivirus programs, anti-malware scanners, and real-time threat detection mechanisms are integral components of operating systems, actively monitoring and mitigating potential malware threats. These security tools employ signature-based detection, behavior analysis, and heuristics to identify and neutralize a wide range of malware, including viruses, worms, Trojans, and ransomware.

Firewalls and network security protocols contribute to the defense of operating systems against external threats. Firewalls monitor and control network traffic, filtering incoming and outgoing data based on predefined security rules. Network security protocols, such as IPsec (Internet Protocol Security), secure communication channels, protecting data as it traverses networks. These measures are essential for preventing unauthorized access, blocking malicious traffic, and fortifying the perimeter defense of operating systems.

Secure boot mechanisms ensure the integrity of the operating system during the startup process, preventing the execution of unauthorized or tampered code. Trusted Platform Module (TPM) technologies and secure boot protocols establish a chain of trust, verifying the authenticity of the operating system's boot components. Secure boot mechanisms are crucial for thwarting attacks that seek to compromise the system at its foundational level, ensuring that only authorized and unaltered operating system components are loaded into memory.

Audit trails and logging mechanisms provide a means to monitor system activities, detect security incidents, and facilitate forensic analysis. Operating systems record relevant events, such as login attempts, system modifications, and access requests, in audit logs. Security Information and Event Management (SIEM) tools can aggregate and analyze these logs to identify patterns indicative of security threats or policy violations. Audit trails play a crucial role in post-incident analysis, helping security professionals understand the nature of security incidents and implement preventive measures.

User awareness and education form an integral part of operating system security, recognizing that human factors contribute significantly to the overall security posture. Educating users about best security practices, the risks of social engineering, and the importance of secure password management enhances the system's resilience against threats. User awareness programs contribute to a security-conscious culture, reducing the likelihood of inadvertent security lapses and fostering a collaborative approach to maintaining a secure operating environment.

Containerization and virtualization technologies offer security benefits by isolating applications and workloads within distinct environments. Containers and virtual machines provide a sandboxed space for applications, preventing them from interfering with each other or accessing unauthorized resources. This isolation enhances the security of the operating system by containing the impact of potential security breaches within individual containers or virtualized instances, minimizing the risk of lateral movement by malicious entities.

The implementation of role-based access control (RBAC) further refines access control mechanisms, aligning user permissions with organizational roles and responsibilities. RBAC ensures that users only have access to the resources and functions necessary for their designated roles, reducing the risk of privilege escalation and unauthorized access. This granular control over user privileges enhances the security posture of the operating system, minimizing the attack surface and limiting the potential impact of security incidents.

Security monitoring and incident response capabilities are essential components of operating system security, enabling proactive threat detection and timely response to security incidents. Intrusion detection systems (IDS) and Security Information and Event Management (SIEM) solutions continuously monitor system activities, identifying anomalies and potential security threats. Incident response frameworks guide security professionals in effectively mitigating security incidents, containing the impact, and implementing corrective measures to prevent future occurrences.

Compliance with security standards and regulations is a crucial aspect of operating system security, especially in environments subject to legal and industry-specific requirements. Adherence to standards such as ISO 27001, NIST (National Institute of Standards and Technology) guidelines, and regulatory frameworks like GDPR (General Data Protection Regulation) ensures that operating systems meet established security benchmarks. Compliance initiatives contribute to the development of robust security policies, procedures, and controls, reinforcing the overall security posture of the operating system.

Security in operating systems extends beyond traditional computing environments to encompass emerging technologies such as IoT devices and edge computing. IoT devices, with their diverse range of sensors and communication capabilities, introduce unique security challenges. Operating systems for IoT must incorporate robust security measures, including secure boot, over-the-air updates, and encryption, to protect against potential vulnerabilities. Similarly, edge computing architectures demand security considerations that balance the need for local processing with the imperative to safeguard against potential threats.

In conclusion, the critical role of security in operating systems is evident in the multifaceted strategies employed to protect against a broad spectrum of threats. From access control and authentication to encryption, malware protection, and secure boot mechanisms, operating system security encompasses a comprehensive framework that safeguards the confidentiality, integrity, and availability of data and system resources. As computing environments evolve and face increasingly sophisticated threats, the ongoing commitment to robust security measures remains essential to maintaining the trust and resilience of operating systems in the digital landscape.

Historical perspectives on security vulnerabilities

Historical perspectives on security vulnerabilities provide a compelling narrative of the evolving challenges and responses within the realm of information technology. The timeline spans the inception of computing systems to the present day, highlighting the persistent and dynamic nature of security threats. In the early days of computing, security concerns were relatively rudimentary, with a primary focus on physical security, as computers were large, centralized machines housed in secure facilities. However, as the technology landscape evolved, so did the nature and complexity of security vulnerabilities.

One of the earliest instances of a security vulnerability dates back to the 1960s with the advent of the first computer viruses. The term "computer virus" was coined by computer scientist Fred Cohen in 1983, but the concept of self-replicating programs that could infect other programs had already manifested itself. The Creeper virus, designed to infect DEC PDP-10 computers, marked the beginning of a new era where malicious code could propagate itself, causing disruptions and raising awareness about the need for protective measures.

The 1980s witnessed the emergence of a series of notable security vulnerabilities and attacks. The Morris Worm, unleashed in 1988 by Robert Tappan Morris, was a landmark incident that highlighted the potential for malware to exploit vulnerabilities and propagate rapidly across interconnected systems. The worm exploited vulnerabilities in Unix-based systems, revealing the susceptibility of early networking infrastructures to widespread attacks. This event led to increased awareness of the need for robust security measures, and it prompted the development of the Computer Emergency Response Team (CERT) to respond to such incidents.

The 1990s saw a proliferation of security vulnerabilities driven by the rapid growth of the internet and the increasing interconnectivity of computing systems. The emergence of the World Wide Web brought new opportunities but also introduced novel attack vectors. The concept of "script kiddies" emerged—individuals with limited technical skills who could exploit pre-existing vulnerabilities using readily available tools. The rise of these less sophisticated but widespread attacks demonstrated the need for comprehensive security strategies, including regular system updates, secure coding practices, and user education.

The early 2000s witnessed a surge in sophisticated cyber threats and a shift toward financially motivated attacks. The infamous Code Red and Nimda worms, both in 2001, exploited vulnerabilities in Microsoft IIS web servers, causing widespread disruptions. Around the same time, the concept of "zero-day vulnerabilities" gained prominence, referring to previously unknown security flaws that attackers could exploit before vendors could develop and deploy patches. The Blaster and Sasser worms in 2003 further underscored the impact of unpatched vulnerabilities, prompting increased emphasis on proactive patch management.

As technology continued to advance, the mid-2000s saw the rise of targeted attacks, often attributed to state-sponsored actors or advanced persistent threats (APTs). Notable instances included the Aurora attacks in 2009, where sophisticated adversaries targeted major corporations, aiming to steal intellectual property and sensitive information. These incidents demonstrated the need for organizations to adopt advanced threat detection mechanisms, enhance network defenses, and implement robust incident response plans to mitigate the impact of targeted attacks.

The increasing prevalence of mobile devices in the 2010s brought forth a new set of security challenges. Mobile operating systems, such as Android and iOS, faced vulnerabilities ranging from app-based threats to operating system exploits. The discovery of vulnerabilities like Stagefright in Android, which could be exploited through malicious multimedia messages, highlighted the need for timely and coordinated security updates across the diverse ecosystem of mobile devices. The intersection of mobile and traditional computing environments introduced novel attack surfaces, emphasizing the importance of holistic security strategies.

The rise of the Internet of Things (IoT) in the late 2010s introduced a myriad of security vulnerabilities stemming from the interconnectedness of devices ranging from smart home appliances to industrial control systems. Insecure default configurations, lack of standardized security practices, and insufficient update mechanisms became prevalent issues. Large-scale Distributed Denial of Service (DDoS) attacks leveraging compromised IoT devices, as seen in the Mirai botnet attacks of 2016, demonstrated the potential consequences of insufficiently secured connected devices and reinforced the urgency of addressing IoT security.

Throughout this historical trajectory, a common theme has been the cat-and-mouse game between security professionals and malicious actors. As security measures evolve, so do the tactics and techniques employed by those seeking to exploit vulnerabilities. The rise of ransomware in the mid-2010s exemplifies this evolution, with attackers encrypting critical data and demanding ransom payments. Notable incidents, such as WannaCry in 2017, underscored the global impact of ransomware attacks, prompting renewed emphasis on robust backup strategies, user awareness, and patch management.

In recent years, supply chain attacks have become a prominent vector for exploiting security vulnerabilities. The compromise of software supply chains, as witnessed in the SolarWinds incident of 2020, demonstrated how adversaries could infiltrate widely used software to gain access to high-profile targets. Such incidents underscore the need for comprehensive security practices not only within organizations but also across the entire software development and distribution lifecycle.

The ever-expanding attack surface and the increasing sophistication of threat actors underscore the continuous nature of the security challenge. Cloud computing, artificial intelligence, and quantum computing present both opportunities and risks, with security professionals facing the task of adapting strategies to these evolving technologies. Quantum computing, for example, poses a potential threat to current cryptographic systems, necessitating the exploration of quantum-resistant encryption methods to secure future communication.

As security vulnerabilities have evolved, so too have the frameworks and standards developed to address them. The Common Vulnerabilities and Exposures (CVE) system, initiated in the late 1990s, provides a standardized method for identifying and naming vulnerabilities. Common Vulnerability Scoring System (CVSS) metrics offer a quantitative measure of the severity of vulnerabilities. Industry-wide collaboration, as seen in organizations like the Open Web Application Security Project (OWASP), fosters the development of best practices and tools for securing software applications.

In conclusion, historical perspectives on security vulnerabilities provide a comprehensive narrative of the challenges faced by the computing industry in safeguarding digital systems. From early instances of viruses and worms to the contemporary landscape of sophisticated cyber threats, the journey has been marked by a continuous quest for robust security measures. The evolution of attack vectors, the emergence of new technologies, and the increasing interconnectedness of systems underscore the dynamic nature of the security landscape. As the digital ecosystem continues to evolve, the historical context serves as a guide for shaping proactive and adaptive security strategies to address the ever-changing threat landscape.

User authentication and authorization

User authentication and authorization are integral components of modern information security, forming a robust framework to control access to digital systems, applications, and resources. Authentication is the process of verifying the identity of an individual or entity seeking access to a system. It ensures that users are who they claim to be, providing a foundational layer of trust in digital interactions. Various authentication methods are employed, ranging from traditional username-password combinations to more advanced biometric measures, multi-factor authentication (MFA), and token-based systems. The objective is to create a secure and reliable mechanism to ascertain the legitimacy of users and prevent unauthorized access.

Username-password authentication is a widespread method where users provide a unique username and a confidential password associated with their account. While simple, this method is susceptible to vulnerabilities such as password guessing, phishing, and credential theft. To enhance security, organizations often enforce password complexity requirements and recommend regular password changes. However, the limitations of this approach have led to the exploration of alternative authentication methods.

Biometric authentication leverages unique physical or behavioral characteristics of individuals, such as fingerprints, facial features, or voice patterns, to verify identity. Biometrics add an additional layer of security by relying on attributes that are challenging to forge or replicate. Advancements in technology have made biometric authentication more practical and accessible, with fingerprint scanners, facial recognition systems, and voice authentication becoming common features in smartphones and other devices. Biometric authentication not only enhances security but also provides a more user-friendly and convenient experience.

Multi-factor authentication (MFA) supplements traditional authentication methods with additional verification steps, requiring users to provide multiple forms of identification. This typically involves a combination of something the user knows (e.g., a password), something the user has (e.g., a physical token or a one-time code sent to a mobile device), and something the user is (e.g., a fingerprint). MFA significantly strengthens the authentication process, mitigating the risks associated with compromised credentials. Popular MFA implementations include time-based one-time passwords (TOTPs), smart cards, and push notifications to mobile devices.

Token-based authentication involves the use of cryptographic tokens to validate a user's identity. These tokens may be physical devices (e.g., USB security keys) or software-based solutions (e.g., mobile apps generating time-sensitive codes). Tokens add an extra layer of security by ensuring that the possession of a specific device or code is necessary for authentication. This method is particularly effective in preventing unauthorized access even if passwords are compromised, as an additional factor (the token) is required for authentication.

As authentication establishes the identity of users, authorization defines the actions and resources they are permitted to access within a system. Authorization is the process of granting or denying permissions based on the authenticated user's identity and defined policies. Role-based access control (RBAC) is a prevalent authorization model where users are assigned roles, and each role is associated with specific permissions. This approach simplifies access management by categorizing users into groups with similar responsibilities and access requirements.

RBAC provides a structured and scalable approach to authorization, but it may not capture the complexity of individual user needs or dynamic access scenarios. Attribute-based access control (ABAC) addresses these limitations by considering various attributes such as user attributes, environmental conditions, and resource attributes to make access decisions. ABAC allows for more granular control over access policies, accommodating diverse user roles and dynamic access requirements in complex environments.

Authorization policies are typically defined through access control lists (ACLs) or policy language statements that specify which users or groups have permission to perform specific actions or access particular resources. These policies are enforced by the system's security mechanisms, ensuring that users only interact with resources in accordance with their permissions. Regular reviews and updates of authorization policies are essential to adapt to changing organizational structures, compliance requirements, and evolving security landscapes.

The principle of least privilege (PoLP) is a foundational concept in authorization, advocating for the restriction of user permissions to the minimum necessary for their roles or tasks. By adhering to the principle of least privilege, organizations reduce the potential impact of security incidents and limit the opportunities for attackers to exploit compromised accounts. Fine-tuning permissions based on job roles or responsibilities aligns with the least privilege principle, creating a more secure and manageable access environment.

Dynamic authorization extends the traditional static authorization models by incorporating contextual information and real-time decision-making. It takes into account factors such as user behavior, device characteristics, and environmental conditions to adapt access permissions dynamically. This approach enhances security by responding to changing risk scenarios and enabling organizations to implement more flexible and adaptive access control policies. Dynamic authorization mechanisms contribute to the resilience of systems against emerging threats and evolving user needs.

OAuth (Open Authorization) is a widely used authorization framework designed for secure delegation of access, often utilized in scenarios involving third-party applications. OAuth allows users to grant limited access to their resources without exposing their credentials directly. The protocol facilitates secure authorization flows between services, ensuring that third-party applications can access specific resources on behalf of the user with their consent. OAuth is commonly employed in scenarios like social media logins, where users grant permission for applications to access their profiles without sharing login credentials.

Authorization also extends to the realm of web security, where web access control mechanisms govern the permissions and restrictions applied to web resources. Cross-Origin Resource Sharing (CORS) is a web security standard that defines how web pages in one domain can request and interact with resources from another domain. CORS policies, implemented in web browsers, prevent unauthorized access to sensitive resources and protect against potential security threats arising from cross-origin requests.

In cloud computing environments, Identity and Access Management (IAM) systems play a central role in managing user identities, authentication, and authorization. Cloud providers offer IAM services that allow organizations to define and enforce access policies for cloud resources. IAM systems integrate with various authentication methods and provide centralized control over user permissions, ensuring secure and compliant access to cloud-based services and data.

The relationship between user authentication and authorization is symbiotic, with effective security practices requiring a seamless integration of both processes. Authentication establishes the identity of users, and upon successful authentication, authorization determines the scope of their access rights. The collective implementation of strong authentication and well-defined authorization policies creates a robust security posture, safeguarding sensitive information, mitigating the risk of unauthorized access, and ensuring compliance with regulatory requirements.

As technology continues to advance, the landscape of user authentication and authorization evolves in response to emerging challenges. Adaptive authentication systems, leveraging artificial intelligence and machine learning, analyze user behavior patterns to detect anomalies and potential security threats. Additionally, the exploration of passwordless authentication methods, such as biometrics and token-based systems, aims to enhance user convenience without compromising security. The ongoing refinement and integration of authentication and authorization practices reflect a commitment to fortifying the foundations of digital security in an ever-changing and interconnected world.

Role-based access control (RBAC) and mandatory access control (MAC)

Role-Based Access Control (RBAC) and Mandatory Access Control (MAC) are two distinct but complementary models within the realm of access control, shaping the landscape of information security by governing the permissions and restrictions placed on users and processes within a computing environment.

Role-Based Access Control (RBAC) is a widely adopted access control model that streamlines the administration of user permissions based on predefined roles. In RBAC, users are assigned specific roles according to their job functions, responsibilities, or organizational roles. Each role is associated with a set of permissions that determine the actions and resources the users in that role can access. This approach simplifies access management by categorizing users into groups with similar responsibilities, reducing the complexity of individually assigning permissions. RBAC provides a structured and scalable method for access control, facilitating efficient administration and auditability. Moreover, RBAC aligns with the principle of least privilege, ensuring that users only possess the minimum necessary permissions for their roles, thereby mitigating potential security risks.

Mandatory Access Control (MAC), on the other hand, is a more stringent and centralized access control model that enforces access policies mandated by a higher authority, typically the system administrator or security policy. In a MAC system, access decisions are based on labels or security clearances assigned to both users and resources. These labels, often represented as security levels or categories, dictate the level of sensitivity or classification associated with the data or system elements. The operating system, acting as the central authority, enforces access policies by comparing the security labels of users and resources, allowing or denying access based on predefined rules. Unlike RBAC, which relies on user roles, MAC introduces a more rigid control mechanism that limits the discretion of individual users and ensures a consistent and centralized enforcement of access policies.

RBAC and MAC serve distinct purposes and are often employed in different contexts, but they can also be integrated to create a comprehensive access control framework. RBAC excels in environments where user roles are well-defined, and the emphasis is on delegation and flexibility in managing access permissions. Organizations with dynamic user structures and evolving job responsibilities find RBAC particularly advantageous. In contrast, MAC is best suited for scenarios where a high degree of control and a strict adherence to security policies are paramount, such as military or government environments with classified information. The integration of RBAC and MAC allows organizations to leverage the strengths of both models, achieving a balance between flexibility and centralized control.

RBAC's strength lies in its ability to simplify the complexity of access control by organizing users into roles, each associated with specific permissions. This model aligns with real-world organizational structures and facilitates efficient management of access rights. However, RBAC may face challenges in adapting to dynamic environments or accommodating fine-grained access control requirements. As organizations grow and roles become more specialized, the administration of RBAC systems can become intricate.

MAC, with its centralized and strict enforcement of access policies, addresses some of the limitations of RBAC by providing a higher level of security and consistency. The reliance on security labels and a predefined hierarchy of access ensures a systematic and controlled approach to information protection. MAC is particularly effective in environments where the sensitivity of data is paramount, and the potential for human error in access management needs to be minimized.

The integration of RBAC and MAC can offer a balanced approach that combines the flexibility of RBAC with the stringent controls of MAC. This hybrid model allows organizations to define roles for users while also incorporating mandatory security labels that determine the sensitivity and classification of data. The synergy between RBAC and MAC enhances the overall security posture, providing a fine-tuned and adaptable access control mechanism. This integration is especially valuable in environments where both organizational structure and data classification are critical considerations.

RBAC and MAC also play vital roles in addressing compliance requirements and regulatory standards. RBAC supports the principle of least privilege, a fundamental concept in many compliance frameworks, ensuring that users have only the minimum permissions required to perform their job functions. This not only enhances security but also contributes to regulatory compliance. MAC, with its strict enforcement of access policies and reliance on security labels, aligns with certain compliance requirements that mandate specific controls and classifications for sensitive data.

While RBAC and MAC contribute significantly to access control, their effectiveness is contingent on proper implementation and ongoing management. In RBAC, regular reviews of user roles and permissions are essential to adapt to organizational changes and evolving security requirements. RBAC systems must also be designed with scalability in mind to accommodate growing user populations and changing job roles. MAC, being more rigid, requires careful planning in defining security labels and access policies. Any adjustments to these labels or policies necessitate meticulous consideration to avoid unintended consequences.

The evolution of access control models, including the integration of RBAC and MAC, is also influenced by technological advancements such as cloud computing, mobile devices, and the Internet of Things (IoT). These technologies introduce new challenges and opportunities for access control, demanding adaptive and innovative solutions. RBAC and MAC need to evolve in tandem with the changing landscape of computing to address emerging threats and support evolving user requirements.

In conclusion, Role-Based Access Control (RBAC) and Mandatory Access Control (MAC) represent pivotal paradigms in access control, each offering distinct advantages and catering to specific security needs. RBAC streamlines access management by organizing users into roles with associated permissions, aligning with organizational structures and providing flexibility. MAC, with its centralized and stringent control, enforces access policies based on security labels, offering a high level of consistency and security. The integration of RBAC and MAC creates a hybrid model that combines the strengths of both, fostering a balanced approach to access control. As the digital landscape continues to evolve, the judicious selection and implementation of access control models become crucial in ensuring the security, integrity, and compliance of information systems.

Techniques for secure data transmission and storage

Secure data transmission and storage are critical facets of information security, playing a pivotal role in safeguarding sensitive information against unauthorized access, interception, or tampering. In the ever-evolving landscape of digital communication and storage, a myriad of techniques and technologies have been developed to address these security concerns and ensure the confidentiality, integrity, and availability of data.

Encryption stands as a cornerstone in securing both data transmission and storage. It involves encoding information in such a way that only authorized parties can decipher it. In the context of data transmission, Transport Layer Security (TLS) and its predecessor Secure Sockets Layer (SSL) protocols have become industry standards for securing communication over networks. These protocols use cryptographic algorithms to encrypt data during transmission, preventing eavesdropping and man-in-the-middle attacks. Similarly, in data storage, techniques like Full Disk Encryption (FDE) or file-level encryption ensure that data is protected even when it is at rest. Advanced Encryption Standard (AES) is widely used for its robust security properties in both transmission and storage scenarios, providing a balance between efficiency and strength.

Public Key Infrastructure (PKI) is another fundamental technique employed to secure data transmission. PKI uses a pair of cryptographic keys – a public key for encryption and a private key for decryption. SSL/TLS protocols often utilize PKI to establish a secure communication channel between a client and a server. The client verifies the server's authenticity using its public key, and a secure session is established through the exchange of encrypted data. Similarly, in secure email communication, Pretty Good Privacy (PGP) leverages PKI to provide end-to-end encryption, ensuring that only the intended recipient can decipher the message.

Hash functions play a crucial role in ensuring data integrity during transmission and storage. A hash function takes input data and produces a fixed-size string of characters, commonly known as a hash value. Any change in the input data results in a completely different hash value. In data transmission, hash functions are used to generate checksums, allowing the recipient to verify the integrity of the received data. In storage, cryptographic hash functions like SHA-256 are applied to data to create a unique identifier, known as a hash, which can be compared to verify the integrity of stored data. Hashing is also integral to password storage, where only the hash of a password is stored, adding an extra layer of security.

Secure data transmission often involves the implementation of Virtual Private Networks (VPNs) to create encrypted tunnels over public networks. VPNs utilize encryption protocols to protect data in transit, making it challenging for unauthorized entities to intercept or manipulate the transmitted information. In addition to traditional VPNs, the advent of technologies like Secure Multipurpose Internet Mail Extensions (S/MIME) and Pretty Good Privacy (PGP) has enhanced the security of email communication, allowing users to encrypt emails end-to-end and authenticate the sender's identity.

Securing data storage encompasses various techniques, including access controls and authentication mechanisms. Access controls restrict and regulate the permissions granted to users or systems attempting to access stored data. Role-Based Access Control (RBAC) and Attribute-Based Access Control (ABAC) are commonly employed models for defining and managing access rights, ensuring that only authorized individuals or processes can access, modify, or delete specific data. Authentication mechanisms, such as username-password combinations or biometric verification, add an extra layer of security by ensuring that only authenticated users can access stored information.

Data backups and redundancy strategies contribute significantly to secure data storage. Regularly backing up data ensures that in the event of data loss, accidental deletion, or a security incident, organizations can recover their information. Redundancy, achieved through techniques like RAID (Redundant Array of Independent Disks), distributes data across multiple storage devices, providing fault tolerance and minimizing the risk of data loss. Cloud storage services further enhance data redundancy and availability by replicating data across geographically distributed servers.

In the context of secure data transmission, the concept of Digital Signatures plays a crucial role in ensuring the authenticity and integrity of messages or documents. Digital signatures are created using asymmetric cryptographic algorithms, where the sender signs the message with their private key, and the recipient verifies the signature using the sender's public key. This process ensures that the message has not been altered during transmission and that it was indeed sent by the purported sender. Digital signatures are widely used in various applications, including email communication, document signing, and software distribution.

Secure Socket Shell (SSH) protocol is an essential tool for secure remote access and data transmission. SSH employs encryption and authentication mechanisms to establish secure communication channels over an unsecured network, enabling users to remotely access and manage systems securely. This is particularly crucial for system administrators who need to perform administrative tasks on remote servers while ensuring the confidentiality and integrity of the transmitted data.

Data anonymization and pseudonymization are techniques applied to protect privacy during data transmission and storage. Anonymization involves removing personally identifiable information (PII) from datasets, ensuring that individuals cannot be readily identified. Pseudonymization involves replacing sensitive identifiers with artificial identifiers, allowing data to be used for specific purposes without directly identifying individuals. These techniques are vital in compliance with privacy regulations such as the General Data Protection Regulation (GDPR) and are widely employed in fields like healthcare and finance.

In the realm of secure data storage, integrity verification through Merkle Trees and hash chains is a technique that ensures the consistency of stored data over time. Merkle Trees, commonly used in blockchain technology, create a hierarchical structure of hash values, allowing users to efficiently verify the integrity of large datasets by checking a single hash value at the top of the tree. Hash chains, on the other hand, link multiple hash values together, forming a chain that verifies the integrity of data blocks sequentially. These techniques provide a means to detect any unauthorized modifications or tampering of stored data.

Secure coding practices and input validation are paramount in preventing security vulnerabilities that could lead to unauthorized access or data breaches. Applications that handle sensitive data must adhere to secure coding guidelines, avoiding common pitfalls such as buffer overflows, injection attacks, and insecure direct object references. Input validation ensures that user inputs are thoroughly checked and sanitized before being processed, preventing malicious inputs from exploiting vulnerabilities and compromising data integrity.

In conclusion, the techniques for secure data transmission and storage constitute a multifaceted approach that addresses the diverse challenges posed by digital communication and information retention. Encryption, hash functions, access controls, VPNs, and digital signatures collectively contribute to the confidentiality, integrity, and authenticity of data during transmission. Secure storage techniques encompass data backups, redundancy strategies, anonymization, pseudonymization, integrity verification, and secure coding practices, ensuring that data is safeguarded against unauthorized access, corruption, or loss. As technology evolves and the threat landscape expands, the continual refinement and integration of these techniques remain imperative in maintaining the resilience and security of data in the digital age.

Overview of encryption algorithms and protocols

The landscape of encryption algorithms and protocols constitutes a diverse and dynamic field that plays a fundamental role in securing digital communications, data storage, and various information systems. Encryption, the process of transforming data into a coded form that can only be deciphered by authorized parties, is a cornerstone of modern cybersecurity. Numerous encryption algorithms and protocols have been developed over the years, each with its unique characteristics, strengths, and applications.

Symmetric key encryption, or secret key encryption, is one of the foundational approaches in cryptography. In symmetric key encryption, the same key is used for both encryption and decryption processes. Widely adopted symmetric key algorithms include the Advanced Encryption Standard (AES), which has become a de facto standard for securing a broad range of applications. AES operates on fixed-size blocks of data and supports key lengths of 128, 192, or 256 bits, providing a balance between efficiency and robust security. The Data Encryption Standard (DES), once a prevalent symmetric key algorithm, has been largely superseded by AES due to its susceptibility to brute-force attacks.

Asymmetric key encryption, or public key encryption, introduces a pair of keys – a public key for encryption and a private key for decryption. This revolutionary concept addresses the key distribution challenge in symmetric key systems. The RSA algorithm, named after its inventors Ron Rivest, Adi Shamir, and Leonard Adleman, is a prominent asymmetric key algorithm widely used for secure data transmission and digital signatures. RSA relies on the mathematical complexity of factoring large prime numbers, ensuring the security of the encrypted communication. Another widely used asymmetric key algorithm is Elliptic Curve Cryptography (ECC), which leverages the mathematical properties of elliptic curves to provide strong security with shorter key lengths compared to traditional asymmetric algorithms.

Hybrid encryption combines the strengths of symmetric and asymmetric encryption, addressing the efficiency and key distribution challenges inherent in each approach. In a hybrid system, a symmetric key is generated for each communication session, providing fast and efficient encryption of data. The symmetric key, in turn, is encrypted using the recipient's public key, ensuring secure key exchange without the need for a shared secret. This hybrid model is commonly employed in secure communication protocols such as Transport Layer Security (TLS) and its predecessor Secure Sockets Layer (SSL), which are integral to securing web communications. TLS and SSL use a combination of symmetric and asymmetric key algorithms to establish secure channels for data transmission over the internet.

Hash functions play a crucial role in ensuring data integrity and authenticity. A hash function takes input data and produces a fixed-size string of characters, known as a hash value. Even a small change in the input data results in a completely different hash value. Cryptographic hash functions, such as Secure Hash Algorithm 2 (SHA-2) and SHA-3, are designed to be collision-resistant, meaning it is computationally infeasible to find two different inputs that produce the same hash value. Hash functions are extensively used in digital signatures, checksums for data integrity verification, and password storage, where only the hash of a password is stored, adding an extra layer of security.

Digital signatures are cryptographic mechanisms that provide a means to verify the authenticity and integrity of digital messages or documents. A digital signature is created by applying a hash function to the message, and the resulting hash value is encrypted with the sender's private key. The recipient can verify the signature using the sender's public key, ensuring that the message has not been altered during transmission and was indeed sent by the purported sender. Digital signatures are widely used in various applications, including email communication, document signing, and software distribution. The Digital Signature Algorithm (DSA) and the Elliptic Curve Digital Signature Algorithm (ECDSA) are examples of widely adopted algorithms for digital signatures.

Secure key exchange protocols are essential components of cryptographic systems, ensuring that parties can establish a shared secret key securely. The Diffie-Hellman key exchange algorithm, a groundbreaking development in cryptography, allows two parties to agree on a shared secret over an unsecured communication channel without exchanging the secret key directly. Diffie-Hellman is widely used in various protocols, including TLS, where it facilitates secure key exchange during the establishment of encrypted connections. The Elliptic Curve Diffie-Hellman (ECDH) variant leverages the mathematical properties of elliptic curves to provide efficient and secure key exchange.

Quantum key distribution (QKD) is an emerging field that addresses the potential threat posed by quantum computers to traditional encryption algorithms. Quantum computers have the capability to efficiently solve certain mathematical problems, such as factoring large numbers, which underpin the security of widely used cryptographic systems. QKD leverages the principles of quantum mechanics to enable secure key exchange between parties, relying on the quantum properties of particles to detect any attempt at eavesdropping. While QKD is still in the experimental stage, it holds promise for establishing quantum-safe communication channels in the era of quantum computing.

Post-quantum cryptography is a proactive response to the anticipated threat posed by quantum computers to existing encryption algorithms. Researchers are actively exploring new cryptographic primitives that are believed to be resistant to quantum attacks. One example is lattice-based cryptography, which relies on the hardness of lattice problems for security. NIST has initiated a standardization process for post-quantum cryptography, inviting proposals and conducting evaluations to identify cryptographic algorithms that can withstand the capabilities of quantum computers.

Homomorphic encryption is an advanced cryptographic technique that allows computations to be performed on encrypted data without decrypting it. This revolutionary concept enables data to remain confidential even during processing, opening new possibilities for secure cloud computing and privacy-preserving data analysis. Homomorphic encryption has applications in scenarios where sensitive data needs to be outsourced for computation without revealing its contents. Fully Homomorphic Encryption (FHE) and Partially Homomorphic Encryption (PHE) are variants that offer varying degrees of computation capabilities on encrypted data.

Zero-knowledge proofs are cryptographic protocols that enable a party to prove the authenticity of certain information without revealing the information itself. These proofs are designed to convince a verifier of the truth of a statement without disclosing any additional details. Zero-knowledge proofs have applications in authentication and privacy-preserving protocols. For example, the Zero-Knowledge Succinct Non-Interactive Argument of Knowledge (zk-SNARK) is a specific zero-knowledge proof used in blockchain technologies like Zcash to provide transaction privacy.

In conclusion, the landscape of encryption algorithms and protocols is characterized by a rich tapestry of techniques that address the multifaceted challenges of securing digital communication and information systems. Symmetric and asymmetric key encryption, hybrid models, hash functions, digital signatures, key exchange protocols, and emerging paradigms like post-quantum cryptography, homomorphic encryption, and zero-knowledge proofs collectively contribute to the robustness of cryptographic systems. As technology advances and security threats evolve, the continuous exploration, refinement, and deployment of these cryptographic techniques remain imperative in preserving the confidentiality, integrity, and authenticity of digital information in an interconnected and dynamic world.

Securing communication channels within the OS

Securing communication channels within an operating system (OS) is a critical aspect of information security, ensuring that data exchanged between various components remains confidential, integral, and protected against unauthorized access. The OS serves as the foundational layer that manages and coordinates communication among different processes, applications, and system components. To fortify these communication channels, a multifaceted approach is essential, encompassing encryption, access controls, authentication mechanisms, and secure protocols.

Encryption stands as a primary defense mechanism for securing communication channels within the OS. It involves the transformation of plaintext data into ciphertext using cryptographic algorithms, making it unreadable to anyone without the appropriate decryption key. Operating systems often implement encryption at various levels, including disk encryption for data at rest and network encryption for data in transit. Full Disk Encryption (FDE) ensures that the entire contents of storage devices, such as hard drives or solid-state drives, are encrypted, safeguarding against unauthorized access in case of physical theft or unauthorized access. Similarly, network protocols like Transport Layer Security (TLS) or its predecessor Secure Sockets Layer (SSL) are instrumental in securing communication over networks, such as when accessing websites or transmitting sensitive data over the internet. These encryption measures ensure that data exchanged within the OS remains confidential, even if intercepted by malicious actors.

Access controls within the OS play a pivotal role in regulating which processes, users, or system components can communicate with each other and access specific resources. Role-Based Access

Control (RBAC) and discretionary access controls are commonly employed models that define and manage permissions based on user roles and predefined policies. RBAC streamlines access management by categorizing users into roles, each associated with specific permissions, reducing the complexity of individually assigning permissions. Discretionary access controls, on the other hand, allow users to set access permissions on resources they own. By implementing these access control models, the OS ensures that only authorized entities can communicate and access specific functionalities, preventing unauthorized users or processes from compromising the integrity of the system.

Authentication mechanisms are integral to verifying the identities of entities involved in communication within the OS. User authentication ensures that individuals accessing the system are who they claim to be, preventing unauthorized users from gaining access to sensitive resources. Common authentication methods include username-password combinations, biometric verification (such as fingerprints or facial recognition), and multi-factor authentication (MFA), which requires users to provide multiple forms of identification. For processes and applications communicating within the OS, cryptographic authentication mechanisms such as digital signatures or API keys may be employed. These authentication measures reinforce the trustworthiness of communication channels, mitigating the risk of malicious entities attempting to impersonate legitimate users or processes.

Secure protocols play a crucial role in establishing and maintaining secure communication channels within the OS. The choice of protocols significantly impacts the security of data exchange. Transmission Control Protocol/Internet Protocol (TCP/IP) is the fundamental set of protocols governing communication over the internet, and its secure variants, such as HTTPS for secure web communication, are widely adopted. Secure File Transfer Protocol (SFTP) and

Secure Shell (SSH) are protocols designed for secure file transfer and remote access, respectively. These protocols implement encryption, authentication, and integrity verification, ensuring that data transmitted within the OS is protected against eavesdropping, tampering, and unauthorized access. Implementing secure protocols ensures the resilience of communication channels in the face of evolving cyber threats.

In the context of interprocess communication (IPC) within the OS, mechanisms such as Inter-Process Communication (IPC) protocols and application programming interfaces (APIs) facilitate communication between different processes or components. The OS must manage IPC securely to prevent unintended access or manipulation of data between processes. Shared memory, message passing, and remote procedure calls are common IPC mechanisms, and securing these channels involves enforcing access controls, encrypting data in transit, and implementing authentication mechanisms to validate the legitimacy of communicating processes. Ensuring the integrity of IPC mechanisms is crucial for preventing security vulnerabilities that could be exploited by malicious actors attempting to compromise the stability and security of the OS.

Virtual Private Networks (VPNs) are employed within the OS to create secure communication channels over untrusted networks, such as the internet. VPNs use encryption and tunneling protocols to establish private and secure connections, allowing users to access resources on a remote network securely. This is particularly important in scenarios where users need to connect to corporate networks or access sensitive data from external locations. VPNs ensure that data transmitted between the user's device and the target network remains confidential and protected from interception by unauthorized entities.

In the realm of cloud computing, where OS instances may interact with cloud services, Identity and Access Management (IAM) systems play a critical role in securing communication channels. IAM systems manage user identities, authentication, and authorization, ensuring that only authorized users or services can access cloud resources. Secure communication between the OS and cloud services involves the use of secure APIs, encryption of data in transit, and adherence to cloud security best practices. The integration of IAM principles within the OS extends the security posture to the cloud environment, maintaining a cohesive and protected communication framework.

Furthermore, the OS must be vigilant against potential threats such as malware, viruses, and other malicious software that could exploit vulnerabilities in communication channels. Antivirus software, intrusion detection systems, and firewalls are essential components in safeguarding the OS against these threats. Regular software updates and patches are crucial for addressing known vulnerabilities and enhancing the overall security of the OS, ensuring that communication channels remain resilient in the face of emerging cyber threats.

In conclusion, securing communication channels within the OS is an intricate and multifaceted undertaking that involves the integration of encryption, access controls, authentication mechanisms, secure protocols, and vigilant protection against emerging threats. These measures collectively contribute to the establishment of a robust security posture, safeguarding data confidentiality, integrity, and availability within the OS environment. As technology advances and cyber threats evolve, the continual refinement and adaptation of these security mechanisms remain imperative to stay ahead of potential vulnerabilities and ensure the trustworthiness of communication channels within the operating system.

Firewalls, intrusion detection, and prevention systems

Firewalls, intrusion detection systems (IDS), and intrusion prevention systems (IPS) constitute integral components of modern cybersecurity, collectively forming a layered defense mechanism to safeguard networks and computing environments against a myriad of cyber threats. A firewall, at its core, is a barrier between a trusted internal network and untrusted external networks, controlling the flow of traffic based on predefined security rules. Network firewalls, often deployed at the perimeter of an organization's network, scrutinize incoming and outgoing data packets, making decisions to allow or block traffic based on specified criteria. Stateful inspection firewalls enhance security by keeping track of the state of active connections and making informed decisions based on the context of the traffic. Additionally, application-layer firewalls focus on the application-level protocols, providing a deeper level of scrutiny to prevent attacks targeting specific applications or services.

Intrusion Detection Systems (IDS) serve as vigilant sentinels within a network, actively monitoring and analyzing network or system activities to detect anomalous patterns indicative of potential security incidents. There are two primary types of IDS: network-based and host-based. Network-based IDS inspect network traffic, identifying suspicious behavior or signatures associated with known attacks. Host-based IDS, on the other hand, analyze activities on individual devices, detecting signs of unauthorized access or malicious activities. Signature-based detection relies on predefined patterns or signatures of known threats, while anomaly-based detection observes deviations from established baselines of normal behavior. The amalgamation of these detection techniques empowers IDS to identify a broad spectrum of security threats, ranging from malware infections to unauthorized access attempts.

Intrusion Prevention Systems (IPS) take the capabilities of IDS a step further by not only identifying but also actively preventing or blocking potential security threats. IPS operate in real-time, using various methods to thwart malicious activities based on the detected patterns or signatures. This proactive approach distinguishes IPS from IDS, as it enables immediate response to potential threats before they can inflict harm on the network or system. Similar to firewalls, IPS employ signature-based and anomaly-based detection methods, leveraging a database of known threats while also adapting to emerging risks by identifying deviations from normal behavior. The integration of IPS into network architecture enhances the overall security posture by adding a preemptive layer of defense against potential cyber threats.

The effectiveness of firewalls, IDS, and IPS lies in their ability to work in concert, forming a cohesive and comprehensive security framework. Firewalls establish a baseline defense by controlling the flow of traffic, allowing only authorized communication to traverse the network. Network-based IDS supplement this by actively monitoring the traffic for suspicious patterns, providing a second layer of defense that can identify potential threats that may have evaded the firewall's initial scrutiny. The incorporation of IPS further fortifies the security infrastructure by not only detecting but also actively preventing malicious activities, creating a triad of defenses that collectively reduce the risk of successful cyber attacks.

Firewalls play a crucial role in enforcing network security policies, which dictate the rules governing the flow of traffic within the network. These policies are meticulously crafted to align with the organization's security objectives, defining which types of communication are permitted or denied. Firewalls employ rule sets that encompass criteria such as source and destination IP addresses, ports, and protocols. By adhering to these policies, firewalls contribute to the creation of a secure network perimeter, mitigating the risk of unauthorized access, data exfiltration, and other network-based attacks. Additionally, firewalls can be configured to provide Virtual Private Network (VPN) support, allowing secure communication over untrusted networks by encrypting data during transmission.

Intrusion Detection Systems serve as vigilant guardians, continuously monitoring network traffic and system activities for signs of potential security breaches. Network-based IDS scrutinize packets flowing through the network, comparing observed patterns against a database of known attack signatures or identifying anomalies that deviate from established baselines. Host-based IDS, deployed on individual devices, scrutinize system logs, file integrity, and application activities to detect signs of compromise or unauthorized access. The correlation of these alerts across multiple devices or network segments enables IDS to provide a holistic view of the security landscape, allowing security teams to swiftly respond to potential threats and mitigate risks before they escalate.

Intrusion Prevention Systems extend the capabilities of IDS by actively intervening to block or mitigate potential threats. IPS operate inline with network traffic, allowing them to take immediate action upon detecting malicious activities. Signature-based prevention involves blocking traffic that matches known threat signatures, while anomaly-based prevention focuses on deviations from normal behavior. This proactive approach empowers IPS to automatically respond to emerging threats, preventing the execution of malicious code, blocking suspicious network traffic, or initiating other predefined actions to neutralize potential security risks. The integration of IPS into the network infrastructure adds a layer of real-time defense, enhancing the overall security resilience of the organization.

The collaboration between firewalls, IDS, and IPS is exemplified in the context of Distributed Denial of Service (DDoS) attacks, a prevalent form of cyber threat. Firewalls can be configured to detect and block traffic patterns associated with DDoS attacks, preventing the flood of malicious traffic from overwhelming network resources. Network-based IDS complement this by continuously monitoring for signs of anomalous traffic indicative of a DDoS attack, allowing for early detection and response. IPS, in turn, can dynamically adjust network configurations or implement rate limiting to mitigate the impact of an ongoing DDoS attack, actively thwarting the malicious activities. This coordinated defense illustrates how the triad of firewalls, IDS, and IPS collaboratively fortify the network against a diverse range of cyber threats.

Furthermore, the evolution of technology has led to the integration of next-generation firewalls (NGFW), which combine traditional firewall capabilities with advanced features such as deep packet inspection, intrusion prevention, and application-level filtering. NGFWs provide enhanced visibility into network traffic, allowing organizations to identify and control applications, users, and content traversing the network. This level of granularity enables more nuanced security policies, ensuring that organizations can enforce policies tailored to specific applications and user behaviors. NGFWs are designed to adapt to the changing threat landscape, offering a proactive defense mechanism against sophisticated cyber attacks.

The synergy between firewalls, IDS, and IPS is crucial in addressing the dynamic and evolving nature of cyber threats. While firewalls establish a fundamental barrier at the network perimeter, IDS continuously monitors for signs of potential security incidents, and IPS takes immediate action to prevent the exploitation of vulnerabilities. This collaborative approach creates a defense-in-depth strategy, reducing the likelihood of successful cyber attacks and minimizing the impact of security incidents.

In conclusion, firewalls, intrusion detection systems, and intrusion prevention systems form an integral triad in the realm of cybersecurity, collectively providing a layered defense mechanism to safeguard networks and computing environments. Firewalls establish a perimeter defense by regulating the flow of traffic based on predefined security policies. Intrusion Detection Systems actively monitor for signs of potential security incidents, identifying anomalous patterns or known attack signatures. Intrusion Prevention Systems extend the capabilities of IDS by actively intervening to block or mitigate potential threats in real-time. The collaborative efforts of these components create a comprehensive defense-in-depth strategy, mitigating the risk of unauthorized access, data breaches, and other cyber threats. As the cybersecurity landscape continues to evolve, the continual refinement and integration of firewalls, IDS, and IPS remain imperative in ensuring the resilience and security of modern computing environments.

Regular updates and patch management

Regular updates and patch management are cornerstones of robust cybersecurity practices, playing a pivotal role in safeguarding information systems, software, and networks against evolving threats and vulnerabilities. The process of keeping software, operating systems, and applications up to date involves applying patches—software modifications designed to address known vulnerabilities, enhance functionalities, and improve overall system stability. This proactive approach is crucial in mitigating the risk of exploitation by cyber adversaries who often target outdated or unpatched software as an entry point for attacks.

Operating systems, being the foundation of computing environments, require frequent updates to address security vulnerabilities, enhance performance, and introduce new features. Operating system updates often include patches for critical security vulnerabilities that, if left unaddressed, could expose systems to various forms of cyber threats such as malware, ransomware, and unauthorized access. Patch management for operating systems involves regularly checking for updates released by the operating system vendors, testing them in a controlled environment to ensure compatibility with existing software, and deploying the patches in a timely manner to all relevant systems across an organization.

Applications and software used in computing environments are equally susceptible to security vulnerabilities, making regular updates and patch management essential. Many cyberattacks exploit vulnerabilities in popular software applications, and vendors routinely release patches to address these weaknesses. Effective patch management for applications involves maintaining an inventory of all software deployed in an environment, monitoring for updates from vendors, and systematically applying patches to eliminate vulnerabilities. This process is critical for reducing the attack surface and enhancing the overall security posture of an organization.

The patch management lifecycle typically involves several stages, starting with vulnerability identification. This stage requires organizations to stay informed about vulnerabilities affecting their software and systems. Vulnerability databases, security advisories, and vendor notifications are valuable sources of information for identifying vulnerabilities. Once a vulnerability is identified, the next stage involves assessment and prioritization. Security teams evaluate the severity of each vulnerability, considering factors such as potential impact on the organization, exploitability, and the existence of known exploits in the wild. Prioritizing patches ensures that the most critical vulnerabilities are addressed promptly.

Testing is a crucial phase in the patch management process to prevent unintended consequences or disruptions to critical systems. Before deploying patches in a production environment, organizations typically conduct testing in a controlled environment to assess the compatibility of patches with existing software and to identify any potential conflicts or issues. Rigorous testing helps mitigate the risk of introducing new problems while attempting to address existing vulnerabilities.

Deployment marks the implementation of tested patches in the production environment. This phase involves rolling out patches to all relevant systems, servers, and endpoints within the organization. Automated patch deployment tools are often employed to streamline this process, ensuring that patches are applied consistently across the entire infrastructure. Additionally, organizations may implement a phased deployment strategy, initially applying patches to less critical systems before progressively rolling them out to more critical components.

Post-deployment monitoring and validation are essential aspects of effective patch management. Continuous monitoring allows organizations to detect any anomalies or issues that may arise after patch deployment. Validation involves confirming that the applied patches have successfully addressed the identified vulnerabilities without introducing new problems. In some cases, security teams may need to conduct post-deployment testing to ensure that critical systems remain stable and secure.

Challenges in patch management are often associated with the need for a delicate balance between applying patches promptly and ensuring system stability. Organizations may face constraints such as the potential impact of patches on custom-developed applications, compatibility issues, or the need for extensive testing in complex environments. Balancing the urgency of patching critical vulnerabilities with the necessity of maintaining system reliability requires careful planning and coordination between IT and security teams.

Automated patch management tools have become integral in addressing the challenges associated with the scale and complexity of modern computing environments. These tools automate various aspects of the patch management lifecycle, including vulnerability scanning, patch testing, and deployment. Automated solutions enable organizations to streamline the patching process, reduce the time between vulnerability disclosure and patch deployment, and enhance overall cybersecurity resilience.

The importance of regular updates and patch management extends beyond individual organizations to the broader cybersecurity ecosystem. Vendors play a crucial role in releasing timely patches to address vulnerabilities in their products. Security researchers and organizations responsible for discovering vulnerabilities contribute to the collective effort to improve cybersecurity by responsibly disclosing vulnerabilities to vendors. Collaboration within the cybersecurity community is essential for developing effective patches, sharing threat intelligence, and collectively defending against evolving cyber threats.

The consequences of neglecting regular updates and patch management can be severe. Unpatched systems are more susceptible to exploitation by malicious actors who leverage known vulnerabilities to gain unauthorized access, compromise data integrity, or launch disruptive attacks. High-profile incidents, such as ransomware attacks exploiting unpatched systems, underscore the critical importance of maintaining an effective patch management strategy. The "WannaCry" ransomware attack in 2017, for instance, exploited a vulnerability in unpatched Windows systems, affecting organizations worldwide and highlighting the widespread impact of inadequate patch management practices.

In addition to addressing known vulnerabilities, organizations must also consider the evolving nature of cyber threats and the need for proactive security measures. This involves adopting a holistic approach to cybersecurity, including continuous monitoring, threat intelligence integration, and a robust incident response plan. While regular updates and patch management are fundamental components of a resilient cybersecurity strategy, they should be complemented by a broader security posture that incorporates proactive threat detection, user education, and rapid incident response capabilities.

In conclusion, regular updates and patch management are indispensable components of effective cybersecurity, serving as a proactive defense against a constantly evolving threat landscape. The patch management lifecycle, encompassing vulnerability identification, assessment, testing, deployment, and post-deployment monitoring, ensures that organizations can promptly address known vulnerabilities without compromising system stability. Automated patch management tools have emerged as valuable assets in streamlining and automating this process, enhancing the efficiency of patch deployment. The collaboration between vendors, security researchers, and organizations contributes to the collective effort to fortify the cybersecurity ecosystem. Neglecting regular updates and patch management exposes organizations to heightened cybersecurity risks, emphasizing the critical importance of maintaining a vigilant and proactive approach to cybersecurity in an interconnected and dynamic digital landscape.

Incident response and recovery strategies

Incident response and recovery strategies are fundamental pillars of cybersecurity, serving as the framework that organizations deploy to detect, respond to, and mitigate the impact of security incidents. An incident in the context of cybersecurity refers to any adverse event or series of events that poses a threat to the confidentiality, integrity, or availability of information systems and data. The objective of incident response is to promptly and effectively manage incidents, limiting damage and reducing recovery time. The incident response lifecycle typically involves preparation, detection and analysis, containment, eradication, recovery, and lessons learned. Organizations must develop and implement comprehensive incident response plans to navigate the complexities of the digital landscape and respond to incidents in a coordinated and structured manner.

Preparation is the initial phase of incident response, involving the establishment of a robust foundation to effectively respond to potential incidents. This includes defining and documenting an incident response plan that outlines the roles, responsibilities, and procedures to be followed during an incident. It also entails creating an incident response team, comprised of individuals with expertise in various areas such as IT, security, legal, and communication. Regular training and drills for the incident response team are essential to ensure readiness, familiarity with procedures, and the ability to adapt to evolving threats. Additionally, organizations need to identify and prioritize critical assets, define communication channels, and establish relationships with external entities such as law enforcement and incident response communities to enhance collective cybersecurity capabilities.

Detection and analysis are central to identifying and understanding security incidents promptly. Organizations deploy a variety of tools and technologies, including intrusion detection systems, security information and event management (SIEM) solutions, and advanced threat intelligence, to monitor network traffic, system logs, and other data sources for signs of suspicious activity. Automated alerts and manual analysis by the incident response team are essential for differentiating between normal and potentially malicious events. The goal is to swiftly identify the scope and impact of the incident, categorize its severity, and prioritize the response efforts accordingly. Continuous monitoring and threat intelligence integration contribute to a proactive approach, enabling organizations to detect and respond to incidents in their early stages.

Containment involves taking immediate actions to prevent the further spread of the incident and mitigate its impact. This may include isolating affected systems, blocking malicious network traffic, or implementing temporary measures to halt the progression of the incident. The incident response team collaborates closely with IT and security personnel to implement containment strategies effectively while minimizing disruption to normal business operations. Decisions made during the containment phase are critical, requiring a balance between limiting the incident's impact and preserving evidence for subsequent analysis and legal or regulatory requirements.

Eradication focuses on removing the root cause of the incident and implementing long-term solutions to prevent its recurrence.

This phase involves a thorough examination of affected systems, identifying vulnerabilities or weaknesses that were exploited, and applying corrective measures such as patches, configuration changes, or system upgrades. Eradication may also involve refining security policies, updating procedures, and enhancing security controls to address systemic issues that contributed to the incident. The goal is not only to remediate the immediate impact but also to fortify the organization's overall cybersecurity posture against similar incidents in the future.

Recovery aims to restore affected systems and services to normal operation, ensuring minimal disruption to business continuity. The incident response team, in collaboration with IT and operational teams, works to verify the integrity of systems, validate the effectiveness of remediation efforts, and gradually bring services back online. Backups play a crucial role in the recovery phase, enabling organizations to restore data and configurations to a pre-incident state. Regularly tested and well-maintained backups are essential to ensure their reliability in the event of an incident. Communication with stakeholders, including employees, customers, and regulatory bodies, is also a key aspect of the recovery phase, managing expectations and providing updates on the status of recovery efforts.

The lessons learned phase is a critical component of incident response, providing an opportunity for organizations to reflect on the incident, evaluate the effectiveness of the response, and identify areas for improvement. This involves conducting a thorough post-incident analysis, documenting findings, and updating incident response plans and procedures based on lessons learned. Communication within the organization and with external stakeholders is essential to share insights gained from the incident and enhance overall cybersecurity awareness. The continuous improvement cycle ensures that incident response capabilities evolve alongside the dynamic threat landscape, incorporating new knowledge and strategies to enhance resilience against future incidents.

Collaboration and communication are foundational principles throughout the incident response and recovery process. Effective communication within the incident response team, with IT and security personnel, and with external entities such as law enforcement or incident response communities are crucial for a coordinated and efficient response. Clear lines of communication help ensure that relevant information is shared promptly, decisions are made collaboratively, and the incident response effort remains focused and effective. Additionally, transparent communication with internal and external stakeholders, including employees, customers, and regulators, builds trust and demonstrates the organization's commitment to addressing and mitigating the impact of the incident.

Incident response and recovery strategies are not static; they require continual refinement and adaptation to stay effective in the face of evolving cyber threats. Threat intelligence feeds, information sharing with industry peers, and participation in cybersecurity communities contribute to staying abreast of emerging threats and enhancing incident response capabilities. Regularly conducting tabletop exercises and simulations allows organizations to test and refine their incident response plans, identify areas for improvement, and enhance the preparedness of the incident response team.

Regulatory compliance and legal considerations are integral aspects of incident response and recovery. Organizations must be aware of and adhere to relevant regulations and legal requirements governing incident reporting, data breach notification, and the protection of sensitive information. Collaborating with legal experts ensures that incident response activities align with legal obligations, preserving evidence for potential legal or regulatory investigations and minimizing the risk of non-compliance.

In conclusion, incident response and recovery strategies are indispensable components of modern cybersecurity, providing a structured and coordinated approach to managing security incidents. The incident response lifecycle, encompassing preparation, detection and analysis, containment, eradication, recovery, and lessons learned, establishes a framework for organizations to respond effectively to cyber threats. Collaboration, communication, continual improvement, and adherence to legal and regulatory considerations are key principles that underpin successful incident response and recovery efforts. As organizations navigate the complexities of the digital landscape, a well-defined and practiced incident response plan is essential for mitigating the impact of security incidents and ensuring the resilience of information systems and data.

Chapter 7: Performance Orchestration: Optimization Techniques and Strategies

Defining and measuring system performance

Defining and measuring system performance is a multifaceted endeavor that encompasses a comprehensive evaluation of how well a computer system or software application executes tasks and handles workloads. System performance is a holistic concept, embracing various aspects such as response time, throughput, resource utilization, and reliability. At its core, performance can be seen as the efficiency and effectiveness with which a system accomplishes its intended functions. The definition of system performance is contingent on the specific goals and requirements of the system, with different applications and environments placing emphasis on distinct performance attributes.

Response time, often considered a fundamental metric of system performance, gauges the time it takes for a system to respond to a user's input or request. It is a crucial aspect of user experience, directly influencing the perceived efficiency and usability of a system. Shorter response times generally correlate with better user satisfaction, especially in interactive applications or services where users expect prompt feedback. For example, in web applications, response time is often measured from the moment a user initiates an action, such as clicking a button, to when the system completes the corresponding task and presents the result.

Throughput is another key dimension of system performance, representing the rate at which a system processes and completes a certain number of tasks over a specific period. Unlike response time, which focuses on individual interactions, throughput provides a broader view of a system's overall capacity and efficiency in handling workloads. Throughput metrics are particularly relevant in scenarios with high transaction volumes, such as database systems, network communication, or batch processing. Effective throughput measurement requires consideration of factors such as the volume and complexity of tasks, system architecture, and resource constraints.

Resource utilization plays a pivotal role in system performance evaluation, encompassing the efficient utilization of hardware resources such as CPU, memory, disk I/O, and network bandwidth. Monitoring resource utilization provides insights into how effectively a system utilizes its available resources to deliver desired performance. Inefficient resource usage can lead to bottlenecks, degradation in response time, and overall degradation in system performance. Resource monitoring tools are employed to assess and optimize the allocation and utilization of resources, ensuring that the system operates efficiently under varying workloads.

Reliability is a critical facet of system performance, reflecting the system's ability to consistently deliver intended functionalities without unexpected failures or downtime. Reliability metrics often include indicators such as Mean Time Between Failures (MTBF) and Mean Time to Recovery (MTTR). A reliable system minimizes disruptions, enhances user satisfaction, and contributes to overall operational stability. Reliability considerations are particularly significant in mission-critical systems, where system failures can have severe consequences.

Defining system performance involves aligning metrics with specific goals, user expectations, and operational requirements. Different applications and contexts may prioritize certain performance aspects over others. For example, a real-time financial trading system may prioritize low latency and high throughput to execute trades swiftly, while a scientific simulation application may prioritize accuracy and efficient resource utilization over rapid response times. Contextualizing performance metrics ensures that the evaluation aligns with the unique demands and objectives of the system in question.

Measuring system performance involves employing a variety of tools, methodologies, and benchmarks to quantitatively assess the identified performance metrics. Performance monitoring tools, such as profilers and monitoring software, capture data on key indicators like CPU usage, memory consumption, and network activity. These tools enable real-time observation and analysis of system behavior under different conditions. Benchmarks, on the other hand, involve running standardized tests to evaluate and compare the performance of a system or component. Benchmark results provide a baseline for understanding system capabilities, identifying potential bottlenecks, and informing optimization efforts.

In the realm of software development, profiling tools are commonly used to analyze code execution and identify performance bottlenecks. Profilers track the execution time of different functions, pinpointing areas of code that consume excessive resources or contribute to prolonged response times. By analyzing the data generated by profilers, developers gain insights into opportunities for code optimization and improvements in resource utilization.

In the context of web applications, tools like Google's PageSpeed Insights or Lighthouse are employed to assess and measure web page performance. These tools evaluate factors such as page load times, rendering speed, and overall user experience. The results guide developers in optimizing web content for faster loading times and improved user satisfaction.

Benchmarking involves the comparison of a system's performance against established standards or other systems. Standardized benchmarks, like the SPEC (Standard Performance Evaluation Corporation) benchmarks for CPUs, provide a consistent framework for evaluating and comparing the performance of hardware and software components. Organizations use benchmark results to make informed decisions about hardware and software configurations, ensuring that the selected components align with their performance requirements.

Cloud service providers offer performance monitoring and analysis tools tailored to their respective platforms. For example, Amazon CloudWatch for Amazon Web Services (AWS) and Azure Monitor for Microsoft Azure provide comprehensive insights into the performance of cloud-based resources. These tools enable users to monitor metrics, set up alarms for predefined thresholds, and gain visibility into resource utilization, helping optimize the performance of applications and services hosted in the cloud.

The measurement of system performance extends beyond individual components to include entire system architectures and networks. Load testing and stress testing are methodologies employed to evaluate how a system performs under varying workloads and stress conditions. Load testing involves simulating normal operating conditions to assess performance, while stress testing involves pushing the system to its limits to identify breaking points and weaknesses. These tests help organizations understand how a system scales, where potential bottlenecks may occur, and how the system behaves under extreme conditions.

In conclusion, defining and measuring system performance is a nuanced and comprehensive undertaking that involves a holistic evaluation of various dimensions, including response time, throughput, resource utilization, and reliability. The definition of system performance is contextual, dependent on the goals and requirements of the specific system or application. Performance measurement encompasses the use of monitoring tools, profiling, benchmarks, and testing methodologies to quantitatively assess how well a system meets its objectives. Whether in software development, web applications, cloud services, or broader system architectures, a systematic and well-informed approach to defining and measuring performance is crucial for optimizing efficiency, enhancing user satisfaction, and ensuring the reliability of computing systems in an ever-evolving technological landscape.

Key indicators for efficiency and responsiveness

Key indicators for efficiency and responsiveness are essential benchmarks used to evaluate the performance and effectiveness of various systems, applications, and processes across diverse domains. Efficiency, in the context of computing and technology, is a measure of how well resources are utilized to achieve desired outcomes, while responsiveness reflects the system's ability to promptly and effectively respond to user interactions or external stimuli. These indicators are critical for assessing the overall functionality and user experience of systems, and they play a pivotal role in guiding optimization efforts and ensuring optimal performance.

One fundamental indicator for efficiency is resource utilization, encompassing the efficient allocation and usage of hardware resources such as Central Processing Unit (CPU), memory, disk space, and network bandwidth. Monitoring and analyzing resource utilization metrics provide insights into how effectively a system utilizes its available resources to execute tasks and handle workloads. High resource utilization may indicate potential bottlenecks, inefficient processes, or the need for resource optimization. Efficient resource utilization contributes to streamlined operations, reduced response times, and improved overall system performance.

Throughput is another key efficiency indicator, representing the rate at which a system processes and completes tasks within a specified timeframe. It provides a quantitative measure of the system's capacity and ability to handle workloads. Throughput is particularly relevant in scenarios with high transaction volumes, such as database systems, network communication, or batch processing. Improving throughput often involves optimizing algorithms, enhancing parallelism, and minimizing contention for shared resources, all of which contribute to increased overall efficiency.

Response time, a crucial indicator for both efficiency and responsiveness, measures the time it takes for a system to respond to user inputs or requests. It directly influences user satisfaction and the perceived performance of a system. Low response times are indicative of an efficient and responsive system, enhancing the user experience. In contrast, prolonged response times may lead to user frustration and impact the overall usability of applications. Optimizing response time involves addressing bottlenecks, improving algorithms, and ensuring efficient resource allocation.

Latency, closely related to response time, is another key indicator for responsiveness, specifically focusing on the delay between the initiation of a request and the receipt of the corresponding response. Low latency is crucial in real-time applications, such as online gaming, video streaming, and financial transactions, where timely responses are imperative. Reducing latency involves minimizing processing delays, optimizing network communication, and adopting technologies like caching and content delivery networks (CDNs) to enhance overall system responsiveness.

Error rates are significant indicators for both efficiency and responsiveness, as high error rates can impact system performance and user satisfaction. Monitoring error rates provides insights into the stability and reliability of a system. Excessive errors may result from issues such as software bugs, network problems, or resource constraints. Identifying and addressing errors promptly contributes to a more efficient and responsive system, preventing disruptions and ensuring a seamless user experience.

Scalability is a critical consideration for both efficiency and responsiveness, especially in dynamic and evolving environments. Scalability measures a system's ability to handle increasing workloads or growing user bases without sacrificing performance. Horizontal scalability, achieved through the addition of more resources or nodes, and vertical scalability, involving the enhancement of existing resources, are strategies to improve scalability. Systems that can scale effectively adapt to changing demands, ensuring sustained efficiency and responsiveness as user requirements evolve.

For web-based applications, page load time is a key indicator that directly influences user experience and satisfaction. Users expect web pages to load quickly, and prolonged load times can lead to increased bounce rates and diminished engagement. Optimizing page load time involves minimizing the size of web assets, leveraging browser caching, and adopting techniques such as asynchronous loading of content. Content Delivery Networks (CDNs) are also employed to distribute content across geographically dispersed servers, reducing latency and improving overall responsiveness.

Transaction time is a critical efficiency and responsiveness indicator in transactional systems, such as e-commerce platforms or financial applications. It measures the time taken to complete a transaction from initiation to confirmation. Efficient transaction processing ensures timely updates to databases, accurate financial reporting, and a positive user experience. Optimizing transaction time involves database tuning, efficient query execution, and minimizing contention for shared resources, contributing to improved overall system performance.

For database systems, query performance is a crucial indicator of efficiency and responsiveness. Slow or inefficient queries can impact the overall performance of applications relying on database interactions. Indexing, query optimization, and database design play vital roles in improving query performance. Monitoring and analyzing query execution times, identifying resource-intensive queries, and implementing optimizations contribute to a more efficient and responsive database system.

In cloud computing environments, resource provisioning and auto-scaling are key strategies to ensure both efficiency and responsiveness. Cloud services allow organizations to dynamically allocate resources based on demand, optimizing costs and ensuring responsive scaling to handle varying workloads. Efficient resource provisioning involves right-sizing instances, leveraging auto-scaling policies, and utilizing cloud-native services to enhance overall system efficiency and responsiveness.

Machine learning models introduce a unique set of indicators for both efficiency and responsiveness. Model inference time, or the time it takes for a model to process and generate predictions on new data, is a critical factor. Optimizing model inference time involves model compression, hardware acceleration, and choosing appropriate algorithms. Additionally, model training efficiency, measured by the time and resources required to train a model, influences the overall efficiency of machine learning workflows.

In conclusion, key indicators for efficiency and responsiveness are multifaceted metrics that guide the evaluation and optimization of various systems and applications. Resource utilization, throughput, response time, latency, error rates, scalability, page load time, transaction time, query performance, resource provisioning, and machine learning model efficiency are among the crucial indicators considered in diverse technological contexts. Balancing and enhancing these indicators contribute to the creation of systems that are not only efficient in resource utilization but also responsive to user inputs, ultimately ensuring a positive user experience and optimal performance across a spectrum of computing environments.

Caching mechanisms and memory compression

Caching mechanisms and memory compression are integral components in the realm of computer systems, playing pivotal roles in enhancing performance, optimizing resource utilization, and improving overall system responsiveness. Caching, a technique rooted in the principle of storing frequently accessed data closer to the point of use, aims to mitigate the latency associated with retrieving information from slower, secondary storage. On the other hand, memory compression involves the compression of data residing in the system's main memory, allowing for more efficient utilization of available RAM (Random Access Memory) and, consequently, enabling the system to handle larger datasets and applications more effectively.

Caching mechanisms are employed to bridge the performance gap between fast-access, volatile memory and slower, persistent storage devices. By maintaining a copy of frequently accessed data in a faster, temporary storage layer, such as cache memory, systems can significantly reduce the time it takes to retrieve information, thereby improving application responsiveness and overall system efficiency. Various levels of caching exist, ranging from hardware-level caches embedded in processors to software-managed caches implemented at the operating system or application level.

At the hardware level, processors often feature multiple cache levels, including L1 (Level 1), L2, and L3 caches. These caches store instructions and data that the CPU is likely to access in the near future, minimizing the need to fetch this information from slower main memory or storage. The hierarchical structure of caches ensures that frequently accessed data is available at different levels, optimizing the trade-off between speed and capacity. Cache management policies, such as Least Recently Used (LRU) or First-In-First-Out (FIFO), dictate how data is selected for retention or replacement in the cache.

Operating systems implement caching at different layers to enhance the performance of file systems, network operations, and application-level data access. File system caches store recently accessed disk blocks in memory, reducing the need for repeated disk reads. Network caches store copies of frequently requested web content, reducing latency and bandwidth usage. Application-level caching, employed by databases and web servers, allows programs to store and retrieve frequently used data from memory, minimizing the computational cost of repeated accesses.

In web applications, caching is a fundamental technique for optimizing content delivery. Web browsers cache static resources, such as images, stylesheets, and scripts, locally on the user's device. This minimizes the need to download these resources with each visit to a web page, resulting in faster page load times and reduced server load. Content Delivery Networks (CDNs) leverage distributed caching to store copies of web content on servers located strategically around the globe, ensuring rapid access to resources from geographically dispersed users.

Memory compression, while distinct from caching, shares the overarching goal of maximizing the efficient use of system resources. In contrast to caching, which involves storing copies of data in faster storage layers, memory compression focuses on reducing the amount of physical memory consumed by actively used data through compression algorithms. This is particularly relevant in scenarios where the system's RAM is a limiting factor, and compressing data allows for more extensive datasets or applications to reside in memory.

Memory compression algorithms aim to identify and exploit redundancy in the data stored in memory. Common techniques include run-length encoding, which represents sequences of repeated values with shorter codes, and dictionary-based compression, which replaces repeated patterns with references to a shared dictionary. When a program attempts to access compressed data, the system decompresses it on-the-fly, ensuring that the application interacts with uncompressed data while saving space in physical memory.

Operating systems employ memory compression as part of virtual memory management to cope with memory pressure and prevent excessive swapping of data between RAM and slower storage devices. When physical memory becomes scarce, the system can compress pages of memory, freeing up space for other active processes. This dynamic approach helps maintain a balance between performance and resource utilization, as memory compression enables the system to retain more data in RAM, reducing the reliance on slower storage devices.

One prominent example of memory compression in modern operating systems is the use of the zswap feature in the Linux kernel. Zswap compresses pages in RAM before swapping them out to the swap space, allowing the system to reclaim memory more efficiently while minimizing the performance impact of swapping. Similarly, Windows operating systems include memory compression mechanisms to optimize memory usage and improve responsiveness.

The integration of caching mechanisms and memory compression into a system's architecture involves careful considerations and trade-offs. Caching strategies require decisions about cache size, eviction policies, and cache coherence mechanisms to ensure consistency between cached copies and the underlying data. Memory compression introduces computational overhead for compression and decompression operations, and the choice of compression algorithms impacts both the compression ratio and the speed of these operations.

In certain scenarios, combining caching and memory compression can yield synergistic benefits. For instance, compressed in-memory caches can enhance the effective capacity of available memory, allowing systems to cache larger datasets without consuming excessive physical memory. This integration requires a nuanced approach, considering factors such as the nature of the data, access patterns, and the computational cost of compression and decompression.

The effectiveness of caching and memory compression extends beyond traditional computing environments to encompass emerging technologies and paradigms. In-memory databases leverage caching and compression techniques to enhance data access speed and accommodate large datasets entirely in RAM. Cloud computing platforms incorporate caching strategies and memory compression to optimize resource utilization in virtualized environments where efficient memory management is critical.

As computing architectures evolve, the demand for efficient caching and memory management mechanisms persists. Non-volatile memory technologies, such as Intel Optane Persistent Memory, introduce new opportunities and challenges for caching and memory compression. These technologies blur the traditional boundaries between volatile and non-volatile storage, prompting innovative approaches to leverage the benefits of fast, persistent memory while addressing the associated complexities.

In conclusion, caching mechanisms and memory compression are essential techniques employed in computer systems to enhance performance, optimize resource utilization, and improve overall system responsiveness. Caching, whether at the hardware or software level, involves storing frequently accessed data closer to the point of use, reducing latency and improving application performance. Memory compression, on the other hand, focuses on dynamically compressing data in RAM to maximize efficient memory usage and prevent excessive swapping. The integration of these techniques requires careful consideration of system architecture, data characteristics, and access patterns, and their application spans a wide range of computing environments, from traditional servers to cloud platforms and emerging technologies. As technology continues to advance, the evolution of caching and memory compression mechanisms will play a pivotal role in shaping the efficiency and responsiveness of future computing systems.

Strategies for minimizing memory leaks

Strategies for minimizing memory leaks are crucial in the development and maintenance of software applications, as memory leaks can lead to resource exhaustion, degraded performance, and system instability. A memory leak occurs when a program allocates memory but fails to release it, resulting in a gradual accumulation of unreleased memory over time. Effectively addressing and preventing memory leaks requires a combination of best practices, tools, and systematic approaches throughout the software development lifecycle.

One fundamental strategy for minimizing memory leaks is adopting a disciplined and proactive coding approach. Developers should adhere to best practices for memory management, emphasizing proper allocation and deallocation of memory resources. Explicitly freeing memory that is no longer needed, using language features like destructors or finalizers, and employing automatic memory management techniques, such as garbage collection in languages like Java or C#, contribute to reducing the likelihood of memory leaks.

Memory leak detection tools play a pivotal role in identifying and addressing memory leaks during the development and testing phases. These tools analyze the runtime behavior of an application, pinpointing instances where memory is allocated but not released. Static analysis tools, such as Valgrind for C and C++, and dynamic analysis tools integrated into modern integrated development environments (IDEs), assist developers in identifying memory leak patterns and understanding the root causes. Regular use of these tools as part of the development workflow helps catch memory leaks early in the development process.

Another effective strategy involves rigorous testing and quality assurance practices. Automated testing frameworks that include memory leak detection capabilities, stress testing, and performance profiling are instrumental in uncovering memory-related issues before software reaches production environments. Test scenarios should encompass a wide range of inputs and usage patterns, simulating real-world conditions to expose potential memory leaks under varying circumstances.

A proactive approach to code reviews can significantly contribute to minimizing memory leaks. Peer code reviews, conducted by experienced developers, provide an opportunity to identify and rectify memory-related issues early in the development lifecycle. Establishing coding standards that explicitly address memory management practices and conducting regular code inspections help create a culture of vigilance against memory leaks within development teams.

The adoption of modern programming languages and frameworks with built-in memory management features can be a strategic choice to minimize memory leaks. Languages like Java, C#, Python, and JavaScript leverage automatic memory management mechanisms, such as garbage collection, to handle memory allocation and deallocation transparently. These languages shift the responsibility of memory management from developers to the runtime environment, reducing the likelihood of manual memory management errors that can lead to leaks.

Incorporating design patterns that promote efficient memory management is another valuable strategy. Object pooling, for example, involves reusing and recycling objects instead of repeatedly creating and discarding them, minimizing the frequency of memory allocation and deallocation. This approach is particularly useful in scenarios where objects are short-lived and frequently used, reducing the chances of memory leaks associated with improper memory cleanup.

Effective logging and monitoring mechanisms are essential for identifying memory leaks in production environments. Application logs, system monitoring tools, and error tracking systems can provide insights into abnormal memory usage patterns, unexpected memory growth, or patterns indicative of memory leaks. Establishing a comprehensive monitoring infrastructure allows organizations to proactively identify and address memory leaks in deployed applications, safeguarding system stability and user experience.

Regularly updating and patching dependencies, libraries, and frameworks is a prudent strategy to minimize memory leaks. Developers should stay informed about updates and releases that address memory-related issues in third-party components. Outdated libraries or frameworks may contain known memory leak vulnerabilities that can be mitigated by incorporating the latest patches and updates.

Memory profiling tools offer a deeper understanding of an application's memory usage patterns and help pinpoint areas susceptible to memory leaks. Profilers, such as VisualVM, YourKit, or Instruments for macOS, provide visual representations of memory allocations, object references, and potential memory leaks during runtime. Utilizing these tools enables developers to identify specific code paths and data structures contributing to memory leaks, facilitating targeted optimizations and fixes.

Implementing proper error handling and recovery mechanisms can prevent memory leaks resulting from unexpected failures. Unhandled exceptions or errors that interrupt the normal execution flow may leave allocated memory unreleased. Robust error handling practices, including resource cleanup in exceptional cases, help ensure that memory is properly released even when unexpected events occur.

Documentation and knowledge sharing within development teams are critical components of a comprehensive strategy for minimizing memory leaks. Developers should document memory management practices, share insights gained from addressing memory-related issues, and maintain a collective awareness of potential pitfalls. This collaborative knowledge-sharing approach contributes to a more informed and proactive team, reducing the likelihood of recurring memory leaks across different parts of the codebase.

Adopting a continuous integration and continuous deployment (CI/CD) pipeline that includes memory leak detection as part of the automated build and testing process is essential. CI/CD pipelines facilitate the early detection of memory leaks in new code changes, preventing the introduction of memory-related issues into production releases. Automated build pipelines can integrate memory leak detection tools to analyze code changes and trigger alerts or prevent deployments if memory leaks are identified.

Code refactoring, when performed with a focus on memory management, can be a strategic approach to minimize memory leaks. Refactoring involves restructuring code to improve readability, maintainability, and performance. Identifying and addressing potential memory leaks during refactoring activities allows developers to enhance the overall quality of the codebase and prevent the accumulation of technical debt associated with memory-related issues.

In conclusion, minimizing memory leaks requires a multifaceted and proactive approach throughout the software development lifecycle. Developers play a central role in adopting disciplined coding practices, leveraging tools for memory leak detection, and embracing testing and quality assurance processes. The integration of memory management best practices into design patterns, the use of modern programming languages with automatic memory management, and the incorporation of monitoring and profiling tools contribute to a holistic strategy for identifying, addressing, and preventing memory leaks. By fostering a culture of awareness, collaboration, and continuous improvement, development teams can create robust and resilient software systems that exhibit optimal memory usage and avoid the detrimental effects of memory leaks in both development and production environments.

Different scheduling algorithms and their impact

Scheduling algorithms play a crucial role in operating systems, influencing the efficiency and performance of computer systems by determining the order in which processes are executed on the CPU. The choice of a scheduling algorithm depends on the system's objectives, workload characteristics, and desired performance metrics. Several scheduling algorithms have been devised, each with its unique characteristics and impact on system behavior.

One of the fundamental scheduling algorithms is the First-Come, First-Served (FCFS) algorithm. In FCFS, processes are executed in the order they arrive in the ready queue. While simple to implement, FCFS can lead to a phenomenon known as the "convoy effect," where short processes get stuck waiting behind long processes, causing inefficient use of CPU time. The impact of FCFS is notable in scenarios where process burst times vary significantly.

To address the convoy effect, Shortest Job Next (SJN) or Shortest Job First (SJF) scheduling algorithms prioritize the execution of the process with the shortest burst time. This minimizes the average waiting time and enhances system efficiency. However, predicting the exact burst time is often impractical, leading to variations like the Shortest Remaining Time First (SRTF) algorithm, which dynamically adjusts scheduling decisions based on the remaining burst time of processes.

Another widely used scheduling algorithm is Round Robin (RR), a preemption-based algorithm that allocates fixed time slices (quantum) to each process in a cyclic manner. RR ensures fair allocation of CPU time among processes, preventing any single process from monopolizing the CPU. While promoting fairness, RR may lead to a higher turnaround time for processes with long burst times due to frequent context switching overhead.

Priority Scheduling assigns priority levels to processes, and the process with the highest priority is selected for execution first. Priority values can be assigned based on factors like waiting time, burst time, or system-defined priorities. While priority scheduling allows for flexible management of process urgency, it may result in "starvation" if lower-priority processes never get the chance to execute. To mitigate starvation, variations like Aging are introduced, where the priority of a process increases over time.

Multi-level Queue Scheduling categorizes processes into multiple queues based on priority levels, and each queue has its own scheduling algorithm. This approach is particularly effective in handling a mix of short and long-term processes with varying priority requirements. The impact of multi-level queue scheduling is evident in its ability to balance the trade-off between responsiveness for short-term tasks and fairness for long-term tasks.

Multilevel Feedback Queue Scheduling extends the idea of multi-level queues by allowing processes to move between queues based on their behavior. Processes that use less CPU time may be moved to higher-priority queues, while those with longer burst times are relegated to lower-priority queues. This adaptive approach caters to the dynamic nature of workloads, providing responsiveness for short processes and fairness for long processes.

The Completely Fair Scheduler (CFS) is designed to provide fair allocation of CPU time among processes in a more deterministic manner. It assigns a "virtual runtime" to each process, and the process with the smallest virtual runtime is selected for execution. CFS aims to distribute CPU time evenly among processes, but it may not be suitable for real-time applications due to its emphasis on fairness over responsiveness.

Real-time Scheduling addresses the timing requirements of time-sensitive applications by guaranteeing that critical tasks meet their deadlines. Fixed Priority Preemptive Scheduling assigns fixed priorities to tasks, and the task with the highest priority is scheduled for execution. Earliest Deadline First (EDF) Scheduling dynamically assigns priorities based on the deadline of each task, ensuring that the task with the earliest deadline is executed next. While real-time scheduling algorithms prioritize meeting deadlines, they may face challenges in handling system overloads and ensuring fairness among non-critical tasks.

In conclusion, the impact of scheduling algorithms is profound in determining the performance, efficiency, and fairness of computer systems. FCFS, SJF, RR, Priority Scheduling, Multi-level Queue, Multilevel Feedback Queue, CFS, and Real-time Scheduling represent a spectrum of approaches, each tailored to specific system requirements. The choice of a scheduling algorithm depends on factors such as the nature of the workload, system responsiveness needs, and the importance of fairness in CPU allocation. Scheduling algorithms continue to evolve to meet the demands of diverse computing environments, and their impact on system behavior remains a critical consideration in the design and optimization of modern operating systems.

Multi-core optimization and parallel processing

Multi-core optimization and parallel processing are fundamental concepts in computer architecture and software development that aim to harness the power of multiple processor cores to improve overall system performance. In the ever-evolving landscape of computing, where the scaling of clock speeds has plateaued, the emphasis has shifted towards leveraging parallelism to meet the increasing demand for computational power. Multi-core processors, which integrate multiple CPU cores on a single chip, have become prevalent in modern computing systems, ranging from personal computers to servers and high-performance computing clusters.

Multi-core optimization involves tailoring software applications and algorithms to effectively utilize the capabilities of multi-core processors. Traditional sequential algorithms, designed to execute instructions in a step-by-step fashion, often struggle to fully exploit the parallelism offered by multi-core architectures. To address this challenge, developers employ parallel programming techniques, such as threading and task parallelism, to decompose tasks into independent subtasks that can be executed concurrently across multiple cores.

Threading is a key mechanism in multi-core optimization, enabling the execution of different threads simultaneously. Threads represent independent streams of execution within a process and can run concurrently on separate cores. Developers use threading libraries, such as POSIX threads (pthreads) in Unix-like systems or the threading support provided by languages like Java and C#, to create and manage threads. By dividing a program into threads that can execute concurrently, developers can take advantage of the parallel processing capabilities of multi-core systems.

Task parallelism is another approach to multi-core optimization, focusing on breaking down a program into independent tasks that can be executed concurrently. Task parallelism allows developers to express parallelism at a higher level, specifying independent tasks without explicitly managing threads. Parallel frameworks and libraries, such as OpenMP and Intel Threading Building Blocks (TBB), provide abstractions for expressing task parallelism, making it more accessible to developers. These frameworks handle the underlying details of thread management and synchronization, allowing developers to focus on designing parallel algorithms.

Parallel processing, in the context of multi-core optimization, extends beyond the boundaries of a single processor core to harness the computational power of multiple cores simultaneously. Parallelism can take different forms, including data parallelism and task parallelism. Data parallelism involves dividing a large dataset into smaller chunks and processing each chunk concurrently. This approach is well-suited for applications that operate on large arrays or matrices, where each core performs the same operation on different portions of the data.

Task parallelism, as mentioned earlier, involves dividing a program into independent tasks that can be executed concurrently. This form of parallelism is more flexible and applicable to a wide range of applications, as it allows developers to express parallelism at a higher level of abstraction. Task parallelism is particularly effective in scenarios where tasks have varied execution times, and the workload can be dynamically distributed among available cores.

The impact of multi-core optimization and parallel processing is evident in various domains, from scientific computing and simulations to data analytics, rendering, and real-time systems. In scientific computing, simulations that involve solving complex mathematical models or running Monte Carlo simulations benefit significantly from multi-core optimization. Parallelizing the computations allows these simulations to complete faster, enabling researchers and scientists to explore larger problem spaces or conduct more extensive experiments.

Data analytics, especially in the context of big data processing, relies heavily on parallel processing to handle vast datasets efficiently. Technologies like Apache Hadoop and Apache Spark leverage parallelism to distribute data processing tasks across a cluster of machines, with each machine utilizing its multi-core architecture. This parallel approach accelerates data processing, enabling organizations to derive insights from large datasets in a timely manner.

Graphics rendering, a computationally intensive task in applications like video games and computer-aided design (CAD), has undergone a transformative impact from multi-core optimization. Modern GPUs (Graphics Processing Units) consist of multiple cores that can process graphical data concurrently, allowing for real-time rendering of complex scenes and simulations. Parallelism is inherent in the architecture of GPUs, and graphics APIs (Application Programming Interfaces) like OpenGL and DirectX provide mechanisms for developers to exploit this parallelism.

Real-time systems, which demand rapid and predictable responses, also benefit from multi-core optimization. Tasks in real-time systems are often parallelized to ensure timely processing of data, especially in applications like autonomous vehicles, robotics, and industrial control systems. The parallel execution of tasks helps meet stringent deadlines and ensures that critical operations are performed in a timely manner.

Despite the potential for performance gains, achieving effective multi-core optimization and parallel processing comes with challenges. Developers must grapple with issues such as data dependencies, race conditions, and synchronization, which can introduce complexities and potential pitfalls. Properly managing these challenges requires a deep understanding of parallel programming principles and careful consideration of the characteristics of the application being parallelized.

Efforts to simplify the process of multi-core optimization have led to the development of parallel programming languages and frameworks. Languages like CUDA (Compute Unified Device Architecture) and OpenCL (Open Computing Language) enable developers to write parallel code specifically for GPUs. Additionally, high-level programming languages like Python with libraries such as NumPy and Dask provide abstractions that hide much of the complexity of parallel programming, making it more accessible to a broader range of developers.

The impact of multi-core optimization extends to the hardware level, influencing the design and architecture of processors. Chip manufacturers increasingly produce multi-core processors with a higher number of cores, leading to the rise of CPUs with four, eight, or even more cores. The trend towards increased core counts reflects a recognition of the importance of parallelism in addressing the computational demands of modern applications.

In conclusion, multi-core optimization and parallel processing represent a paradigm shift in computing, where the focus has shifted from increasing clock speeds to harnessing the power of multiple cores. Threading, task parallelism, data parallelism, and parallel programming frameworks are essential components of multi-core optimization. The impact of these techniques is evident across diverse domains, from scientific computing and data analytics to graphics rendering and real-time systems. As computing technology continues to advance, the effective utilization of multi-core architectures remains a critical aspect of software development and system design, influencing the performance and responsiveness of applications in an increasingly parallel and interconnected world.

Improving file access speed and data retrieval

Improving file access speed and data retrieval is a critical aspect of optimizing the performance of computer systems, impacting the efficiency and responsiveness of applications across various domains. File access speed is intimately linked to the underlying storage architecture, file system design, and the strategies employed for reading and writing data. Data retrieval, on the other hand, encompasses a broader scope, involving not only file access but also database queries, network requests, and other mechanisms for fetching information. To enhance file access speed and data retrieval, a multifaceted approach is required, addressing aspects such as storage technology, file system optimizations, caching mechanisms, indexing, compression, parallelism, and network efficiency.

At the foundational level, the choice of storage technology significantly influences file access speed and data retrieval. Traditional Hard Disk Drives (HDDs) have been widely used for storage, but their mechanical nature introduces latency in accessing data due to physical read/write heads and spinning platters. Solid State Drives (SSDs), with no moving parts, offer significantly faster read and write speeds, reduced seek times, and improved random access performance. Leveraging SSDs or emerging storage technologies, such as NVMe (Non-Volatile Memory Express), accelerates file access and data retrieval by providing faster data transfer rates and lower access latencies.

File system design plays a crucial role in optimizing file access speed. File systems organize and manage data on storage devices, and their efficiency directly impacts read and write operations. Techniques like block allocation strategies, file indexing, and metadata optimization influence file access performance. Journaling file systems, such as ext4 or NTFS, enhance data reliability but can introduce some overhead. Alternatively, log-structured file systems like F2FS (Flash-Friendly File System) are designed with SSDs in mind, providing efficient data retrieval and write performance for flash-based storage.

Caching mechanisms are fundamental to improving file access speed and data retrieval. Caches store frequently accessed data in a faster, volatile memory layer, reducing the need to fetch data from slower storage. Operating system-level caches, such as the buffer cache, keep recently accessed disk blocks in memory, speeding up subsequent reads. Application-level caches, like those implemented in web browsers or database systems, store frequently used data or query results, enhancing response times and reducing the load on underlying storage.

Indexing is a key strategy for optimizing data retrieval in both file systems and databases. Index structures, such as B-trees or hash indexes, provide quick access paths to specific data points, minimizing the time required to locate and retrieve information. In databases, creating indexes on columns frequently used in queries accelerates data retrieval operations. However, there is a trade-off between the benefits of indexing and the additional storage overhead, as indexes consume space and can impact write performance.

Compression techniques contribute to improved file access speed and data retrieval by reducing the size of stored data, leading to faster transfer times and reduced storage requirements. While compression may introduce some computational overhead during the compression and decompression processes, the benefits in terms of storage efficiency and data transfer speed often outweigh these costs. Compression algorithms, such as gzip or LZ4, are commonly used in scenarios where storage space is a premium, or network bandwidth is a limiting factor in data retrieval.

Parallelism is a powerful strategy for accelerating data retrieval from both storage devices and databases. Parallel file access involves dividing a large file or dataset into smaller chunks and reading or writing them concurrently, leveraging the capabilities of multi-core processors or distributed computing environments. Parallel database queries distribute the workload across multiple processors or nodes, enabling faster retrieval of information from large datasets. Efficient parallelism requires careful consideration of data dependencies, synchronization, and load balancing to fully exploit the available computational resources.

Network efficiency is a critical factor in optimizing data retrieval, especially in scenarios involving distributed systems or cloud-based storage. Reduced latency and increased bandwidth contribute to faster data transfers across networks. Content Delivery Networks (CDNs) employ distributed caching and optimized routing to deliver web content closer to end-users, minimizing latency and accelerating data retrieval. Network protocols, such as HTTP/2 or QUIC, enhance the efficiency of data transfer by reducing connection overhead and allowing for multiplexing multiple streams over a single connection.

In-memory computing is a transformative approach to improving data retrieval speed by storing frequently accessed data directly in memory, eliminating the need for disk or network I/O. In-memory databases, caching systems like Redis, and in-memory file systems leverage the speed of volatile memory to provide rapid access to data. The main challenge with in-memory computing is the limitation of available memory capacity, making it suitable for datasets that can fit entirely in RAM.

Efficient data structures contribute significantly to file access speed and data retrieval. Well-designed data structures, such as hash tables, trees, and linked lists, influence the efficiency of searching, insertion, and deletion operations. Algorithms that operate on these data structures can be optimized for specific access patterns, leading to improved retrieval times. Choosing the right data structure for a given application scenario is essential for achieving optimal data access performance.

Pre-fetching and speculative execution strategies are employed to anticipate future data access patterns and proactively load relevant data into memory. By predicting which data will be accessed next, pre-fetching mechanisms reduce the latency associated with waiting for data to be loaded from slower storage. This approach is particularly beneficial in scenarios where predictable access patterns exist, allowing the system to make informed decisions about pre-loading data to enhance overall retrieval speed.

Load balancing mechanisms play a crucial role in optimizing data retrieval in distributed systems. Uneven distribution of data or queries across multiple nodes can lead to suboptimal performance. Load balancers distribute incoming requests evenly among available resources, preventing individual nodes from becoming bottlenecks.

In cloud environments, auto-scaling and load balancing services dynamically adjust resources based on demand, ensuring efficient data retrieval even in dynamically changing workloads.

Efforts to improve file access speed and data retrieval also involve leveraging specialized hardware accelerators. Graphics Processing Units (GPUs) and Field-Programmable Gate Arrays (FPGAs) are used to offload specific computational tasks, such as data processing or encryption, from the CPU, accelerating overall system performance. These accelerators excel in parallel processing tasks, making them suitable for scenarios where parallelism is a key factor in data retrieval optimization.

In conclusion, optimizing file access speed and data retrieval is a multifaceted endeavor, involving considerations ranging from storage technology and file system design to caching mechanisms, indexing, compression, parallelism, and network efficiency. The choice of strategies depends on the specific characteristics of the application, the nature of the data, and the performance requirements. As computing technology continues to advance, the quest for faster and more efficient data access remains a driving force in the design and optimization of systems across various domains.

Reducing fragmentation and optimizing storage

Reducing fragmentation and optimizing storage are essential aspects of enhancing the efficiency, performance, and longevity of storage systems in computer architectures. Fragmentation, both at the file and disk level, can lead to suboptimal read and write performance, increased storage space wastage, and accelerated wear on storage devices. Addressing fragmentation involves employing various strategies such as defragmentation, wear leveling, compression, and the use of advanced file systems. Additionally, optimizing storage encompasses a broader set of practices, including efficient data organization, tiered storage, data deduplication, and the adoption of emerging storage technologies.

Defragmentation is a key technique to combat fragmentation at the file system level. Over time, as files are created, modified, and deleted, free space becomes scattered across the storage medium. Defragmentation processes rearrange the fragments of files, consolidating free space and ensuring that files are stored in contiguous blocks. This reduces seek times during file access and improves overall read and write performance. Automated defragmentation utilities, integrated into many operating systems, help maintain file system integrity by regularly reorganizing data on the storage device.

Wear leveling is a critical strategy for optimizing the lifespan and performance of NAND flash-based storage devices, such as Solid State Drives (SSDs). NAND flash memory has a finite number of program/erase cycles before it becomes unreliable. Wear leveling algorithms distribute write and erase cycles evenly across the memory cells, preventing certain cells from wearing out faster than others. This ensures that the entire storage medium wears uniformly, extending the lifespan of the SSD and optimizing its performance over time.

Compression is employed as a means of optimizing storage by reducing the physical space occupied by files. By encoding data in a more space-efficient format, compression minimizes the amount of storage required for a given set of files. This not only conserves storage space but can also improve read and write speeds, especially in scenarios where the bottleneck is the storage transfer rate. However, the trade-off involves increased computational overhead for compression and decompression operations, and the effectiveness of compression depends on the nature of the data being stored.

File systems play a pivotal role in both reducing fragmentation and optimizing storage. Advanced file systems, such as ZFS (Zettabyte File System) or Btrfs (B-Tree File System), incorporate features like copy-on-write, checksums, and data deduplication. Copy-on-write ensures that new data is written to a different location, reducing fragmentation and enhancing data integrity. Checksums enable error detection, preventing data corruption. Data deduplication identifies and eliminates duplicate data, conserving storage space. These file system features collectively contribute to improved storage efficiency and reliability.

Efficient data organization involves placing frequently accessed data in faster storage tiers, such as SSDs, and less frequently accessed data in slower, high-capacity storage tiers, such as Hard Disk Drives (HDDs). This tiered storage approach, known as storage tiering, optimizes overall system performance by aligning storage resources with the access patterns of different types of data. Automated storage tiering systems dynamically move data between tiers based on its usage, ensuring that the most relevant data resides in the fastest storage medium at any given time.

Data deduplication is a technique aimed at optimizing storage by identifying and eliminating redundant copies of data. In scenarios where multiple instances of the same data exist, deduplication mechanisms store a single copy and maintain references to that copy for subsequent occurrences. This reduces the physical storage footprint and minimizes the amount of data that needs to be backed up or transferred across networks. Deduplication is commonly used in backup systems, virtualized environments, and storage appliances to enhance storage efficiency.

Emerging storage technologies, such as Non-Volatile Memory Express (NVMe) and Storage Class Memory (SCM), contribute to storage optimization by providing faster data access speeds and lower latencies compared to traditional storage interfaces. NVMe, designed specifically for flash-based storage, reduces command overhead and leverages parallelism to maximize throughput. SCM, which includes technologies like Intel Optane, combines the speed of volatile memory with the persistence of storage, offering a new class of high-performance storage solutions.

Storage virtualization is a strategy that abstracts the physical storage infrastructure, allowing multiple storage devices to be managed as a single, virtualized pool. This abstraction simplifies storage management, enables efficient utilization of storage resources, and facilitates features such as thin provisioning. Thin provisioning allocates storage capacity on demand rather than pre-allocating it, preventing over-provisioning and optimizing storage utilization.

RAID (Redundant Array of Independent Disks) configurations contribute to storage optimization by combining multiple disks into a single logical unit for improved performance, redundancy, or a combination of both. RAID levels, such as RAID 0 (striping for performance), RAID 1 (mirroring for redundancy), and RAID 5 (striping with parity for a balance of performance and redundancy), provide various trade-offs to meet specific storage optimization requirements. RAID configurations are widely used in storage arrays to enhance data protection, performance, and availability.

Cloud storage services offer an alternative approach to optimizing storage by offloading data to remote servers managed by cloud providers. Cloud storage solutions, such as Amazon S3, Microsoft Azure Blob Storage, or Google Cloud Storage, provide scalable and cost-effective storage options. These services often include features like data redundancy, automatic backups, and flexible storage tiers to accommodate diverse storage needs. Cloud storage also enables seamless scalability, allowing organizations to adapt their storage capacity to changing requirements.

Tape storage, though considered a traditional medium, remains relevant for long-term archival and backup purposes. Tape libraries offer high-capacity, cost-effective storage solutions with lower power consumption compared to disk-based systems. Tape storage is often used in conjunction with hierarchical storage management (HSM) systems, where infrequently accessed data is moved to tape storage to optimize costs and overall storage efficiency.

Efforts to optimize storage also involve the implementation of data lifecycle management strategies. By categorizing data based on its lifecycle stage (e.g., hot, warm, cold), organizations can apply different storage and access policies. Frequently accessed "hot" data may reside on high-performance storage, while less frequently accessed "warm" or "cold" data may be stored on slower, cost-effective storage mediums. This approach ensures that storage resources align with the changing access patterns of data over time.

Storage encryption contributes to both security and storage optimization by safeguarding data from unauthorized access. Encrypted storage ensures that even if physical storage devices are compromised, the data remains protected. The use of hardware-accelerated encryption, as found in modern storage devices, minimizes the impact on read and write performance. Encryption is particularly crucial in compliance-driven environments where data confidentiality is a top priority.

In conclusion, reducing fragmentation and optimizing storage are integral components of enhancing the efficiency, performance, and longevity of storage systems. Defragmentation, wear leveling, compression, advanced file systems, tiered storage, data deduplication, emerging storage technologies, storage virtualization, RAID configurations, cloud storage, tape storage, data lifecycle management, and storage encryption collectively form a comprehensive toolkit for achieving storage optimization. The choice of strategies depends on specific use cases, performance requirements, and the evolving landscape of storage technologies. As organizations continue to grapple with growing data volumes, optimizing storage remains a dynamic and crucial aspect of modern computing infrastructures.

Overview of tools for performance analysis

An overview of tools for performance analysis reveals a diverse ecosystem designed to assess and optimize the efficiency of software applications, hardware systems, and entire computing environments.

These tools play a crucial role in identifying bottlenecks, analyzing resource utilization, and uncovering opportunities for improvement. Performance analysis encompasses various aspects, including application profiling, system monitoring, debugging, and benchmarking. A comprehensive set of tools is available for developers, system administrators, and performance engineers, each catering to specific needs and domains.

Application profiling tools form a cornerstone of performance analysis, providing insights into the runtime behavior of software. Profilers capture information about function execution times, memory usage, and code paths, helping developers identify performance hotspots and optimize critical sections of their code. Popular profiling tools include Intel VTune Profiler, which supports a wide range of processors and offers advanced performance analysis features. For Java applications, tools like YourKit and VisualVM provide real-time profiling capabilities, allowing developers to identify memory leaks, CPU bottlenecks, and inefficient code patterns.

System monitoring tools are essential for gaining visibility into the performance of an entire computing environment. These tools track resource usage metrics such as CPU utilization, memory consumption, disk I/O, and network activity. Prominent system monitoring tools include Nagios and Zabbix, which offer comprehensive dashboards and alerting mechanisms. For Unix-like systems, top and htop provide real-time views of system resource utilization. Additionally, tools like Perf on Linux or Windows Performance Monitor offer low-level insights into kernel-level activities, enabling users to diagnose system-level performance issues.

Debugging tools play a crucial role in performance analysis by helping developers identify and resolve software defects that impact performance. Traditional debuggers like gdb (GNU Debugger) provide a powerful command-line interface for stepping through code, inspecting variables, and setting breakpoints. Integrated Development Environments (IDEs) such as Visual Studio and IntelliJ IDEA offer graphical debugging interfaces with features like watch lists, variable inspection, and memory debugging. Memory debugging tools like Valgrind on Linux or AddressSanitizer help detect memory leaks, invalid memory accesses, and other memory-related issues.

Benchmarking tools are instrumental in assessing the performance of hardware, software, or entire systems under specific workloads. These tools generate standardized tests and metrics to evaluate and compare performance across different configurations. Popular benchmarking tools include Geekbench, which assesses CPU and GPU performance across various platforms, and SPEC (Standard Performance Evaluation Corporation) benchmarks, which provide industry-standard benchmarks for evaluating system performance in areas like CPU, graphics, and energy efficiency. Benchmarking tools assist in making informed decisions about hardware upgrades, software optimizations, and overall system configurations.

Profiling tools specific to web applications offer insights into the performance of web pages, including loading times, resource utilization, and rendering speed. Google Chrome DevTools and Mozilla Firefox Developer Tools include built-in profilers for analyzing web page performance. Lighthouse, an open-source tool from Google, not only audits web page performance but also provides recommendations for improvement. For server-side performance analysis of web applications, tools like New Relic and AppDynamics offer application performance monitoring (APM) solutions, allowing developers to identify performance bottlenecks in server-side code.

Network monitoring tools are essential for analyzing the performance and efficiency of network infrastructure. Wireshark, a widely used packet analyzer, allows users to capture and inspect the data traveling over a network. Network monitoring solutions like SolarWinds and Nagios Network Analyzer provide comprehensive insights into bandwidth usage, network latency, and device health.

These tools are crucial for diagnosing connectivity issues, optimizing network configurations, and ensuring the smooth operation of distributed systems.

Container orchestration platforms, such as Kubernetes, have given rise to specialized performance analysis tools tailored for containerized environments. Tools like cAdvisor (Container Advisor) provide real-time monitoring of container resource usage, helping users understand the performance characteristics of containerized workloads. Kubernetes-native monitoring solutions like Prometheus and Grafana offer a robust ecosystem for collecting, querying, and visualizing performance metrics within Kubernetes clusters. These tools are essential for optimizing resource allocation, scaling, and overall containerized application performance.

For parallel and distributed computing environments, specialized tools are designed to analyze and optimize the performance of parallelized code and distributed systems. OpenMP and MPI (Message Passing Interface) profiling tools, like Score-P and Scalasca, help users understand the performance of parallelized applications by providing insights into thread synchronization, communication overhead, and load balancing. Apache Hadoop and Apache Spark, widely used for distributed data processing, come with built-in tools for monitoring and optimizing distributed job performance.

In the realm of database performance analysis, tools address the unique challenges associated with querying, indexing, and overall database efficiency. MySQL and PostgreSQL, two popular relational database systems, provide built-in performance analysis tools such as EXPLAIN for query execution plans. NoSQL databases like MongoDB offer tools like MongoDB Compass for visualizing query performance and optimizing indexing strategies. Dedicated database performance monitoring solutions, such as Percona Monitoring and Management (PMM) or DataDog, provide comprehensive insights into database health, query performance, and resource utilization.

Cloud-based performance analysis tools cater to the growing trend of deploying applications in cloud environments. Cloud providers like Amazon Web Services (AWS), Microsoft Azure, and Google Cloud Platform offer native tools for monitoring and optimizing cloud resources. AWS CloudWatch, Azure Monitor, and Google Cloud Monitoring provide centralized dashboards for tracking resource usage, setting up alerts, and analyzing the performance of cloud-based services. Third-party tools like Datadog and New Relic extend performance analysis capabilities to multi-cloud and hybrid cloud environments.

Real-time analytics tools offer the capability to analyze and visualize performance data in real-time, enabling quick decision-making and proactive issue resolution. ELK Stack (Elasticsearch, Logstash, Kibana) is a popular open-source solution for real-time log analysis, allowing users to aggregate and visualize log data for performance troubleshooting. Splunk, a commercial real-time analytics platform, offers features for monitoring and analyzing machine data, providing insights into application and system performance.

Containerized environments, microservices architectures, and serverless computing have given rise to observability tools that go beyond traditional monitoring. Observability tools, including Jaeger and Zipkin for distributed tracing, Prometheus for metric collection, and Grafana for visualization, allow users to gain deep insights into the behavior of complex, distributed systems. These tools facilitate root cause analysis, performance optimization, and overall system reliability in modern, dynamic application landscapes.

In conclusion, the landscape of tools for performance analysis is vast and diverse, reflecting the complexity and diversity of modern computing environments. Application profiling, system monitoring, debugging, benchmarking, web performance analysis, network monitoring, container orchestration, distributed computing, database performance analysis, cloud-based tools, real-time analytics, and observability solutions collectively form a comprehensive toolkit for developers, system administrators, and performance engineers. The choice of tools depends on specific use cases, requirements, and the evolving nature of technologies, ensuring that users have the necessary resources to analyze, optimize, and enhance the performance of their applications and systems.

Real-time monitoring and profiling techniques

Real-time monitoring and profiling techniques are integral components of modern computing systems, providing continuous insights into the performance, health, and behavior of applications, infrastructure, and networks. In the dynamic and fast-paced landscape of computing, where rapid decision-making and immediate issue resolution are paramount, real-time monitoring and profiling play a pivotal role in ensuring system reliability, optimizing resource utilization, and enhancing overall user experience.

Real-time monitoring involves the continuous observation and collection of performance metrics, events, and status updates from various components within a system. This ongoing process allows stakeholders to gain immediate visibility into critical aspects of system behavior. One of the fundamental elements of real-time monitoring is the collection of metrics related to system resources, such as CPU utilization, memory usage, disk I/O, and network activity. Monitoring tools like Prometheus, Grafana, and Nagios enable organizations to create comprehensive dashboards that provide real-time visualizations of these metrics, facilitating quick identification of anomalies or performance bottlenecks.

Profiling techniques complement real-time monitoring by offering detailed insights into the execution and behavior of software applications. Application profiling in real-time involves capturing data related to function execution times, memory usage, and code paths during the runtime of an application. Tools like YourKit, VisualVM, and Intel VTune Profiler provide developers with real-time profiling capabilities, enabling them to identify performance hotspots, memory leaks, and inefficiencies in their code. Profiling helps developers understand how their code behaves under different conditions, facilitating the optimization of critical sections and the enhancement of overall application performance.

Distributed tracing is a specialized form of profiling that has gained prominence in microservices architectures and other distributed systems. Tools like Jaeger and Zipkin enable the tracking of requests as they traverse through various microservices, providing a holistic view of the entire request lifecycle. Distributed tracing in real-time allows organizations to identify latency issues, track down bottlenecks, and understand the flow of requests across multiple components. This capability is crucial in ensuring the responsiveness and reliability of complex, distributed applications.

Real-time monitoring and profiling extend beyond the application layer to encompass network monitoring, ensuring the efficient and secure operation of communication channels. Network monitoring tools, including Wireshark, SolarWinds, and Nagios Network Analyzer, capture and analyze network traffic in real-time. These tools provide insights into bandwidth usage, latency, packet loss, and device health, enabling administrators to promptly detect and resolve network issues. In a world where connectivity is crucial, real-time network monitoring is essential for maintaining the integrity and performance of communication infrastructures.

Web performance monitoring focuses specifically on the user experience of web applications, assessing factors such as page load times, rendering speed, and resource utilization. Real-time web performance monitoring tools, like Google PageSpeed Insights, New Relic Browser, and Dynatrace, continuously assess the performance of web pages from the end-user perspective. By monitoring real-time metrics related to web performance, organizations can identify and address issues that impact user satisfaction, ensuring optimal responsiveness and a positive user experience.

In the context of containerized environments and microservices architectures, real-time observability tools have emerged as crucial components for understanding the behavior and interactions of complex, distributed systems. Tools like Prometheus, Grafana, and Kubernetes-native solutions offer real-time insights into the health, performance, and resource utilization of containers and microservices. Real-time observability enables organizations to dynamically adapt to changing conditions, scale resources based on demand, and quickly respond to issues, ensuring the robust operation of containerized applications.

Security monitoring in real-time is vital for detecting and responding to security incidents promptly. Security information and event management (SIEM) tools, such as Splunk, ELK Stack, and QRadar, enable organizations to collect, correlate, and analyze security-related events in real-time. These tools provide a comprehensive view of the security posture, allowing security teams to identify potential threats, investigate incidents, and implement timely remediation measures. Real-time security monitoring is essential in today's threat landscape, where cyberattacks can occur rapidly and with significant impact.

Real-time analytics leverage data processing and analysis techniques to derive insights from streaming data sources in real-time. Technologies like Apache Kafka, Apache Flink, and Apache Storm enable organizations to process and analyze data as it is generated, allowing for immediate decision-making based on current information. Real-time analytics is particularly valuable in scenarios where timely insights can influence business decisions, such as financial trading, online advertising, and predictive maintenance.

Cloud providers offer native real-time monitoring solutions to users deploying applications in cloud environments. Amazon Cloud-

Watch, Azure Monitor, and Google Cloud Monitoring are examples of cloud-native tools that provide real-time insights into the performance and health of cloud-based resources. These tools allow organizations to monitor virtual machines, databases, and other cloud services in real-time, facilitating efficient resource management, cost optimization, and the identification of performance bottlenecks.

Log analysis in real-time involves the continuous processing and interpretation of log data generated by applications and systems. ELK Stack (Elasticsearch, Logstash, Kibana), Splunk, and Graylog are widely used real-time log analysis tools. These platforms enable organizations to centralize log data, search and analyze logs in real-time, and set up alerts for specific events. Real-time log analysis is crucial for identifying anomalies, troubleshooting issues, and ensuring the operational integrity of applications and systems.

In the realm of hardware and infrastructure, real-time monitoring is essential for ensuring the health and performance of servers, storage devices, and networking equipment. Hardware monitoring tools, such as Open Hardware Monitor and Dell OpenManage, provide real-time insights into hardware components, temperatures, voltages, and fan speeds. These tools allow administrators to detect hardware failures, preemptively address potential issues, and optimize the overall reliability of the underlying infrastructure.

The adoption of real-time monitoring and profiling techniques is driven by the need for organizations to maintain a proactive stance in addressing performance, security, and operational challenges. The integration of these techniques into the fabric of software development, system administration, and operational processes enables organizations to respond swiftly to changing conditions, identify emerging issues, and optimize the performance of their applications and infrastructure in a continuous and iterative manner. As computing environments become more complex and dynamic, real-time monitoring and profiling emerge as indispensable tools for ensuring the reliability, responsiveness, and security of modern systems.

Chapter 8: Beyond the Horizon: Future Trends in Operating System Design

Integration of AI and machine learning in OS design

The integration of Artificial Intelligence (AI) and Machine Learning (ML) in operating system (OS) design represents a transformative paradigm shift that extends the traditional role of operating systems from mere resource management to intelligent decision-making and adaptability. This convergence of AI and OS design introduces a new era where operating systems can leverage advanced algorithms, predictive analytics, and self-learning mechanisms to enhance efficiency, security, and user experience across a wide range of computing environments.

One fundamental aspect of integrating AI and ML into OS design is the optimization of resource management. Traditional operating systems allocate resources based on predefined rules and static configurations. However, by incorporating machine learning algorithms, operating systems can adaptively optimize resource allocation in real-time, taking into account dynamic workloads, application priorities, and user behavior. ML models can analyze historical resource usage patterns, predict future demands, and dynamically adjust resource allocations to maximize overall system performance and responsiveness.

The application of AI and ML extends to the realm of power management, particularly in the context of mobile devices and energy-efficient computing. Operating systems equipped with machine learning capabilities can analyze patterns of user behavior, application usage, and power consumption to intelligently optimize power profiles. By predicting user preferences and adapting power management strategies accordingly, these systems can extend battery life, reduce energy consumption, and create a more sustainable computing environment.

Security is a paramount concern in modern computing, and the integration of AI and ML in OS design brings forth innovative approaches to threat detection, prevention, and response. Traditional antivirus and intrusion detection systems rely on signature-based approaches, which may struggle to keep pace with the rapidly evolving landscape of cyber threats. AI-driven security features in operating systems can employ machine learning models to detect anomalous behavior, identify previously unknown threats, and proactively respond to security incidents in real-time. Behavioral analysis, anomaly detection, and predictive modeling become integral components of OS security, enhancing the overall resilience of the system.

User experience is another domain where AI and ML integration in OS design can make a substantial impact. Personalization of user interfaces, adaptive recommendations, and context-aware interactions become achievable through machine learning algorithms that analyze user preferences, usage patterns, and contextual information. Operating systems can dynamically adjust interface elements, suggest relevant applications or content, and tailor the user experience based on individual behaviors, creating a more intuitive and user-friendly computing environment.

The management of system updates and patches is a critical aspect of OS security and stability. AI and ML can be leveraged to optimize the update process by predicting the impact of updates on system stability, identifying potential compatibility issues, and determining the optimal timing for installations based on user behavior patterns. This intelligent update management ensures that the OS remains secure and up-to-date without disrupting user workflows or causing unexpected issues.

In the domain of file and data management, AI-powered features can enhance search capabilities, content organization, and data accessibility. Operating systems can employ natural language processing algorithms to understand user queries, making file searches more intuitive and efficient. ML models can learn user preferences and automatically organize files based on usage patterns, reducing clutter and streamlining data management tasks. Furthermore, intelligent data caching mechanisms can anticipate user needs, preloading frequently accessed data into memory for faster access.

Edge computing, characterized by processing data closer to the source of generation, benefits significantly from the integration of AI and ML in operating systems. Edge devices often operate with limited resources, requiring intelligent resource allocation, data processing, and decision-making at the edge. OS designs that incorporate machine learning capabilities enable edge devices to perform tasks such as real-time analytics, pattern recognition, and decision-making locally, reducing latency and enhancing the overall responsiveness of edge computing systems.

The design of autonomous systems, including self-driving vehicles and drones, relies heavily on AI and ML. Operating systems for such systems must integrate sophisticated machine learning models to process sensor data, make real-time decisions, and adapt to dynamic environments. These AI-driven OS designs enable autonomous systems to learn from experience, refine their behavior over time, and operate safely and efficiently in complex scenarios.

Concurrency and parallelism, essential aspects of modern computing with multi-core processors and distributed systems, can be optimized through the integration of AI and ML in OS design. Machine learning algorithms can analyze application workloads, identify parallelization opportunities, and dynamically allocate computing resources to maximize parallel processing efficiency. This adaptive approach to concurrency management ensures optimal utilization of available resources and enhances the overall performance of parallelized applications.

The adoption of AI and ML in OS design also brings forth challenges related to transparency, interpretability, and ethical considerations. As machine learning models make decisions that impact system behavior, it becomes crucial to provide mechanisms for users to understand and interpret these decisions. Ethical considerations, such as bias in AI algorithms and the responsible use of user data, must be addressed to ensure that AI-driven OS designs prioritize fairness, transparency, and user privacy.

In conclusion, the integration of AI and Machine Learning in operating system design represents a paradigm shift that transcends the traditional boundaries of resource management. These intelligent OS designs bring forth adaptive resource allocation, proactive security measures, personalized user experiences, efficient edge computing, and optimized concurrency management. As computing environments continue to evolve, the symbiotic relationship between AI and OS design promises to redefine the capabilities of operating systems, ushering in an era of intelligent, self-learning, and adaptive computing systems. The ongoing exploration of this intersection between AI and OS design holds the potential to revolutionize how we interact with and harness the power of computing technology.

Quantum computing implications for operating systems

The advent of quantum computing brings forth a paradigm shift in the landscape of computing, with profound implications for operating systems (OS) that form the foundational layer of computer architectures. Quantum computing harnesses the principles of quantum mechanics, allowing for the representation and manipulation of information using quantum bits or qubits. As quantum computers advance in capabilities, the implications for operating systems become multifaceted, touching upon aspects of security, algorithm design, resource management, and the very foundations of computational theory.

One of the most significant implications of quantum computing for operating systems lies in the realm of security. The widely-used cryptographic protocols that underpin secure communication on classical computers, such as RSA and ECC, rely on the complexity of certain mathematical problems for their security. However, quantum algorithms, notably Shor's algorithm, have the potential to efficiently factor large numbers and solve discrete logarithm problems, threatening the security of these classical cryptographic systems. Quantum-resistant cryptographic algorithms and protocols, such as those based on lattice cryptography or hash-based cryptography, must be integrated into operating systems to safeguard sensitive data and communications in the post-quantum era.

Quantum computers introduce a novel computing model that challenges classical algorithmic paradigms. As a result, the development and integration of quantum algorithms become a crucial consideration for operating systems. Quantum algorithms, designed to leverage the unique capabilities of quantum computers, can potentially outperform their classical counterparts in certain tasks, such as factoring large numbers, searching unsorted databases, and solving certain optimization problems. Operating systems need to accommodate the execution of quantum algorithms, possibly through specialized quantum programming interfaces, to harness the full potential of quantum computing for specific computational tasks.

Quantum computing's impact on resource management within operating systems is also a significant consideration. Quantum computers exhibit unique characteristics, such as superposition and entanglement, that challenge classical notions of memory and processing. Quantum bits can exist in multiple states simultaneously, leading to complex interactions between quantum and classical information. Operating systems must adapt their resource management strategies to effectively utilize the hybrid quantum-classical systems that may emerge, where classical and quantum processors work in tandem, sharing computational tasks in a coherent and efficient manner.

Quantum computing introduces the concept of quantum parallelism, where quantum algorithms can process multiple possibilities simultaneously. This has implications for the design of parallel and distributed computing frameworks within operating systems. Quantum-inspired algorithms, such as those for optimization and machine learning, may require new paradigms for managing concurrency and parallelism. Operating systems must evolve to efficiently coordinate and orchestrate the execution of quantum and classical algorithms in a coherent and synchronized manner, optimizing overall system performance.

The nature of quantum computation also challenges traditional programming models and languages. Quantum algorithms are expressed in quantum programming languages, often utilizing quantum gates and circuits to represent quantum operations. Operating systems need to provide support for these quantum programming languages and ensure seamless integration with classical programming languages. This integration should enable developers to build applications that leverage both classical and quantum computation, potentially unlocking new capabilities and solving problems that were previously deemed intractable.

Quantum computing's impact on communication protocols is a crucial aspect for operating systems to address. Quantum key distribution (QKD) offers a theoretically secure method for key exchange, leveraging the principles of quantum mechanics to detect eavesdropping attempts. Operating systems must integrate QKD protocols into their networking and communication stacks to establish secure communication channels in a quantum-aware environment. Quantum-safe communication protocols are essential for ensuring the confidentiality and integrity of data transmissions in a world where quantum computers pose a threat to classical cryptographic systems.

The scalability of quantum computers poses challenges and opportunities for operating systems. As quantum processors scale up in terms of the number of qubits and coherence times, operating systems must adapt to manage the increasing complexity of quantum systems. Quantum error correction, a crucial aspect of large-scale quantum computation, introduces additional computational overhead. Operating systems need to incorporate mechanisms for error correction and fault tolerance to ensure the reliable execution of quantum algorithms. Quantum processors may become integral components of hybrid computing architectures, and operating systems must efficiently orchestrate the collaboration between quantum and classical processors.

Quantum machine learning is an emerging field that explores the synergy between quantum computing and machine learning algorithms. Quantum computers have the potential to accelerate certain machine learning tasks, such as linear algebraic computations and optimization problems. Operating systems must accommodate the integration of quantum machine learning libraries and frameworks, enabling developers to leverage quantum-enhanced machine learning algorithms. This integration opens avenues for solving complex problems in artificial intelligence and data analytics that were previously computationally prohibitive.

Quantum sensors and quantum-enhanced sensing technologies further expand the scope of quantum computing implications for operating systems. Quantum sensors leverage quantum entanglement and superposition to achieve unprecedented levels of precision in measurements. Operating systems must provide support for quantum sensor data acquisition, processing, and integration into applications. This integration has implications for fields such as quantum-enhanced imaging, quantum metrology, and quantum sensing, where quantum computers and sensors work in tandem to extract valuable information from physical systems.

Quantum cloud computing services, where quantum processors are made available as part of cloud infrastructure, introduce new challenges and opportunities for operating systems. Operating systems must facilitate seamless integration between classical and quantum cloud resources, enabling users to harness the power of quantum computing through standard cloud interfaces. Quantum cloud services may require specialized resource management and scheduling algorithms within operating systems to optimize the allocation of quantum processing units and ensure fair access for users across diverse application domains.

Ethical considerations surrounding quantum computing, such as the responsible use of quantum algorithms and the potential societal impacts of quantum technologies, also demand attention from operating systems. As quantum computing capabilities advance, operating systems must embed ethical principles into their design, addressing issues related to data privacy, algorithmic fairness, and the responsible deployment of quantum technologies. Operating systems play a pivotal role in ensuring that quantum computing is harnessed for the benefit of society while minimizing potential risks and ethical concerns.

In conclusion, the integration of quantum computing into operating systems represents a monumental shift that transcends classical computational paradigms. Quantum-safe cryptography, quantum algorithm integration, resource management in hybrid quantum-classical systems, adaptation to quantum programming models, communication protocol security, scalability challenges, quantum machine learning, quantum sensors, cloud integration, and ethical considerations collectively shape the implications of quantum computing for operating systems. As quantum technologies progress from theoretical concepts to practical implementations, operating systems must evolve to embrace the unique challenges and opportunities posed by the quantum realm, paving the way for a future where classical and quantum computing seamlessly coexist and complement each other.

The rise of containerized applications

The rise of containerized applications signifies a transformative shift in the landscape of software development, deployment, and infrastructure management. Containerization, driven by technologies like Docker and Kubernetes, has emerged as a cornerstone in modern application development practices, offering a portable, scalable, and efficient approach to building, packaging, and running software. This paradigm shift represents a departure from traditional monolithic architectures towards a microservices-oriented model, where applications are decomposed into smaller, independently deployable units encapsulated within lightweight containers. The multifaceted impact of containerization encompasses aspects of development workflows, operational efficiency, resource utilization, scalability, and the overall agility of software delivery pipelines.

From a developer's perspective, containerization introduces a fundamental shift in how applications are constructed and packaged. Containers encapsulate an application along with its dependencies, libraries, and runtime environments in a standardized, isolated unit. This ensures that an application runs consistently across various environments, from a developer's laptop to production servers, eliminating the notorious "it works on my machine" challenge. Docker, the de facto standard for containerization, provides developers with a unified packaging format and tools for building, sharing, and deploying containers. This uniformity simplifies the development process, accelerates application onboarding, and streamlines collaboration across development teams.

Containerization facilitates the adoption of microservices architectures, where applications are decomposed into modular, independently deployable services. Each microservice runs within its own container, enabling teams to develop, deploy, and scale services independently. This decoupling of services promotes flexibility, allowing organizations to choose the most suitable technologies for each microservice and update individual components without affecting the entire application. Kubernetes, the popular container orchestration platform, plays a pivotal role in managing the deployment, scaling, and operation of containerized microservices, providing a resilient and automated infrastructure for modern application architectures.

Operational efficiency is a key driver behind the rise of containerized applications. Containers encapsulate applications and their dependencies in a lightweight, isolated manner, enabling consistent behavior across diverse environments. This consistency simplifies the configuration and management of infrastructure, reducing the likelihood of conflicts between different components of an application stack. The immutability of containers, combined with declarative configuration through tools like Docker Compose and Kubernetes manifests, promotes reproducibility and eliminates configuration drift, ensuring that applications run predictably in any environment.

Resource utilization is optimized through containerization, as containers share the host operating system's kernel while maintaining isolation at the application level. This shared kernel approach significantly reduces the overhead associated with virtualization, allowing for higher density of application instances on a single host. Containers boot quickly and have lower resource overhead compared to traditional virtual machines, making them ideal for dynamic and scalable workloads. The ability to deploy and scale containers rapidly, coupled with efficient resource utilization, enhances the overall efficiency and responsiveness of applications in both development and production environments.

Scalability is a defining characteristic of containerized applications, aligning with the demands of modern, cloud-native architectures. Containers provide a lightweight and portable unit of deployment, making it straightforward to scale applications horizontally by adding or removing container instances. Kubernetes, with its robust orchestration capabilities, automates the scaling of containerized services based on predefined policies, resource utilization, or external triggers. This dynamic scalability allows organizations to respond rapidly to changing workloads, ensuring that applications can seamlessly handle varying levels of demand, from minimal traffic to peak usage.

The rise of containerized applications has redefined the continuous integration and continuous delivery (CI/CD) pipeline, introducing efficiencies at every stage of the software delivery lifecycle. Containers encapsulate not only the application code but also its dependencies, runtime, and configuration, creating a consistent environment from development through testing to production. CI/CD tools, such as Jenkins, GitLab CI, and Travis CI, integrate seamlessly with containerization technologies, enabling automated testing, building, and deployment of containerized applications. This streamlined CI/CD process enhances the speed, reliability, and repeatability of software releases, fostering a culture of rapid iteration and experimentation.

Containerization accelerates the adoption of DevOps practices by promoting collaboration and communication between development and operations teams. The consistency between development and production environments, facilitated by containers, reduces friction and enables smoother handovers between these two traditionally siloed domains. DevOps teams leverage container orchestration platforms like Kubernetes to automate deployment, scaling, and management tasks, allowing them to focus on strategic initiatives rather than routine operational tasks. The marriage of containerization and DevOps principles results in faster, more reliable deployments, increased collaboration, and improved overall system reliability.

The flexibility offered by containerization extends to hybrid and multi-cloud deployment scenarios. Containers encapsulate applications and their dependencies in a standardized format, making them agnostic to the underlying infrastructure. This portability allows organizations to deploy containerized applications seamlessly across on-premises data centers, public clouds, and hybrid environments. Kubernetes, with its cloud-agnostic nature, enables consistent management and orchestration of containers regardless of the underlying infrastructure, providing organizations with the freedom to choose the most suitable hosting environment for their workloads.

Security considerations play a crucial role in the rise of containerized applications. Containers provide a level of isolation between applications and the host system, but ensuring the security of containerized workloads requires a comprehensive approach. Container security tools, such as Docker Security Scanning and Clair, help identify vulnerabilities within container images. Kubernetes provides features like Pod Security Policies to enforce security best practices at the orchestration level. The declarative nature of container orchestration also enhances security by enabling the definition of security policies as code, ensuring consistent application of security measures across environments.

The rise of containerized applications has catalyzed the evolution of infrastructure as code (IaC) practices. Container orchestration platforms, particularly Kubernetes, treat infrastructure configurations as code, allowing developers and operators to define and version infrastructure using declarative manifests. This approach aligns with the broader trend of infrastructure automation, enabling organizations to manage infrastructure at scale, provision resources on-demand, and maintain consistency between development, testing, and production environments.

The modularity introduced by containerization fosters a vibrant ecosystem of containerized applications and services available through container registries. Public container registries, such as Docker Hub and Google Container Registry, serve as repositories for sharing, distributing, and discovering container images. Organizations leverage private container registries to manage their proprietary images securely. This ecosystem accelerates software development by enabling the reuse of containerized components, fostering collaboration, and promoting the development of standardized, interoperable solutions.

Containerization has become instrumental in the evolution of serverless computing, a cloud computing model where applications are developed and executed in a stateless, event-driven manner. Serverless platforms, such as AWS Lambda and Azure Functions, utilize containers to encapsulate and execute individual functions. Containers provide the isolation required for secure and scalable execution of functions while enabling rapid scaling based on demand. The integration of containerization and serverless computing represents a convergence of technologies that simplifies the deployment and management of event-driven, scalable applications.

In conclusion, the rise of containerized applications marks a pivotal transformation in the way software is developed, deployed, and managed. Containerization, driven by Docker, Kubernetes, and related technologies, introduces consistency, efficiency, scalability, and agility to modern application architectures. From developers' local environments to production deployments in hybrid and multi-cloud scenarios, containers provide a standardized and portable unit of deployment. The impact of containerization resonates across the entire software delivery lifecycle, enhancing collaboration, accelerating release cycles, and enabling organizations to navigate the complexities of modern, cloud-native computing environments. As the containerization ecosystem continues to evolve, it is poised to shape the future of software development and infrastructure management, driving innovation and empowering organizations to meet the demands of an ever-changing technological landscape.

Impact on OS architecture and deployment

The impact of modern technological trends on operating system (OS) architecture and deployment is a dynamic and multifaceted landscape that reflects the evolving demands of contemporary computing environments. One of the prominent influences on OS architecture is the paradigm shift towards containerization. Container technologies, exemplified by Docker and Kubernetes, have redefined how applications are packaged, deployed, and managed. OS architectures are adapting to accommodate the lightweight, portable nature of containers, which encapsulate applications and their dependencies in isolated units. This shift towards container orchestration platforms has necessitated changes in OS kernels and system components to support the efficient and secure execution of containerized workloads.

Furthermore, the rise of microservices architectures, closely intertwined with containerization, has implications for OS deployment strategies. Traditional monolithic applications are giving way to modular, independently deployable microservices, each encapsulated within its container. This decentralization of application components poses challenges and opportunities for OS deployment models, as they need to support the seamless coordination and scaling of microservices across distributed environments. OS architectures are evolving to embrace the principles of service discovery, load balancing, and dynamic provisioning to facilitate the deployment and management of microservices.

The prevalence of cloud computing has also left an indelible mark on OS architectures and deployment practices. Cloud-native

OS designs prioritize compatibility with cloud services, allowing seamless integration with popular cloud platforms such as Amazon Web Services (AWS), Microsoft Azure, and Google Cloud Platform. These OS architectures emphasize flexibility, scalability, and the ability to seamlessly transition workloads between on-premises data centers and various cloud providers. Cloud-native OS deployments often leverage container orchestration platforms like Kubernetes to optimize resource utilization and provide a consistent environment across diverse cloud and on-premises infrastructures.

Security considerations have become paramount in OS architecture and deployment strategies. The increasing sophistication of cyber threats demands robust security postures, prompting OS designers to integrate advanced security features. OS architectures are incorporating mechanisms for secure boot, runtime integrity checking, and isolation between applications and the OS kernel. Enhanced access controls, mandatory access controls (MAC), and capabilities like AppArmor and SELinux contribute to securing OS deployments. Additionally, OS deployment practices are evolving to emphasize the importance of timely security updates, patch management, and vulnerability assessments to mitigate potential risks.

The advent of edge computing has introduced new dimensions to OS architectures and deployment models. Edge computing involves processing data closer to the source of generation, reducing latency and enabling real-time decision-making. OS architectures for edge computing prioritize lightweight, efficient designs that can run on resource-constrained devices. Deploying OS instances at the edge requires considerations for reliable connectivity, robust security, and the ability to manage distributed deployments seamlessly. Edge OS architectures often incorporate features like edge gateways, edge orchestration, and support for heterogeneous edge devices to address the unique challenges posed by edge computing environments.

Furthermore, the evolution of hardware architectures, especially the proliferation of accelerators like Graphics Processing Units (GPUs) and Field-Programmable Gate Arrays (FPGAs), has influenced OS designs. OS architectures are adapting to harness the computational power of accelerators for tasks such as machine learning, scientific simulations, and high-performance computing. Deployment strategies for GPU-intensive workloads, for example, necessitate specialized OS configurations to ensure optimal utilization and efficient scheduling of GPU resources.

The integration of Artificial Intelligence (AI) and Machine Learning (ML) into OS designs represents a transformative aspect. AI-driven OS features, such as intelligent resource management, automated anomaly detection, and predictive maintenance, are becoming integral components of modern OS architectures. OS deployment strategies must consider the inclusion of AI algorithms for optimizing system performance, enhancing security, and providing a more adaptive and responsive computing environment.

The rise of serverless computing introduces a paradigm shift that influences OS architectures and deployment models. Serverless platforms abstract away the infrastructure layer, allowing developers to focus on writing code without managing the underlying OS or server instances. OS architectures for serverless computing often involve lightweight, ephemeral instances that execute individual functions on-demand. Deployment strategies revolve around packaging and deploying these functions independently, with OS components abstracted and managed by the serverless platform. This shift towards serverless computing impacts how OS designers think about resource provisioning, scaling, and the overall abstraction of infrastructure.

Hybrid cloud environments, where organizations operate across both on-premises data centers and various cloud providers, pose unique challenges for OS architecture and deployment. OS designs must support seamless integration between on-premises infrastructure and multiple cloud environments, necessitating compatibility with hybrid cloud management tools and orchestration platforms. Deployment strategies in hybrid environments require a balance between centralized management and distributed control, ensuring consistent operation across diverse infrastructures.

Additionally, the rise of quantum computing introduces novel challenges and opportunities for OS architectures. Quantum computers, with their unique computational models, demand specialized OS designs that can manage and orchestrate quantum workloads alongside classical computing resources. Deployment strategies for quantum-ready OS architectures involve considerations for interoperability, security, and the integration of quantum algorithms into existing application workflows.

In conclusion, the impact of contemporary technological trends on operating system architecture and deployment is characterized by adaptability, security enhancements, and the need for flexibility in diverse computing environments. Containerization, microservices, cloud computing, edge computing, AI integration, serverless computing, hybrid cloud, hardware accelerators, and quantum computing collectively shape the evolution of OS designs. The dynamic interplay between these trends necessitates a continual reevaluation and adaptation of OS architectures and deployment practices to meet the evolving demands of the computing landscape. Operating systems are not merely static entities but dynamic components that evolve in response to the ever-changing needs of applications, users, and the broader technological ecosystem.

Operating systems in the era of distributed computing

In the era of distributed computing, operating systems (OS) are undergoing a profound transformation to meet the challenges and opportunities presented by distributed architectures, cloud computing, and the rise of interconnected devices. Traditional monolithic operating systems, designed for single machines, are evolving into distributed operating systems that orchestrate the seamless interaction of resources across multiple nodes. The shift towards distributed computing architectures, where tasks are executed across a network of interconnected machines, necessitates a rethinking of OS designs to provide scalability, fault tolerance, and efficient resource utilization.

Distributed operating systems are characterized by their ability to manage and coordinate computations, data storage, and communication across a network of interconnected nodes. Cloud computing, a prominent manifestation of distributed computing, relies on OS architectures that can dynamically allocate and de-allocate resources, scale applications on demand, and ensure reliability in the face of failures. Operating systems in this context are tasked with managing virtualized infrastructure, containers, and serverless computing environments, orchestrating the deployment and execution of applications across diverse cloud platforms.

The rise of microservices architectures, an integral part of distributed computing, has further implications for OS design. Microservices involve breaking down monolithic applications into smaller, independently deployable services that communicate over a network. Distributed OS architectures need to facilitate the deployment, scaling, and coordination of these microservices, often leveraging container orchestration platforms like Kubernetes. The OS must support the dynamic nature of microservices, where instances can be created, scaled, or terminated based on fluctuating workloads.

Security considerations in distributed operating systems become paramount as computing resources span multiple nodes and potentially traverse diverse networks. These OS architectures incorporate features such as secure communication protocols, encryption, and robust access controls to ensure the confidentiality and integrity of data in transit and at rest. Distributed OS designs also address the challenges of identity management, authentication, and authorization in a decentralized environment, where resources may be owned and operated by different entities.

The proliferation of edge computing introduces another dimension to distributed operating systems. Edge computing involves processing data closer to the source of generation, reducing latency and enabling real-time decision-making. OS architectures for edge computing prioritize lightweight, efficient designs that can run on resource-constrained devices. These distributed OS instances at the edge need to seamlessly integrate with centralized cloud resources, ensuring a cohesive and responsive computing environment across the distributed edge-cloud continuum.

Moreover, the era of distributed computing is marked by the advent of the Internet of Things (IoT), where a myriad of interconnected devices generates and consumes data. Operating systems play a critical role in managing the diversity of devices, communication protocols, and data streams in IoT environments. Distributed OS designs for IoT must support edge computing capabilities, handle intermittent connectivity, and ensure the security of data exchanged between devices, all while managing the heterogeneity of device architectures and capabilities.

In distributed systems, OS architectures must tackle the challenges of consistency, availability, and partition tolerance, often referred to as the CAP theorem. Ensuring data consistency in the face of network partitions or failures, providing high availability of services, and accommodating partition tolerance are critical considerations in the design of distributed operating systems. Techniques like distributed consensus algorithms (e.g., Paxos, Raft) and eventual consistency models are employed to navigate these challenges, influencing the core principles of OS architectures.

The integration of Artificial Intelligence (AI) and Machine Learning (ML) into distributed operating systems represents a transformative aspect. AI-driven OS features, such as intelligent resource management, automated anomaly detection, and predictive maintenance, are becoming integral components of modern distributed OS architectures. These AI-driven features enhance the adaptability and responsiveness of distributed systems, optimizing resource allocation and ensuring efficient operation across dynamic and heterogeneous environments.

Containerization technologies, exemplified by Docker, have become fundamental building blocks in distributed operating systems. Containers encapsulate applications and their dependencies, providing a consistent and portable unit of deployment across distributed environments. Orchestrating the deployment and scaling of containers is often managed by container orchestration platforms like Kubernetes, which itself requires a distributed OS foundation. Distributed OS architectures need to seamlessly integrate with container runtimes, manage container orchestration, and provide a resilient infrastructure for containerized applications.

Security concerns in the era of distributed computing extend beyond traditional notions of perimeter defense. Operating systems must incorporate robust security measures to protect against threats such as distributed denial-of-service (DDoS) attacks, data breaches, and unauthorized access to distributed resources. Concepts like zero-trust security, where trust is never assumed based on network location, become essential in distributed OS designs. Additionally, the use of encryption, secure bootstrapping, and secure communication channels are integral components of a comprehensive security posture in distributed systems.

The orchestration and management of distributed storage systems are pivotal aspects of modern OS architectures. Distributed file systems, object storage, and data storage solutions like Apache Hadoop or Apache Cassandra require OS support for efficient data replication, consistency, and fault tolerance. Operating systems must manage the distributed storage layer, ensuring that data is reliably stored, retrieved, and maintained across multiple nodes while adapting to changing workloads and storage requirements.

The adoption of serverless computing, where functions are executed in a stateless and event-driven manner, further influences the landscape of distributed operating systems. Serverless platforms abstract away the infrastructure layer, and OS architectures must adapt to the ephemeral and event-driven nature of serverless workloads. Distributed OS designs for serverless computing often involve lightweight instances that execute individual functions on-demand, with the OS components abstracted and managed by the serverless platform.

Hybrid cloud environments, where organizations operate across both on-premises data centers and various cloud providers, pose unique challenges for distributed OS architectures. OS designs must support seamless integration between on-premises infrastructure and multiple cloud environments, necessitating compatibility with hybrid cloud management tools and orchestration platforms. Distributed OS deployment strategies require a balance between centralized management and distributed control, ensuring consistent operation across diverse infrastructures.

In conclusion, the era of distributed computing is shaping the evolution of operating systems into dynamic, adaptable, and resilient platforms that can seamlessly manage the complexities of interconnected, heterogeneous environments. From orchestrating containerized workloads to supporting microservices architectures, securing distributed systems, managing edge computing, navigating the challenges of IoT, integrating AI-driven features, and enabling hybrid cloud deployments, distributed operating systems play a pivotal role in shaping the future of computing. The ongoing evolution in OS architectures reflects a commitment to addressing the demands of a distributed computing landscape, where connectivity, scalability, security, and adaptability are paramount considerations. As the technological landscape continues to evolve, distributed operating systems will remain at the forefront, driving innovation and providing the foundational framework for the distributed computing ecosystems of the future.

Edge computing challenges and solutions

Edge computing, a paradigm that involves processing data closer to the source of generation, presents a spectrum of challenges and demands innovative solutions to fully harness its potential. One of the foremost challenges in edge computing lies in the heterogeneity of devices and infrastructure at the edge. Unlike centralized cloud environments, edge computing encompasses a diverse range of devices with varying computational capabilities, storage capacities, and communication protocols. This heterogeneity necessitates adaptive and lightweight solutions in both hardware and software to ensure seamless integration and interoperability across the edge ecosystem. Edge devices, ranging from sensors and actuators to powerful edge servers, demand a flexible and scalable architecture that accommodates this diversity while optimizing resource utilization.

Latency, a critical factor in many edge computing applications, poses a significant challenge. In scenarios where real-time decision-making is paramount, latency must be minimized to ensure timely responses. Edge computing solutions must address the latency challenge by optimizing communication protocols, implementing edge caching mechanisms, and leveraging edge data processing capabilities. Edge nodes equipped with sufficient computational power can perform data processing locally, reducing the need to transmit large volumes of raw data to centralized cloud servers. This approach mitigates latency and enhances the responsiveness of applications, especially in use cases such as autonomous vehicles, industrial automation, and augmented reality.

The security and privacy concerns associated with edge computing are substantial and demand comprehensive solutions. Edge devices often operate in uncontrolled environments, making them susceptible to physical tampering, unauthorized access, and various cyber threats. Securing edge devices requires robust hardware security measures, secure boot processes, and encryption mechanisms to safeguard data in transit and at rest. Moreover, edge computing applications frequently involve sensitive data, necessitating privacy-preserving techniques such as on-device data anonymization and encryption. Edge security solutions must encompass access controls, identity management, and intrusion detection mechanisms tailored to the unique challenges posed by decentralized edge environments.

Edge computing introduces the challenge of managing distributed infrastructure efficiently. Unlike traditional centralized data centers, edge deployments consist of numerous geographically dispersed nodes, each with its own set of resources and management requirements. Edge infrastructure management solutions must address issues such as dynamic scalability, remote updates, and automated provisioning while ensuring high availability and fault tolerance. Technologies like edge orchestration platforms and containerization play a crucial role in streamlining the deployment and lifecycle management of applications across distributed edge environments. Additionally, decentralized monitoring and management tools are essential for maintaining the health and performance of edge nodes.

Another challenge in edge computing is the limited bandwidth and unreliable connectivity that may be prevalent in some edge environments. Edge devices may operate in remote or resource-constrained locations with intermittent network connectivity. This constraint poses challenges for transmitting large volumes of data to centralized cloud servers. Edge solutions must incorporate strategies like edge caching, data compression, and adaptive communication protocols to optimize bandwidth usage. Furthermore, edge computing architectures can leverage edge fog computing, where intermediate nodes act as relays for data transmission, reducing the dependency on direct communication with centralized cloud servers.

The lifecycle management of edge applications introduces complexities that demand streamlined solutions. Edge deployments often consist of numerous devices, each requiring software updates, security patches, and application changes. Managing the lifecycle of edge applications involves addressing challenges related to version control, rollback mechanisms, and automated update processes. Edge computing solutions must incorporate efficient deployment strategies, over-the-air updates, and compatibility checks to ensure a seamless and secure application lifecycle. Edge orchestration platforms, capable of managing the deployment and updates of applications across diverse edge nodes, play a pivotal role in simplifying edge application lifecycle management.

Data governance and compliance become intricate challenges in edge computing environments, particularly in industries with stringent regulatory requirements. Edge devices may generate and process sensitive data, and adhering to data privacy regulations is paramount. Edge solutions must include mechanisms for enforcing data governance policies, ensuring that data is handled in compliance with legal and industry-specific regulations. Techniques like edge-based encryption, secure data sharing protocols, and audit trails can contribute to achieving data governance and compliance in distributed edge environments.

The diversity of edge use cases demands domain-specific optimizations and customization, posing a challenge for creating generic edge computing solutions. Edge applications span a wide range of industries, from healthcare and manufacturing to smart cities and agriculture, each with unique requirements and constraints. Building edge solutions that cater to these diverse use cases requires a modular and customizable approach. Edge computing platforms must offer flexibility for developers to tailor applications to specific domains while providing reusable components that address common challenges, such as connectivity, security, and data management.

Energy efficiency is a critical concern in edge computing, particularly for battery-powered devices and remote edge nodes with limited power sources. Edge devices often operate in environments where power consumption is a primary constraint. Energy-efficient algorithms, low-power hardware architectures, and dynamic power management strategies are crucial for optimizing the energy efficiency of edge devices. Edge solutions should prioritize mechanisms for intelligent workload distribution, allowing tasks to be processed on devices with available resources and low power consumption. Additionally, edge computing platforms must support energy-aware scheduling and optimization techniques to prolong the operational life of battery-powered devices.

The dynamic nature of edge environments introduces challenges in achieving resilience and fault tolerance. Edge nodes may operate in harsh conditions, experience hardware failures, or face transient network disruptions. Edge computing solutions must incorporate mechanisms for fault detection, isolation, and recovery to ensure continuous operation. Techniques like edge clustering, where multiple nodes collaborate to share workloads and provide redundancy, contribute to achieving fault tolerance in edge environments. Moreover, edge applications need to implement strategies for stateful recovery, ensuring that critical data and application states are preserved during transient failures.

The integration of artificial intelligence and machine learning at the edge introduces complexities related to model deployment, inference efficiency, and continuous learning. Edge devices may have limited computational resources, requiring optimization techniques for deploying and executing machine learning models efficiently.

Edge solutions must support on-device model training, allowing devices to adapt to changing data patterns and requirements without relying on centralized cloud training. Edge computing platforms should facilitate the seamless deployment and management of machine learning models across diverse edge nodes while considering the privacy implications of processing sensitive data locally.

In conclusion, the challenges in edge computing are diverse and multifaceted, spanning issues of heterogeneity, latency, security, infrastructure management, limited bandwidth, lifecycle management, data governance, customization, energy efficiency, resilience, and the integration of artificial intelligence. Addressing these challenges demands innovative and holistic solutions that take into account the unique characteristics of edge environments. As the field of edge computing continues to evolve, the development of comprehensive frameworks, standards, and best practices will be crucial in fostering a resilient and efficient edge ecosystem that unlocks the full potential of decentralized computing for a wide range of applications across industries.

Predictive security measures and AI-driven defenses

Predictive security measures and AI-driven defenses represent a paradigm shift in the field of cybersecurity, leveraging advanced technologies to proactively identify and mitigate emerging threats. The traditional reactive approach to cybersecurity, relying on signature-based detection and post-incident response, is increasingly complemented by predictive measures that anticipate and preemptively counteract potential security risks. Artificial Intelligence (AI) plays a pivotal role in this evolution, offering the capability to analyze vast datasets, recognize patterns, and make intelligent decisions in real-time. Predictive security, enabled by AI-driven defenses, encompasses a range of strategies and technologies designed to anticipate, adapt, and autonomously respond to the dynamic landscape of cyber threats.

One key aspect of predictive security is threat intelligence analysis, where AI algorithms sift through massive volumes of data to identify patterns indicative of potential cyber threats. Machine learning models, trained on historical threat data, analyze current network traffic, user behavior, and system logs to detect anomalies and deviations from normal patterns. By identifying subtle indicators of compromise or unusual activities, predictive security measures can raise alerts or take preventive actions before an actual security incident occurs. This predictive approach enhances the overall resilience of systems by staying ahead of evolving threats and minimizing the window of vulnerability.

AI-driven predictive analytics also extends to the realm of vulnerability management. Traditional vulnerability assessments often involve periodic scans and assessments, but predictive security employs continuous monitoring and dynamic risk assessments. AI algorithms can analyze the security posture of systems and applications in real-time, predicting potential weaknesses and vulnerabilities based on emerging threats and the evolving threat landscape. This allows organizations to prioritize and address vulnerabilities proactively, reducing the likelihood of exploitation by malicious actors.

Behavioral analytics, powered by machine learning, is another critical component of predictive security. By establishing a baseline of normal user behavior, AI algorithms can identify deviations and anomalies that may indicate unauthorized access or compromised accounts. Predictive security measures utilize these behavioral insights to detect insider threats, credential misuse, or unusual activities that may precede a cyberattack. By recognizing patterns associated with malicious behavior, AI-driven defenses can initiate response actions, such as user account lockdowns or alerting security teams, before significant damage occurs.

In the context of endpoint security, predictive measures leverage AI to detect and respond to potential threats at the device level. Endpoint protection platforms utilize machine learning models to analyze the behavior of applications and processes on endpoints, identifying indicators of compromise or malicious activity. Predictive endpoint security can proactively quarantine or remediate compromised devices, preventing the lateral movement of threats within the network. Additionally, AI-driven threat hunting capabilities enable security teams to identify and mitigate emerging threats before they escalate.

The integration of predictive security measures with threat hunting workflows underscores the proactive nature of modern cybersecurity strategies. Threat hunting involves actively searching for signs of compromise within an organization's network and systems. AI-driven threat hunting tools can analyze historical data, identify patterns indicative of advanced persistent threats (APTs), and uncover subtle indicators of compromise that may elude traditional security controls. This predictive threat hunting approach allows organizations to stay one step ahead of sophisticated adversaries by anticipating their tactics, techniques, and procedures.

In the domain of network security, predictive measures leverage AI to enhance intrusion detection and prevention capabilities. Machine learning models can analyze network traffic patterns, identify anomalous behavior, and detect potential signs of a cyberattack in real-time. Predictive network security solutions can dynamically adjust firewall rules, block malicious IP addresses, or initiate automated responses to mitigate ongoing threats. By predicting potential attack vectors and adapting defenses accordingly, organizations can strengthen their resilience against evolving cyber threats.

Predictive security extends to the identification and mitigation of phishing attacks, a prevalent vector for cyber threats. AI-driven solutions can analyze email content, user behavior, and communication patterns to identify phishing attempts in real-time. Predictive phishing defenses leverage machine learning to detect subtle indicators of phishing, such as email spoofing or socially engineered messages, and can automatically quarantine or flag suspicious emails before they reach end-users. This proactive approach helps organizations prevent successful phishing attacks, safeguarding sensitive information and maintaining the integrity of communication channels.

In the era of cloud computing, predictive security measures are essential for protecting cloud-native environments and applications. AI-driven cloud security solutions continuously monitor cloud workloads, configurations, and user activities to identify potential risks and misconfigurations. Predictive cloud security can anticipate and respond to unauthorized access, data exposure, or other cloud-related threats by leveraging machine learning models that understand the normal behavior of cloud environments. By proactively addressing cloud security challenges, organizations can ensure the integrity and confidentiality of their data in the cloud.

The convergence of predictive security measures with incident response capabilities is a hallmark of modern cybersecurity resilience. AI-driven incident response enables organizations to automate and orchestrate response actions based on predictive analytics. When a potential security incident is identified, predictive security solutions can autonomously initiate predefined response actions, such as isolating compromised devices, blocking malicious domains, or updating security policies. This automated response capability not only reduces the time to contain threats but also minimizes the manual workload on security teams, allowing them to focus on more strategic aspects of threat mitigation.

Adversarial machine learning, where malicious actors attempt to manipulate or evade AI-driven security defenses, poses a unique challenge. Predictive security measures must be resilient to adversarial attacks, employing techniques such as model diversification, anomaly detection, and continuous retraining to adapt to evolving threats. Adversarial machine learning defenses ensure that AI-driven security models maintain their effectiveness in the face of sophisticated attempts to deceive or circumvent predictive security measures.

Ethical considerations and transparency in the deployment of AI-driven predictive security measures are crucial aspects of responsible cybersecurity practices. Organizations must ensure that AI models used in cybersecurity are fair, unbiased, and do not inadvertently discriminate against certain groups. Transparent and explainable AI models help build trust among security professionals, enabling them to understand how predictions are made and facilitating collaborative decision-making between human experts and AI-driven systems.

In conclusion, predictive security measures, powered by artificial intelligence, represent a transformative approach to cybersecurity that goes beyond traditional reactive defenses. By harnessing the capabilities of machine learning, predictive security enables organizations to anticipate, adapt, and autonomously respond to emerging cyber threats. From threat intelligence analysis to behavioral analytics, vulnerability management, endpoint security, and incident response, AI-driven defenses enhance the overall resilience of cybersecurity postures. As the cyber threat landscape continues to evolve, the integration of predictive security measures becomes increasingly essential, offering organizations a proactive defense strategy to stay ahead of sophisticated adversaries and safeguard their digital assets.

Adapting OS security to evolving cyber threats

Adapting operating system (OS) security to the ever-evolving landscape of cyber threats is an ongoing and dynamic challenge that requires a multifaceted approach. The relentless advancement of cyber threats, ranging from sophisticated malware and ransomware attacks to complex vulnerabilities and zero-day exploits, demands constant vigilance and adaptation in OS security strategies. At the core of this adaptive process is the recognition that security is not a static state but an ongoing journey, requiring continuous assessment, innovation, and proactive measures to mitigate risks and respond effectively to emerging threats.

One fundamental aspect of adapting OS security involves staying abreast of the latest threat intelligence. This requires establishing robust mechanisms for gathering, analyzing, and disseminating information about new and emerging cyber threats. OS security teams need to be plugged into global threat intelligence networks, collaborating with cybersecurity organizations, government agencies, and industry peers to gain insights into evolving attack vectors, tactics, and techniques. Continuous monitoring of the threat landscape allows OS security professionals to anticipate potential risks and proactively fortify defenses against emerging threats.

Vulnerability management is a critical component of adapting OS security. Operating systems are complex software ecosystems prone to vulnerabilities that can be exploited by malicious actors. A proactive approach involves regular vulnerability assessments, patch management, and timely updates to address known vulnerabilities. Automated tools and processes can assist in identifying and prioritizing vulnerabilities based on their severity and potential impact. The adaptive nature of OS security is exemplified by the ability to rapidly respond to newly discovered vulnerabilities, releasing patches and updates to close potential avenues of exploitation before they can be weaponized by cyber adversaries.

In the context of the dynamic threat landscape, OS security must extend beyond reactive measures to embrace proactive and predictive strategies. Behavioral analytics, powered by artificial intelligence and machine learning, can play a crucial role in detecting anomalies and deviations from normal patterns of user behavior or system activity. By establishing baselines and continuously monitoring for deviations, OS security systems can identify potential indicators of compromise and malicious activities that may precede a full-scale cyber attack. Predictive security measures enable preemptive responses, allowing organizations to disrupt potential threats before they manifest into security incidents.

The integration of threat hunting into OS security practices further underscores the adaptive nature of cybersecurity. Threat hunting involves actively searching for signs of compromise within the OS environment, seeking out indicators of advanced persistent threats (APTs) or stealthy adversaries. This proactive approach involves skilled analysts leveraging threat intelligence, behavior analytics, and other advanced techniques to identify potential threats that may have eluded automated security measures. OS security teams must embrace a hunter mentality, continuously refining their methodologies to stay ahead of adversaries who are constantly evolving their tactics.

As modern operating systems become increasingly interconnected and interdependent, the concept of Zero Trust Security becomes paramount. Traditional perimeter-based security models are no longer sufficient, and OS security must adopt a Zero Trust approach, assuming that no entity—whether internal or external—should be inherently trusted. Implementing micro-segmentation, least privilege access controls, and continuous authentication are integral components of a Zero Trust Security model. This adaptive paradigm requires ongoing evaluation and adjustment of security policies based on the evolving threat landscape and the dynamic nature of user activities within the OS environment.

In the face of sophisticated cyber threats, OS security must also grapple with the challenge of defending against advanced persistent threats (APTs). APTs are characterized by stealth, persistence, and a targeted focus on compromising specific organizations or individuals over an extended period. Adapting OS security to combat APTs involves a combination of advanced detection mechanisms, threat intelligence sharing, and incident response strategies. Security teams must assume a proactive stance, assuming that determined adversaries are continually evolving their tactics, and continuously refining defense strategies to detect and thwart these persistent threats.

The integration of DevSecOps principles into the software development lifecycle is a key adaptive strategy for OS security. Embedding security practices within the development process ensures that security considerations are not an afterthought but an integral part of the software development pipeline. Continuous integration and continuous delivery (CI/CD) pipelines can incorporate security testing, static code analysis, and vulnerability scanning to identify and remediate security issues early in the development lifecycle. This adaptive approach helps address security concerns at the root, reducing the likelihood of deploying insecure code into production environments.

Ensuring the resilience of OS security also involves a robust incident response and recovery framework. Despite the best preventive measures, security incidents may still occur. An adaptive incident response strategy encompasses pre-defined playbooks, continuous tabletop exercises, and simulations to prepare security teams for a swift and effective response. Post-incident analysis, lessons learned, and continuous improvement are essential components of an adaptive incident response framework. By learning from each incident, OS security can evolve to better anticipate, detect, and mitigate future threats.

In the age of cloud computing, OS security must extend its adaptive strategies to encompass the unique challenges posed by cloud environments. Cloud-native security involves understanding the shared responsibility model, where cloud service providers and customers have distinct responsibilities for security. OS security practices must adapt to leverage cloud-native security controls, implement secure configurations, and address the challenges of data visibility, identity management, and compliance in the cloud. Embracing DevSecOps practices in cloud environments further facilitates the integration of security into the development and deployment lifecycle.

The adaptive nature of OS security also requires a strong focus on user awareness and education. Social engineering attacks, phishing attempts, and other forms of user manipulation are prevalent in the cyber threat landscape. OS security strategies must incorporate ongoing user training, awareness campaigns, and simulated phishing exercises to educate users about potential threats and instill a security-first mindset. An adaptive security culture involves empowering users to recognize and report suspicious activities, creating a collective defense against evolving cyber threats.

The regulatory landscape also plays a crucial role in shaping adaptive OS security practices. Compliance with industry-specific regulations and data protection laws requires OS security teams to stay informed about evolving compliance requirements. Adapting security controls and policies to align with regulatory changes ensures that organizations not only protect their systems from cyber threats but also meet legal and compliance obligations. The adaptive interplay between OS security and regulatory compliance underscores the need for a holistic and evolving approach to cybersecurity governance.

The integration of threat intelligence sharing and collaboration with the broader cybersecurity community is a fundamental aspect of adaptive OS security. Cybersecurity is a collective effort, and information sharing about emerging threats, vulnerabilities, and attack techniques is paramount. OS security teams must actively participate in Information Sharing and Analysis Centers (ISACs), industry forums, and collaborative initiatives to exchange threat intelligence. By contributing and consuming threat intelligence, OS security can stay ahead of emerging threats and collectively strengthen the cybersecurity posture of the entire ecosystem.

In conclusion, adapting operating system security to evolving cyber threats requires a comprehensive, proactive, and adaptive approach that goes beyond traditional security paradigms. The dynamic nature of the cyber threat landscape necessitates continuous monitoring, threat intelligence analysis, vulnerability management, and the integration of advanced technologies such as AI-driven predictive analytics. Embracing a Zero Trust Security model, incorporating DevSecOps principles, preparing for advanced persistent threats, and fostering a security-aware culture are integral components of adaptive OS security. The collaboration with the broader cybersecurity community, compliance with regulatory requirements, and a strong incident response framework further contribute to the adaptability and resilience of OS security in the face of ever-evolving cyber threats.

Shaping the future of user interfaces

Shaping the future of user interfaces (UI) is a captivating journey that intertwines technological innovation, human-centered design, and the evolving ways in which individuals interact with digital systems. Over the years, UIs have evolved from command-line interfaces to graphical user interfaces (GUIs), touch-based interfaces, and voice-controlled interactions. The future promises a continuation of this transformative trajectory, driven by emerging technologies that blend the physical and digital realms seamlessly. Central to this evolution is the concept of natural user interfaces (NUIs), where interactions with digital systems mimic real-world experiences, transcending traditional input devices and redefining the relationship between humans and technology.

The advent of augmented reality (AR) and virtual reality (VR) technologies represents a paradigm shift in UI design. AR overlays digital information onto the physical world, enriching the user's perception of reality. VR immerses users in entirely virtual environments. Both AR and VR challenge traditional UI conventions by introducing spatial computing, gestural controls, and three-dimensional interfaces. The future of UIs lies in creating immersive and intuitive experiences that leverage AR and VR to seamlessly integrate digital elements into our physical surroundings or transport users to entirely new realms.

Gesture-based interactions stand at the forefront of reshaping UIs, offering a hands-on and intuitive approach to controlling digital devices. With advancements in computer vision and depth-sensing technologies, users can now interact with UI elements through gestures, hand movements, and even facial expressions. This paradigm shift extends beyond traditional touchscreens, empowering users to manipulate digital content in the air or on surfaces. Gesture-based UIs cater to a more dynamic and expressive user experience, fostering a sense of direct engagement with digital information.

Voice interfaces have become ubiquitous, driven by the proliferation of smart speakers, virtual assistants, and natural language processing (NLP) capabilities. The future of UIs embraces voice interactions as a primary mode of communication with digital systems. Conversational interfaces, powered by AI, not only respond to voice commands but also understand context, anticipate user needs, and engage in meaningful dialogues. As speech recognition technology advances, voice interfaces are poised to become more accurate, context-aware, and seamlessly integrated into various devices and applications.

The advent of haptic technology introduces a tactile dimension to UIs, enabling users to feel and interact with digital content. Haptic feedback, such as vibrations or simulated textures, enhances the sense of touch in virtual environments or when interacting with touchscreens. The future envisions more sophisticated haptic interfaces that provide nuanced feedback, enabling users to perceive textures, temperatures, or even the resistance of virtual objects. Haptic

UIs promise a more immersive and multisensory digital experience, bridging the gap between the physical and digital realms.

Brain-computer interfaces (BCIs) represent a frontier in UI design, allowing users to interact with digital systems using their thoughts. BCIs translate neural signals into actionable commands, opening possibilities for hands-free and direct mental control of devices. While still in its early stages, the potential impact of BCIs on the future of UIs is profound. Imagine navigating interfaces, typing messages, or controlling smart devices with nothing but your thoughts. The development of BCIs holds the promise of empowering individuals with disabilities and unlocking new dimensions of human-computer interaction.

The rise of wearable devices marks a shift towards UIs seamlessly integrated into our daily lives. Smartwatches, augmented reality glasses, and other wearables introduce glanceable interfaces that provide information at a glance without the need for extensive user interaction. The future of wearable UIs involves refining form factors, enhancing display technologies, and leveraging biometric data to create unobtrusive yet informative interfaces. Wearable UIs aim to seamlessly blend into our routines, offering contextual information and actionable insights without disrupting the flow of daily activities.

The Internet of Things (IoT) further extends the canvas of UI design, as everyday objects become interconnected and capable of digital interaction. Ambient interfaces, embedded in our environments, enable users to interact with a multitude of interconnected devices seamlessly. The future of IoT UIs envisions a cohesive and context-aware ecosystem where smart homes, connected cars, and intelligent cities offer a harmonized user experience. Voice commands, gestures, and contextual awareness will play pivotal roles in navigating and controlling the expansive IoT landscape.

Personalization and adaptive UIs are key elements in shaping the future of user interfaces. AI and machine learning algorithms analyze user behavior, preferences, and contextual data to tailor interfaces to individual needs. Adaptive UIs anticipate user intent, dynamically adjust layouts, and offer personalized content, creating a more fluid and user-centric experience. The future envisions UIs that not only respond to explicit user commands but also anticipate desires, proactively offering information and services tailored to individual preferences.

Ethical considerations in UI design become increasingly prominent as technology embeds itself deeper into our lives. Designing inclusive interfaces that cater to diverse user needs, ensuring accessibility for individuals with disabilities, and mitigating biases in AI-driven interfaces are crucial aspects of responsible UI design. The future demands a commitment to ethical and inclusive practices, fostering interfaces that empower users, respect privacy, and contribute positively to the human experience.

The evolution of UIs is inseparable from the broader trend of digital transformation, where technology becomes an integral part of our personal and professional lives. The future of UIs extends beyond individual devices or applications, envisioning a seamless and interconnected digital ecosystem that adapts to user preferences, anticipates needs, and fosters intuitive interactions. The interplay of emerging technologies, innovative design principles, and a human-centered approach will continue to shape the future of user interfaces, offering immersive, intuitive, and inclusive experiences that redefine the boundaries between humans and technology.

Human-centric design principles in future OS development

In the landscape of future operating system (OS) development, human-centric design principles emerge as guiding beacons, shaping the evolution of digital environments towards seamless integration with human needs, behaviors, and aspirations. As technology advances, the focus shifts beyond the mere functionality of operating systems to a profound understanding of users, their diverse contexts, and the intricate interplay between individuals and the digital realm. Human-centric design principles reflect a commitment to enhancing user experiences, fostering inclusivity, and empowering individuals to interact with technology in intuitive, meaningful, and personalized ways.

One paramount principle in future OS development revolves around user empowerment. Empowering users entails providing them with tools and interfaces that align with their cognitive processes, preferences, and proficiency levels. Future OSs envision interfaces that adapt to users' skillsets, catering to both novices and experts. Adaptive UI elements, contextual guidance, and personalized settings contribute to an OS that not only serves as a digital tool but also as a platform that accommodates diverse user capabilities and fosters a sense of mastery and control.

The concept of inclusivity takes center stage in the human-centric OS of the future. Inclusive design aims to create digital environments that consider the needs of users with diverse abilities, ensuring that technology is accessible to everyone. Future OSs prioritize features such as screen readers, voice commands, and customizable interfaces to cater to individuals with visual, auditory, or motor impairments. Inclusivity also extends to diverse cultural and linguistic contexts, fostering a global digital ecosystem where users from different backgrounds can engage with technology in a manner that resonates with their cultural perspectives.

Seamless integration of technology into the fabric of daily life is a core tenet of human-centric OS development. The future envisions OSs that operate in the background, intelligently anticipating user needs and proactively offering relevant information and services. Ambient computing, where devices collaboratively respond to user context and intent, becomes a hallmark of future OSs. Whether it's a smart home adjusting settings based on user preferences or a wearable device seamlessly integrating with daily activities, the goal is to create an OS that complements human experiences without imposing unnecessary cognitive burdens.

Personalization emerges as a fundamental aspect of human-centric OS design, recognizing that each user is unique and that their digital experiences should reflect this individuality. Future OSs leverage artificial intelligence and machine learning algorithms to understand user behavior, preferences, and habits. This deep understanding facilitates the creation of adaptive interfaces, personalized content recommendations, and context-aware interactions. By tailoring the OS experience to individual users, future systems aim to not only meet functional needs but also resonate with users on a personal level, creating a more meaningful and engaging digital environment.

Transparency and user agency are integral principles in the human-centric OS of the future. Users should have a clear understanding of how their data is used, what algorithms govern system behavior, and the implications of their interactions with the OS. Future systems prioritize transparency in data handling, algorithmic decision-making, and privacy controls. Moreover, user agency is emphasized, allowing individuals to customize privacy settings, control data sharing, and influence the behavior of the OS. The goal is to create an environment where users feel informed, in control, and confident in their digital interactions.

The concept of digital well-being becomes a cornerstone in the design philosophy of future OSs. Acknowledging the impact of technology on mental health and overall well-being, human-centric OS development focuses on features that promote a healthy balance between digital engagement and real-life experiences. Tools for managing screen time, notifications that respect focused work periods, and features that encourage breaks and physical activity are integrated into the OS to foster a harmonious relationship between users and their digital devices. The aim is to prioritize the user's mental and emotional health, ensuring that technology serves as a positive enabler rather than a source of stress or distraction.

Collaborative and cooperative computing principles are envisaged as essential in future OS development. The digital landscape is increasingly characterized by collaboration, whether in the context of remote work, online learning, or virtual teamwork. Future OSs prioritize features that facilitate seamless collaboration, offering integrated communication tools, real-time document sharing, and collaborative editing capabilities. The OS becomes a facilitator of teamwork, breaking down digital silos and providing a cohesive environment where users can seamlessly transition between individual and collaborative tasks.

Security and privacy are paramount considerations in the human-centric OS of the future. Recognizing the growing concerns about data breaches, cyber threats, and the misuse of personal information, future OSs prioritize robust security features and privacy controls. End-to-end encryption, secure biometric authentication, and granular privacy settings empower users to safeguard their digital identities. The OS acts as a guardian, ensuring that users can trust the system to protect their sensitive information and provide a secure digital environment for their interactions.

Environmental sustainability emerges as a conscientious principle in human-centric OS development. As technology becomes an integral part of daily life, the ecological impact of digital systems is a growing concern. Future OSs emphasize energy efficiency, sustainable practices in data centers, and features that encourage environmentally conscious behaviors. Whether through optimizing power consumption, promoting recycling of electronic devices, or minimizing carbon footprints, the OS becomes a catalyst for users to contribute to a more sustainable and environmentally friendly digital future.

Continuous learning and adaptability define the trajectory of the human-centric OS. The future envisages operating systems that evolve in response to user feedback, emerging technologies, and changing societal needs. Regular updates introduce new features, refine existing functionalities, and address vulnerabilities, ensuring that the OS remains relevant, secure, and aligned with user expectations. This iterative and adaptive approach reflects a commitment to continuous improvement, acknowledging that the digital landscape is dynamic, and the OS must evolve in tandem with the evolving needs of its users.

In conclusion, human-centric design principles in future OS development transcend the traditional boundaries of functional utility, emphasizing a holistic and empathetic approach to technology. Empowering users, fostering inclusivity, seamlessly integrating technology into daily life, personalization, transparency, digital well-being, collaborative computing, security, privacy, environmental sustainability, and a commitment to continuous learning collectively shape the envisioned OS of the future. Grounded in the understanding that technology should enhance, not overshadow, the human experience, these principles pave the way for operating systems that serve as enablers of positive, meaningful, and user-centric digital interactions.